KERI

with David Byrne

www.**HERO**BOOKS.digital

HERO BOOKS

PUBLISHED BY HERO BOOKS
1 WOODVILLE GREEN
LUCAN
CO. DUBLIN
IRELAND

Hero Books is an imprint of Umbrella Publishing
First Published 2021
Copyright © David Byrne 2021
All rights reserved

A CIP record for this book is available from the British Library

ISBN 9781910827390

Cover design and formatting: jessica@viitaladesign.com
Ebook formatting: www.ebooklaunch.com
Photographs: Sportsfile and *Kerry's Eye*

★ DEDICATION ★

To all those who have worn the
famous green and gold

★ CONTENTS ★

★ ACKNOWLEDGEMENTS ★

HEADING UP TO the All-Ireland final replay between Kerry and Dublin in September 2019 I remember overhearing an elderly Kerry fan expressing his delight that he wasn't missing his local evening Vigil Mass, as it had been changed so as not to clash with the big game.

At the same time, another avid Kerry football fan Fr Mossie Brick of Castleisland stated, 'Football is the religion at the moment', and he wasn't far off.

They say football *is like* a religion in the Kingdom, and to me that day was a clear indication of this certainly being the case.

As a kid, getting to watch Kerry games while I was on school holidays in beautiful Ballyheigue was a huge part of my childhood summers. Even though a hurling stronghold, the grá for football in the North Kerry pocket where I spent many a summer's day was clear to see.

We have hurling in Limerick, my native county, but for me football in the Kingdom is a passion on another level that is alive in the hearts, minds and daily lives of the public. Football is a language in Kerry, and seeps into every aspect of life.

I believe this is showcased in the wonderful stories shared in this book, as 30 legends speak long and passionately about their lives on the field, and far beyond the white lines.

With this in mind, it has been an absolute pleasure and a total privilege to be able to bring you this book, and help the thousands of Kerry football supporters throughout the world recall such wonderful days.

Days selected by the heroes themselves from seven wonderful decades for Kerry football.

FIRST OF ALL, this book would not have been possible without those 30 Kerry football legends who gave their time during what was a difficult period for many. And not only did they share their amazing stories, they did so with such friendliness, humour and generosity. I am truly grateful for their time and courtesy in chatting, reminiscing, laughing and looking back so fondly on their days in green and gold – and for some, their days in their beloved club colours.

I could have included many more top players who wore the most famous football jersey in the country, but this book isn't an effort at putting together a list of the Top 30 – rather, it is an attempt to share a wide range of stories, and as many great days as possible which this county has had in the past seven decades from a broad range of footballers from throughout the county.

It is one handful of the greatest Kerry footballers ever.

Their stories will hopefully make this book an enjoyable experience for Kerry supporters at home, and throughout the world.

I couldn't be more thankful to Liam Hayes and the fantastic team at Hero Books for this opportunity, and their generous support throughout this process. I am indebted to Liam for trusting me in undertaking the task of selecting the 30 legends and revealing their chosen 'days'. My many thanks also to my fantastic colleagues at *Kerry's Eye*, especially Padraig Kennelly and Kerry Kennelly, Ger Colleran, who supported me in this venture from the get-go.

I am also particularly thankful to the game's amazing administrators, the men and women who do the heavy lifting in all of our clubs, and who kindly took the time to put me in touch with many of the legends who feature in this book. Their help and advice at the outset of this project set this journey on a wonderful and exciting pathway, resulting in the culmination of what I hope will prove to be an enjoyable read for many.

Almost finally, and most importantly!

My wonderful girlfriend Kate was more than patient as I embarked on this journey and was my rock throughout the writing of this book, often having to listen to me excitedly repeating the brilliant stories over and over again. It was a thoroughly enjoyable but tough task writing this book during a global pandemic, and I'm sure it wasn't easy for Kate having to put up with me taking over our apartment throughout several lockdowns. For this, I am forever grateful.

From the start, Kate's parents Paudie and Anne – avid Kerry supporters –

were second to none in their advice. Their input has been invaluable. To my own parents Mike and Teresa, your lifelong support from an early age has got me to this point in life, and made all of this possible. Similarly, the encouragement from my two younger brothers Adam and Shane, and my extended family and friends, is always greatly appreciated.

Finally, let me pay tribute to every single person who has volunteered their time for the good of gaelic games in Kerry. Without this heroic band of loyal supporters and volunteers, the 30 men in this book openly admit that they wouldn't have a story to tell. Your work doesn't go unnoticed and really is for the betterment of life in the Kingdom.

The fact that six of the 30 players interviewed chose a club game as the 'Game of their Life' further highlights the importance of the parish and the club, still, in the modern world of the GAA.

I sincerely hope you enjoy this. I simply was in a privileged position to bring these wonderful memories to life. This book is about the glory of the famous green and gold jersey, and all those who have gone before us.

Kerry Abú!

David Byrne
October 2021

MICK O'DWYER
(& SEÁN MURPHY)

KERRY 3-7 GALWAY 1-4
All-Ireland SFC Final
Croke Park
SEPTEMBER 27, 1959

Mick O'Dwyer being inducted into the GAA Hall of Fame at the GAA Museum in Croke Park in 2014.

★ **KERRY:** J Culloty; J O'Shea, N Sheehy, T Lyons; **Seán Murphy**, K Coffey, **M O'Dwyer (0-1)**; Mick O'Connell, Seamus Murphy; D McAuliffe (2-2), T Long, P Sheehy; D Geaney, John Dowling (0-2), T Lyne (0-2). Subs: Jack Dowling for Lyons, Moss O'Connell for Mick O'Connell, G McMahon (1-0) for Geaney.

★ **GALWAY:** J Farrell; J Kissane, S Meade, M Greally; M Garrett, J Mahon, S Colleran; F Evers (1-0), Mattie McDonagh; J Young (0-2), S Purcell (0-2), Michael 'Hauleen' McDonagh; M Laide, F Stockwell, J Nallen. Subs: S Keeley for Nallen, P Dunne for Greally.

THE ACTION

IN WHAT BECAME known as 'The Seán Murphy All-Ireland', the old triumphed over the new at Croke Park as Kerry's traditional catch-and-kick style gained an overwhelming vote of confidence from almost 86,000 in attendance.

Kerry won easily with goals by Dan McAuliffe (two) and Garry McMahon, securing the Kingdom's third of three All-Ireland football titles in the 50s.

In a dry and sunny, but windy day for football, the game quite inexplicably lacked the atmosphere associated with such occasions. Even when the game struggled to get going, Kerry always looked more likely to prevail.

Early long-range points from John Dowling gave Kerry a dream start, and no doubt settled the nerves but it was Galway who struck the net first with a goal coming in the fifth minute. In a cluster, the ball broke to Frank Evers and the Galway midfielder was quick to snatch the rare opportunity, hitting the bouncing ball on the half-volley from close range. The west had awakened.

From the moment Dan McAuliffe levelled the scores in the 10th minute, however, Dr Eamonn O'Sullivan's charges never looked back.

In addition to being the better balanced team throughout the field, Kerry also had the game's two really outstanding individual performers in right half-back Seán Murphy and centre-forward cum-midfielder Tom Long. Murphy had his greatest hour; he popped up to achieve rescue work in the most unlikely of places.

It was level at half-time – 0-5 to 1-2 – but midway through the second-half Kerry hammered home two goals and a point to take a lead of 2-7 to 1-3. During this three-minute spell of total aberration by the Galway defence, the element of doubt as to the ultimate result was removed and a most unmemorable final fizzled out like the dampest of squibs.

When substitute Gary McMahon screwed a ball goal-wards from 30 yards and it went in off the post, within seconds of his arrival on the scene, it was evident the Sam Maguire Cup was once more booked for a trip to the Kingdom.

★★★★★

66

THE FINAL AGAINST Galway in 1959 stands out for me. I was the first person from Waterville to play in and win an All-Ireland. We had a great team back then. We had Mick O'Connell, Seán Murphy, Kevin Coffey, Paudie Sheehy, John Dowling… all these fellas. They were all great players.

It is a game I'll always remember because I was dropped from the minor panel for the All-Ireland final in 1954 and I had to come back from that disappointment to get on this team. There was great satisfaction in that.

But there is also a great feeling in winning your first All-Ireland.

Seán Murphy was playing right half-back that day and no matter where he went the ball followed him. He was playing on a young fella by the name of 'Hauleen' McDonagh, who Seán had a wonderful game on. Seán was on top of his game that day.

He gave one of the finest exhibitions I've seen by any player in Croke Park. It was one of those days when everything just went right for him. That *happens* sometimes.

But to be able to bring the Sam Maguire Cup back to Waterville as the first ever person from the village to win the All-Ireland was most enjoyable, to be honest.

I was playing on a man by the name of Joe Young; a fine footballer.

I played well and I scored a point as well in that final. Normally half-backs didn't do that. I enjoyed the way I went out and played. Of course, at that time the job of a wing back was to try and keep your man scoreless for the hour; that was the big thing.

Nowadays, it is the case of… *How many scores can you get?*

If you want to be able to play both types of a game, you have to be able to play both as a back and as a forward. I think all forwards should play in the full-back line at some stage of their lives because they are going to have to be coming back in games, as well as going forward.

When I look back on my footballing career, it was very satisfying to be directly involved in 21 senior All-Ireland football finals and 15 National League finals, both as a player and a manager.

Another man who stands out was Mick O'Connell... an exceptional player. He was an outstanding player... the likes of whom we'll never see again. But then again, you go through every era and you get outstanding players. Now it is young Clifford... not long ago it was the 'Gooch'... before that it was Maurice Fitzgerald. There was Jack O'Shea before that as well. He had some engine on him. He was unreal.

There is always some shining star on the Kerry team. Going back to my time, it was O'Connell. There is always *some* fella. All those players were exceptional talents... class players.

I never thought I'd be so involved in so many important games. You generally have maybe 10 years and you finish... and go and get out, but I was so lucky to have had such a wonderful time and to be highly involved. To actually be involved in all those All-Ireland finals is just something that you could only dream of. It wasn't because of myself or anything, it was because of the marvellous fellas that came through to us.

I never thought I'd get involved in management when I was playing.

I managed a team in 1974 and then Ger McKenna asked me would I take over Kerry. I didn't want to take over, but I did reluctantly. It came to autumn and I said I'd give it a couple of months anyway... *See how it goes.*

But it all came together then.

In the first 12 months we won an All-Ireland... and it wasn't too easy to get out then. It all happened after that!

I don't know if it is all about the manager. The manager helps alright, but it is *all about* the quality of the players.

I was dead lucky that a wonderful bunch of players came through in 1974 and '75. That was a great bunch of players... and '75 was an unbelievable year. To think that the average age of that team at that time was 21 and a half... and to go on and win an All-Ireland senior football final. It was some achievement. But I could never have imagined what happened after that.

Then, of course, we did the four in-a-row, but we could have quite easily done nine years. We lost the Munster final in 1983 to Cork by a point. We lost the five in-a-row final to Offaly by a point. If we had won the two of them we'd have gone on to win nine All-Irelands in-a-row.

The quality of player was there!

That's what won those All-Irelands for Kerry.

It was evident from when that bunch of players came in at a very young age that they were a very close group, and that lasted for about 12 years.

It was an unusual thing, yet it was a team that had won three under-21s… we had a great opportunity because of those great friendships.

I was completely enthralled by the game of football.

I'd go to games every day of the week to watch players. I travelled all over the country just to see games. The interest was there, there is no doubt about that.

Then, of course, when we were having so much success, it keeps you going all of the time.

Winning the All-Ireland with such a young team in '75… *I'll never forget that day!*

To be very honest, as it was happening in front of my eyes… I couldn't believe it. They always played attractive football. They were only all young fellas so I told them Croke Park was just another pitch with a stand and a terrace, and to just go out and do the job.

I do look back on it with great pride.

But all those players who came through had to be coached and managed by juvenile coaches along the way; in club teams, and in county teams. All those people involved at underage level make all the difference.

After Kerry, I really enjoyed my time at Laois, Wicklow, Kildare… and Clare as well.

It was really enjoyable because they are so keen in all of those counties to do well. There are a lot of very good players in a lot of those so-called 'weaker counties'. All you can do is fall in and give a bit of guidance. If you do that, you will achieve a certain amount.

You might not be winning everything, but you can be close and that is the important thing. Sure, you win some and you lose some, but to be able to get to the top and stay around the top, that's the most important thing of all.

99

SEÁN MURPHY

Dr Seán Murphy (left) and Tommy Doyle, two sons of Camp, with 10 All-Ireland victories between them to remember forever.

"

I WENT TO Coláiste Íosagáin in Ballyvourney and we won everything.

Everything!

Everything that was to be won, for the first time ever. My brother and I were midfield and we were quite prominent in the whole series of matches with the school through 1949... we would have gone on to win the Hogan Cup that year, but the bishops decided they'd cancel the competition right there and then.

We were terribly disappointed.

They cancelled it because they figured that the seminarians were getting a taste of life outside of the priesthood and they were losing candidates for the priesthood by allowing matches outside of the county.

But, in 1949, we'd won everything... Munster colleges... which was a big one to win. We beat Tralee, and Tralee were *unbeatable*. The seminary in Killarney was *unbeatable*, but we beat the whole lot of them and won the Munster colleges title.

In 1949 also, I went on to play in an All-Ireland minor final with Kerry, after we'd beaten Dublin in Tralee. Dublin were really on top of us that day; they had a fantastic minor team.

They came out with towels around their necks, onto the pitch in Tralee, trying to intimidate us. A whole lot of that team playing that day had already won All-Irelands – Tim O'Mahony was one of them.

We beat Dublin, then, in the senior All-Ireland some time later. Kerry hadn't won an All-Ireland from 1946 on… we were being beaten every year. I think it all started for Kerry by getting to the minor All-Ireland final against Armagh in 1949.

We were leading by two points with about three minutes to go and there was a '50' awarded to Kerry, but it didn't go over the bar. There was a fella called John McKnight playing for Armagh; he was very prominent for years in the Armagh county team, and he was a champion sprinter. He got the ball and… in double-quick time… they were *very fast*…they put the ball in the back of our net, and they won the All-Ireland.

During that time, there was a Kerry newspaper called the *Kerry Champion*. The newspaper, after the minor All-Ireland semi-final against Dublin, had an article… and you will see in the second paragraph, it says… *Murphy takes over.*

That was me!

I'm quoting this because history repeated itself years later in the 1959 All-Ireland final, after which I got Footballer of the Year.

But I believe that the renaissance for Kerry started on that day in 1949… the All-Ireland minor semi-final in Tralee. It was a point in time that seemed to rejuvenate Kerry and brought them back to what they were.

We won the minor All-Ireland in 1950.

In the interval between the minor All-Ireland win in 1950 and the '53 senior All-Ireland, which we won, I won the junior All-Ireland with Kerry. So, I had a minor, junior and senior All-Ireland. That was the beginning of my career.

I have to say the game that I remember best of all would be the 1959 All-Ireland against Galway.

It was a more fulfilling All-Ireland for me. I really should have given up football by then because I was a medical student in my final year. I came into work the next day after beating Galway and I was holding a retractor. There was a surgeon that I was working with as a junior doctor…. and he looked me straight in the face and said, 'The day that you can't come to work and hold a retractor for me, you are no good to me'.

And I thought… *All the money my mother has spent on me on all my studies!*

I decided there and then to retire from football, but I was influenced. My brother Seamus had come along then, and I was influenced really to maybe help him win a couple of All-Irelands. Then he influenced me to come back.

Seamus won the 1959 All-Ireland with me – he was midfield. I just felt that there was something that I thought maybe would be a benefit to both of us, but to him particularly, so I kept going for another few years.

I went on then until 1961, when we were beaten by Down in the All-Ireland semi-final.

I was only 27 when I retired.

Before that All-Ireland against Down, I had my appendix removed… six weeks before that game. I should have never played.

The *Game of My Life* has got to be the 1959 All-Ireland final.

It's got to be.

Because of that game, I got selected on the Team of the Century, and I got on the Team of the Millennium… and I got the Caltex Footballer of the Year trophy.

Some people call the 1959 All-Ireland… *The Seán Murphy All-Ireland.*

By definition almost, I have to say that *that* was *the game.* There are many things that stimulated my memory to think of that particular year… and that particular game. We went to America on a trip… everything seemed to happen that year.

That game is imprinted on my mind. It is 62 years ago now, but what I remember particularly is the training we did under Eamonn O'Sullivan. He was a marvellous football trainer. The personnel on the team changed so much at the time. If you look at the teams in 1953, '55, and '59, there are only about two or three who played a full career… myself, Paudie Sheehy and Tadhgie Lyne.

We lost Jackie Lyne and Tom Ashe… we lost a whole lot of footballers.

Galway were tipped to win again. Kerry were never seen to be very hot favourites during my time. We won against the odds during the whole 50s era. If you saw the headlines in the papers and one write-up by Paul Russell… he was a great Kerry footballer and he tipped Galway to win.

He particularly chose 'Hauleen' McDonagh, who was playing on me, and said that McDonagh would win the game for them.

But he didn't.

Mick O'Connell got injured during the first-half. Without Mick O'Connell, Kerry appeared to be very much a beaten side. He was such a dominant figure in football, particularly in Kerry, and the very fact that he got injured and the shuffling they did to counteract that… it didn't appear that it was a winning move.

But it was eventually. We did win it.

Seán Purcell was a magnificent footballer for Galway… and they had Jack Mahon. They were a superb team, that Galway team. Top class footballers.

Of course, they went on to win three All-Irelands in-a-row a few years afterwards; that will tell you how good they were.

I wasn't surprised that they were being tipped to beat us in the All-Ireland final because they were a special group that came together… almost like a college team that stays together and goes from colleges to the minors, juniors… to the senior county team.

I remember the way that game went. Seamus was midfield with O'Connell, and he played very well.

From the start, the Galway kick-out just kept coming out to my wing – I was playing right half-back. Time after time after time again, it seemed to drop into my hands.

I had never experienced that before. You would maybe win two kicks against one kick for the opposing left half-forward in a game, but that particular day it seemed to me that the ball was destined for my hands.

I was never one of these modern attacking half-backs. I reckoned myself that the proper way to deliver a ball from the half-back line to our half-forward line was to have a trajectory of about 45 degrees. I remember telling both Dan McAuliffe, who was left full-forward, and Tadhgie Lyne, who was left half-forward, that every time I got the ball I would kick it… and I would try and drop it about three or four yards, maybe five yards, ahead of them… so they could collect it running.

That was something I had perfected long before the All-Ireland final.

If you get that type of trajectory what it does is – and it is something I think is missing today with all these toe-to-hand footballers – it gives half-forwards a better chance.

If you go toe-to-hand, you are giving the opposing backs plenty of time to put their arms around the half-forwards; it's what they do. By the time the ball arrives the half-forward is overpowered or overwhelmed.

There is a scientific formula that says… *For every action there is an equal and opposite reaction.* Therefore, I reckon that if a half-back – I am particularly talking about half-backs, but this applies right through the whole team – is fighting for the ball, gets the ball, has the opportunity to deliver it where he wants to… then you don't give the backs time to tie the forwards down.

Then they can manoeuvre and Tadhgie Lyne was an expert at spotting that from 50 or 60 yards. He was terrific. And Dan McAuliffe was a bustling full-forward that scored goals and points equally.

There was that plan of action that I can remember in that game.

Kerry and Dublin was also a big game in 1955, but I didn't regard that as my finest hour. A lot of people say that was an epoch-making event, to beat Dublin; that it was more than just beating a Dublin team. *There was more than just football at stake.*

I could deliver a ball from 80 to 100 yards, and I was ambidextrous… left or right.

But I practiced getting distance and accuracy into my kicking with the idea of being able to drop the ball within five yards of the half-forward or the full-forward, so that he could collect it on the run, having already lost his marker.

I used to drop the ball… and I used to lean and kick it at an angle. When I was young, every fella used to kick it as high as they could, and used to think the higher it went… *The better.* They used to shout… 'The highest today!'

But I thought that was ridiculous. You didn't gain any territory that is of any advantage to you. It is like a golf swing… if you can get the ball at the end of the swing there is much more power in it.

There were a lot of skills like that *that* I don't think people developed. They don't develop them today. They just seem to be totally committed to running the ball into the back of the net at the other end. It is all about possession and keeping the ball nowadays.

I studied the whole thing, *and I still do.*

I can see why Kerry are being beaten. They have too many footballers that can weave and find their way up the field, but eventually they run into a cul-de-sac… when the team should have scored a point already!

If they parted with the ball earlier, they would have scored a point and they'd be walking back to their position waiting for the kickout. They are committing that sin almost every time they get the ball.

When I was playing for Kerry, we were very committed without having the coaching and various back-ups that the teams have now.

I used to walk miles with hobnail boots in the evenings because I didn't want anybody seeing me do it on the road.

I used to climb up the mountains during the day, very often with a gun and our sheep dog; spend all day up on the hills, just walking along Caherconree and the hills around Camp. We were very fit.

Paddy 'Bawn' Brosnan used to be fishing, and some fellas were working farms. We were taken in for two weeks for a training camp under Eamonn O'Sullivan, and he said it to me one day that what the training was doing was giving the lads an opportunity to convert the muscle that they were using in their various work… to muscle we could use playing football.

He had a theory that he wouldn't allow any of us to go swimming. He had a theory that you develop what they call contrary muscles that were no good to you playing. So he concentrated on what he thought were the muscles that would help us to win.

There was something instilled in us… I played in five senior All-Irelands; we won three… but even the ones we lost, I couldn't see us being beaten the morning of the game. I think we felt that we would beat everyone and win every All-Ireland.

I felt that on my day, *nobody can beat me…* it was as simple as that.

I don't know if that was everybody's experience but that was my experience. We had a confidence which I think was embedded deeply in the consciousness of the players. It wasn't superficial.

Though you wouldn't think it to look at us…. we didn't *look* very confident.

Out on the field, Dublin would jump and run, and the northern teams would be running around before the match and whatnot. The Kerry team used to slouch onto the field, and just watch the other team, and beat them; not the whole time obviously.

There was that type of insolence about the whole thing – no respect for the other team.

When I was playing, everyone was given certain sections on the pitch to look after. It was introduced by Dr Eamonn, and there was no other way we knew how to play football.

We never really had a tactical meeting. Everybody knew his job.

And you felt that in the game. John Joe Sheehan was a marvellous footballer. To see him going up, catching the ball, and just turning around and putting it over the bar; he knew what to do as a centre-forward.

And there was no laxness. The midfielders were allowed a latitude of running which nobody else was.

I think that is missing today. There is confusion… they are all running, running… *running*. They delay so much that they lose the ball. It is the dispossession rate that I can't understand.

When our crowd got the ball, they weren't hanging around. The ball was in safe hands – nobody took it away. There was very little dispossession in the teams I played in.

Every footballer, no matter who he is, he's got the energy to last the hour, that's for sure, but then if he's being dispossessed and he is trying to claw back the ball and whatnot, he can run out of steam very easily. We're still only amateur footballers, never forget that.

If you can drift that ball 50 or 60 yards out of the half-back line… into the half-forwards, that's very, *very* energy conserving. These basic principles all apply but nobody talks about them… but that was Dr Eamonn; he was technical. He had a reason for everything.

That's why Kevin Heffernan didn't play up to his usual high standard against Kerry in 1955; he drifted outfield… but Ned Roche stayed in there. And when Heffernan came back in, Roche dominated and won their tussle in the square.

Camp is the most peculiar place in that you have a population of about 200, and you've a hell of a lot of All-Ireland medals for a small place. It is only a crossroads.

We had Tim O'Donnell, who had four All-Irelands, Charlie O'Sullivan with another four All-Irelands… Denny O' Shea, he'd one All-Ireland… my brother Seamus had won four All-Irelands, I have three… and Tommy Doyle – one of the best footballers Kerry ever turned out – has seven.

Tommy Doyle was a marvellous footballer – never got enough credit really. He had *everything*. I thought he was one of the best centre-backs ever. He was wonderful.

My father Jackie was a great influence for us. He was a head-teacher from Ballydavid, west of Dingle. He won a junior All-Ireland with Kerry in 1928, and I think it was he who made football the top choice in what games you played in school… ahead of sprinting or any other sport. And I think that is reflected in the number of All-Ireland medals for such a small place.

My father was the founding member of Dingle GAA Club. He was a great supporter of Dingle… that's why I wanted to play with them.

My brother Pádraig won a junior All-Ireland with Kerry, and my brother Tom won a minor All-Ireland with me. The four of us – myself, Pádraig, Seamus, and Tom – won an All-Ireland in some shape, and I won all three… minor, junior, and senior.

I would have always played with Dingle, given the opportunity, but when Castlegregory had a club we couldn't play with Dingle. They couldn't field a team at one time, and I said straightaway that I was going playing with Dingle! I played with Dingle then for a couple of years… a few years after I had stopped playing with Kerry.

When I was in college, you could double up… play with the college and play with your club back home. When they made a list of the college footballers I was always classified as playing with Castlegregory, which I was at the beginning.

One day with Castlegregory, we were playing Strand Road… and Dan O'Keeffe was the goalie for Strand Road. There was a fella from the Maharees – there was a big family of them there – and they put him in full-forward. His job was to bury Dan O'Keeffe, so every time the ball was coming in, this fella went in and, of course, Danno would sidestep him… and the fella would end up in the back of the net. The next time he finished up in the back of the net, he really went for Danno… and Danno stayed where he was. Danno gave him an elbow into the gob; he made a mess of him.

It was a different world back then.

I saw a row on the sideline another day!

There was a fella from Camp; he was a fanatic supporter of Camp. We were playing Castlegregory this day, and the next thing there was a hullabaloo. There in the corner was this fella with the pump for his bicycle… and he was belting another fella with the pump.

Different world.

We won the Lower Senior League three years in-a-row from 1949 to '51.

Maharees beat us the fourth year.

Camp had a dance hall, and the Maharees footballers, the whole lot of them, arrived at our hall with their medals pinned to their jackets. That was dangerous.

What used to happen with all these places was, you'd have a very ordinary team… but there would be one fella who'd played for Kerry and won a couple of All-Irelands. That was like signing a death notice!

One day we were playing Dingle, and the ball was running out to the sideline. I was running towards the ball and I got there first… when I was tripped from behind. I couldn't believe it, this fella started kicking me on the ground… left, right, and centre.

I caught his leg…. before he damaged me.

There was another fella called Jack Walsh. He was a chemist in Dingle, and he got the ball, and he put it under his arm and he looked around to see where I was. He charged to hit me with a belt of a shoulder. Well anyway, I met him with a shoulder.

What a wham that was!

The next thing, there were two or three more of them shouldering me all over the place. You could get killed playing with teams like that if you were an inter-county man.

I certainly look back on it all with huge pride.

Being named in the right half-back position on the Football Team of the

Century and on the Team of the Millennium were extremely proud moments.

Technically, they chose you for a position over a 100 years' timeline. That to me was an honour. You were competing with a lot of great names in football; players from Cavan, Roscommon, Galway and Dublin.

I didn't expect it, I'll be quite honest about it. I thought that the players that were playing the game at that particular time left a greater imprint in the minds of the population at large.

It was one part of my life and, like everything else I have accomplished, I turned the key on it and left it there. I got on with my life.

I have enjoyed meeting with fellas and chatting with them, but it is an amateur game. It never superimposed itself on my life, but it was always there; it is what the Americans would call a 'talking piece'.

It was very pleasurable and it was a subject that didn't do anybody any harm.

The influence of teachers and the church was very prevalent in these teams. Going to Mass and that type of thing was terribly important to them.

Paddy 'Bawn' Brosnan never went to bed without getting down on his knees and saying his prayers; and we stayed in some rough hotels. There was I suppose… and I wouldn't call it deeply religious, but an *influence* there which didn't do anyone any harm.

Football made life very pleasurable.

It had an innocence about it.

Football fulfilled a life existence. There was a place for it in your life and if you hadn't that… *What would you have?*

99

MICHAEL GLEESON

SPA 1-11 KILCUMMIN 1-6
O'Donoghue Cup Final
Fitzgerald Stadium, Killarney
AUGUST 26, 1966

Michael Gleeson (right) with former Spa teammates, Fr Michael O'Donoghue, John Kelly and Jim Gleeson, in 2016 at the 50-year anniversary reunion celebrating the 1966 O'Donoghue Cup win.

★ **SPA:** M Kissane; D Doolan, J Morris, J Gleeson (0-2); J Batt Cronin, D O'Sullivan (0-3), M O'Donoghue; P Casey, T Morris; B Fenton, **M Gleeson (0-5)**, M Cronin (0-1); S Moynihan, P Dennehy (1-0), J Kelly.

★ **KILCUMMIN:** P O'Connor; J Coffey, G Moriarty, D O'Donoghue; B Doolan, James Sheehan, J Keane; T Sheehan (0-5), Johnny Sheehan; P Doolan, Joe Sheehan, B Kelly (1-1); M Moriarty, M O'Leary, D Dwyer.

THE ACTION

THIS HISTORIC GAME continues to be talked about in the parish of Spa, even to this day.

In what was a tough battle and a big struggle against near neighbours Kilcummin, a cracking Paddy Dennehy goal was enough to ensure the O'Donoghue Cup was on its way to Spa for the first time in what was the club's first year as a senior team.

Spa's famous victory was made all that bit more memorable considering the club's significant decline in the 50s.

The club's earliest success was in 1949 when they won the East Kerry senior league. Spa reappeared in a league final three years later, but a combination of emigration, the retirement of several senior players – and having just a small pool of underage players coming through – led to decline setting in from 1952 onwards. The club became temporarily defunct in 1959 and players joined the recently formed St Finan's Hospital team.

The senior club was inactive for a number of years, but Trojan work off the field allowed the game of football to flourish with the local national schools playing a crucial role in the future revival of Spa GAA Club. The success of the senior team in 1966 certainly can be attributed to the efforts of Naomh Mhuire – an amalgamation of Lissivigeen, Tiernaboul, Loughquittane, and Loreto national schools – in local school competitions.

The club was revived just four years before they won the O'Donoghue Cup.

Heading into the semi-final against Rathmore, and the final against Kilcummin, Spa were boosted by the fact they could now avail of the services of star inter-county players Donie O'Sullivan, and Michael Gleeson due to the beginning of school and college holidays, while Pat Casey and Johnny Doolan, who had been abroad on navy duty, had returned to action.

With O'Sullivan performing brilliantly at centre-back, Spa had an early control on the game and tightened their grip when experienced full-forward Dennehy burst through the Kilcummin defence to score the decisive goal. Spa were kingpins of East Kerry, and frantic scenes and celebrations into the early hours rewarded the heroic players.

★★★★★

"

THE MOST IMPORTANT game in my life was with my own club, Spa.

There used to be a club there in the late-40s and early-50s, but the club went out of existence due to a lack of numbers, and emigration, which was rife then, of course.

In my formative years there was no club in our area, so I had no Spa minor team to play with if I wanted to be in contention for the Kerry minors. So… *We were kind of lost.* We were dependent on trying to get a game with Killarney town teams, if we were deemed good enough.

And then some of us – when Spa totally disbanded in 1959 – joined a club which was known as St Finan's, which was attached to St Finan's Hospital.

Johnny Culloty – Kerry captain in 1969 – played with them, as did Weeshie Fogarty. They were a transient kind of a team, and they went out of existence in the mid-60s.

I was in college in Dublin at the time playing with Erin's Hope so I had no individual club to come home to. Although, I would have had an involvement with East Kerry.

But then, unknown to me, some football activist in the Spa area decided to reform the senior team in 1966. They played a couple of early games, again unknown to me as I was in Dublin. They won one game, they lost the next… and then they won the third one. I don't know how some of us then became available – Donie O'Sullivan, myself, Pat Casey, who'd been away, and Johnny Doolan.

Donie was also in Dublin at the time but he'd been playing with Dr Crokes in Killarney. But when Spa reformed, he transferred – he'd be from the heartland of Spa, right beside where the Spa field is now. There was no field back then, in that formal sense, only the goodwill of a neighbour.

We were informed, and we came down – it was probably summer holidays. We played a semi-final and got to the final of the O'Donoghue Cup, a wonderful competition.

We beat Kilcummin in the final.

That was the most transformative game in my life because it meant now I had a base in the Killarney parish from a football perspective.

It did two things.

It gave me *a club* and it reinvigorated the rural community that we, in a general sense, call Spa.

Had that not happened – I qualified as a teacher in 1967 from St Patrick's College and I started teaching in Finglas in Dublin – I more than likely would have joined Erin's Isle in Finglas. That would have meant I'd have disappeared forever from the Kerry landscape.

The victory defined me… and gave me the opportunity to play with my own club and to represent my own community, and thereafter to represent East Kerry… and to represent Kerry. Had Spa not been victorious in that game against Kilcummin, it is possible that the team would have faded away again. But winning that established us as a credible team in the eyes of all other clubs in East Kerry.

We reinforced that the following Easter Sunday when we beat Gneeveguilla in a subsidiary competition to the O'Donoghue Cup.

That gave us respectability.

Thereafter, we were not always victorious, but we were always considered a challenging opposition. We went on to win seven O'Donoghue Cups.

That game against Kilcummin gave us a reason to believe… *We are Spa people. We have our own club, and we have our own community.*

That has been of huge importance for that entire area ever since. To see the magnificent clubhouse and field that is there now is an enormous testament to what a community can do when it focuses on itself and is creative and developmental.

That would be the game for me, that is at the very apex of what is important to me from a sporting point of view. I would not have played for Kerry if it wasn't for that victory. It dictated the course of my playing career, and it led to winning the All-Irelands in 1969 and '70 with Kerry.

Playing in an All-Ireland was a childhood ambition realised.

I'm quite sure the game against Kilcummin was maybe not of the highest standard from a football perspective… *One never knows when one is playing.*

Paddy Dennehy got the defining goal, and we had Donie O'Sullivan starring, particularly in the second-half at centre-back. Donie was the driving force in that victory and remained for many years thereafter. He was a vitally important man in the Kerry set-up.

To a large extent as well, those players from that era remained my lifelong friends, and that bond would still be very strong. Sadly, some of them are gone.

The team also contained my brother Jim. He scored two vital points in that game even though he'd normally be a corner-back.

Playing half-forward that day was a man called Brian Fenton, whose son Brian is now fairly well-known in GAA circles wearing the sky blue of Dublin. Brian's brother Denis would have been part of the panel.

A Kerry game that meant most to me was winning the All-Ireland in 1969.

I was No 13, playing on the captain of the Offaly team – a man called John Egan, who is now deceased.

He became a very great friend because when I was working in Finglas in Dublin I stayed in Glasnevin, and John Egan and his wife Betty owned a very large guesthouse around the corner from where I lived. We met on occasions – he was a very fine man. He was part of that legendary full-back line along with Greg Hughes and Paddy McCormack… the famous trio. The three of them were still there in 1969.

I got the opening score of the game for Kerry. After that, any ball I got I tried to pass it off to a better placed colleague.

The sense of both relief and joy at achieving one's childhood ambition was enormous. Once the cup was presented – that was an era when the public came onto the field – I went across the field and met my brother.

In exhaustion, I just collapsed into his arms because of the amount of energy and time, both emotional and physical, one puts into a game like that.

There was a degree of disappointment for me at the start of that game because my club colleague Donie O'Sullivan was not selected for the final. But he was most encouraging to me before the game.

It was a great era because East Kerry were going strong as well at the time. Another game that would have meant a lot to me was East Kerry winning the first All-Ireland Club title. I was lucky enough to be captain of that team.

It was a huge reaffirmation for the Spa club that two players were on the first 21 of that winning All-Ireland team – Donie O'Sullivan and myself. That really reaffirmed the existence of the club and the people in their belief in the club, and I presume it gave them encouragement to go on.

That belief was reinforced when Donie was the captain when Kerry beat Meath in the All-Ireland final in 1970. Unfortunately, he was unable to finish that game. He had to go off with a hamstring injury. I was able to go up and accept the cup.

The overwhelming joy in 1970 when the cup came home to Spa, and when we visited the local schools, left an indelible influence on minds in the locality and was a huge inspiration for the young generation to continue playing the game.

The game continues to thrive in the area and there is that very definite link between club and county. The club meant an enormous amount to both Donie and myself, particularly given the circumstances in which the club was resurrected.

I think that's what always defined us along the way.

I worked in Dublin until 1974 and Donie until about '71. We tried very hard to always get home to Kerry at the weekends for the games that were being played... and there were *a lot* of games. We suffered from an early burnout in a way. Travelling up and down to Dublin under pressure is not fun. It might be alright leading up to an All-Ireland final, but doing it weekend after weekend was very demanding.

That game against Meath in 1970 was a very special final. It was an 80-minute final. And Donie being captain was extra-special. It is a game that is particularly remembered for a goal from Din Joe Crowley, who is now deceased... a dramatic goal after he soloed through.

I had sneaked in a goal earlier, which probably made victory fairly secure, but Din Joe's goal made it absolutely certain that we were going to win it. That is classed as one of the better games. There weren't too many more 80-minute finals.

Brendan Lynch, a retired psychiatric doctor, who played that day, played in a 60-minute, a 70-minute and an 80-minute final – the only player in the country to have done that. He played in a 60 minute final in 1968 when Kerry were beaten by Down.

I think one of the great marvels of the game is the way, when one pulls on the county jersey one totally forgets which club any player belongs to. We are all in it together.

I remember in 1970, East Kerry were playing the county final against Waterville the Sunday after the All-Ireland final. Waterville would have had two of the players on the winning Kerry team… Mick O'Dwyer and Mick O'Connell. But we had full support for one another on the field, and I think that is a wonderful bond in a county.

That's something very strong in Kerry always, historically as well, even going back to the era of the Civil War… playing of the game and wearing the Kerry jersey was a great healing process in the county post-Civil War.

That was always so true, and I would be very proud that that is still so.

Six of that Kerry team are dead – some of them passed away quite young. But I still have enormous respect for all of them as individuals, not just as footballers, but as people as well… *A very fine bunch of people.*

Should the hour ever come, I'd have no hesitation in ringing any one of them if I wanted help or advice, or support in any way. I know it would be there and I know they'd feel exactly the same way.

Football certainly was of some help to me politically when I ran for election for the Council, because there is that wonderful bond and friendship. People might say to me, 'Sure I remember you playing for East Kerry… or I remember the day we beat ye in the semi-final of the O'Donoghue Cup'. It is a wonderful bond within the county and still is, and I hope it will always remain so.

The most important thing in my life, next to one's own immediate home, is the Spa community. It is where I'm at, as they say in the modern lingo. It is where I know I have mutual friendship and where there is mutual respect, and that is all because of that victory in 1966.

Had that not happened, I mightn't have even come back down from Dublin to teach in Killarney. I could have become established in Finglas and played with Erin's Isle. The principal of the school in Finglas, a lovely man named Eddie Devlin, was very involved in the club. He sent me a note one day and said, 'Michael, if you would consider playing with Erin's Isle, we'd be delighted. I won't say any more about it, I'll just leave it up to you!'

I'm quite sure that would have happened had Spa not reformed in the Spring of '66. It was the seed that was sown that day that defined whatever football I played thereafter. If there is anything going to be put on my headstone, Spa will be first.

We are part of Killarney parish but there is still that rural element to it, so trying to protect and maintain our identity is of enormous importance because it will be very easy to become lost in the context of a major commercial town like Killarney.

Every time I see the Spa clubhouse and the magnificent three fields that they have now, I am filled with pride, especially coming from an era when we had a field with no dressing-rooms due to the generosity of a local farmer for a couple of pounds a year. It was of huge importance to me and it still is. I have nephews and nieces who are involved with the club and it is a wonderful thing to see, that continuity.

In the Spa context, there are four schools – Tiernaboul, Loughquittane, Loreto, and Lissivigeen. Away back in the 50s, in about 1954, a man called Tadhg O'Sullivan came as principal to Lissivigeen school. He was native to the area, up near where the Spa field is now. He was a great teacher and a huge football follower.

A local farmer, just deceased aged 99, let us use what was called his bog field. That was the genesis of the resurrection.

Every lunchtime we would go up to the bog field and Tadhg would be there.

In an East Kerry schools competition, these four schools would play together and always be beaten by the town team. Of course, this reinforced the importance of coming back and getting our own back sometimes. Internal rivalries are very important. That was a defining moment. *One thing leads to another. The chain is never ending.*

I would have been one of the very few players who came from a void, in the sense of having no club. If Spa had existed in the early-60s, I probably would have played minor and won an All-Ireland or two. But I had no place to showcase what I could do. Kerry did win the 1962 and '63 All-Irelands – they would have been my years as a minor. Kerry also won their first under-21 All-Ireland in 1964.

I remember in New York once, somebody came up to me in Gaelic Park and said, 'You're from the Spa'. That meant so much to me!

My senior Kerry career would not have happened except for the miracle of the rebirth in '66, and from that… *Everything grew.*

GER O'KEEFFE

KERRY 2-5 GALWAY 1-8
All-Ireland MFC Final
Croke Park
SEPTEMBER 27, 1970

Losing at minor and under-21 level gave Kerry a fierce hunger that presented itself in 1975 (Ger O'Keeffe is at the right on the front row before the All-Ireland final against Dublin) and never left Mick O'Dwyer's brilliant team.

★ **KERRY:** P O'Mahoney; B O'Shea, J Clifford, J Deenihan; D Healy, M O'Sullivan (0-1), **G O'Keeffe (1-0)**; P Lynch (0-1), J Long (0-1); C O'Connell (1-0), P Brosnan, G Power; G Dillon, J Egan, J Murphy (0-2). Subs: T McEllistrim for O'Shea, G Browne for Murphy.

★ **GALWAY:** PJ Higgins; S Cloonan, A Marren, S Campbell; PJ Burke, M Geraghty, J Corcoran; P Silke, T O'Connor; J Lardner, M Rooney (0-2), M Burke; I Barrett (1-1), M Walsh, J Tobin (0-5). Sub: J Meehan for Walsh.

THE ACTION

GER O'KEEFFE POPPED up with a rare goal from the half-back line to save Kerry blushes right at the death to earn a replay against a resilient Galway at Croke Park.

Featuring future household names such as John Egan, Mickey Ned O'Sullivan, Ger Power, Jimmy Deenihan, Ger O'Keeffe and Paudie O'Mahoney, Kerry mounted a dramatic comeback from being four points down in the dying minutes to ensure a dramatic finish. The Kingdom, fighting for their first minor All-Ireland title in seven years, turned the game on its head in the space of two minutes.

A curtain-raiser to Kerry senior footballers' convincing seven-point All-Ireland final win over Meath, the first-half was a low-scoring affair and level at half time at 0-2 apiece. Scores came a little more frequently after the restart – midway through the second-half it was Kerry who held the narrowest of margins, 0-4 to 0-3. With 17 minutes to go, however, it looked like a Galway win was on the cards, but a goal from Cahersiveen's Christy O'Connell – a great effort which hit the underside of the crossbar and bounced down over the line – sparked the game into life.

The title looked like it was heading west six minutes from time when Iomar Barrett blasted home from close range, despite being closely marked by Batt O'Shea, John Clifford, and Jimmy Deenihan. Galway led by four points (1-7 to 1-3) with just over five minutes remaining on the clock.

Credit to the young Kerry footballers. From a John Long '50', O'Keeffe towered above the Galway defence to sublimely punch the ball into the back of the net. In dramatic fashion, Long grabbed his fifth point of the afternoon a minute later when he sent over the equalising point from an angled free.

Paudie Lynch burst through the Galway defence for a great point to put Kerry one up but with only 30 seconds to play Barrett shot the equalising point. The final whistle came with the kickout. In the thrilling replay, Galway edged out Kerry by 1-11 to 1-10 to capture the title, the winning point coming in the last minute.

★ ★ ★ ★ ★

66

A GAME THAT stands out for me is the minor All-Ireland final defeat in 1970. We drew the first game... I got a goal near the end to bring it to a replay. I was taken off then with an eye injury the second day. Galway won the replay.

Our years together playing minor, and then playing under-21, were really the making of that famous 1975 senior team. It all started with that minor team.

I was carted off in the replay... that's the *bad memory*. The *good memory* was getting the draw.

If you look at the sequence of events that really transformed Kerry at that time... we lost to Galway in that All-Ireland minor final in 1970, we lost to Galway again in an under-21 final in '72, and then we beat Mayo in the All-Ireland under-21 final in '73. Out of that 1973 team came a pile of players who played in 10 All-Ireland finals. It was a time when we all seemed to advance together from young boys to men, very quickly... then culminating in winning the All-Ireland in 1975. It was in the making from 1970, really.

Somebody sent me on a photograph of a programme recently.

We played Tyrone and beat them 2-14 to 0-12 in the National League in 1974. Ger Power was right half-back, my brother Tony was centre half-back, I was left half-back, John O'Keeffe was midfield... and you had Mikey Sheehy playing corner-forward. There were five of us from Austin Stacks playing with Kerry at the same time.

At that stage, all the older Kerry players who had played in the period of time from 1969 to '74 were all slipping by, and you had this new crop of players coming through.

It was an exciting time because of the fact that there were a lot of athletes... *And fellas who fancied themselves as athletes.* We had PE teachers, and we had a lot of people who were very interested in sport. Really, with this young generation, we were all interested in winning, but we were *also* interested in training hard and reaching our full potential.

Rather than a specific game, to me it was... *That period of time*...which was absolutely fantastic.

It was a phenomenal time for our club too.

The club would probably have been more successful if the county team wasn't so successful, because sometimes we ended up playing county finals a week after All-Ireland finals and things like that, which was really unfair on the club.

I played junior for Kerry as well.

It was a kind of a transition. You were going through the various stages of life and going through the various stages of your football career. At that time, I had played National League for Kerry in 1972, '73, and '74 – we won the three National Leagues, even though we'd lost to Cork in the 1973 and the '74 Munster finals.

There was a bit of learning to be done as well. In that transition period the older players were fading and the younger fellas probably weren't getting enough of a go; I suppose the selectors and the management at the time felt we were a bit young, but as a group of young players at that time... *We were raring to go.*

You'd John Egan, Mickey Ned O'Sullivan, Paudie Lynch, Paudie O'Mahoney, Jimmy Deenihan, myself, John O'Keeffe and Ger Power. We'd a huge crop of players at that time raring to go. It was extraordinary that such a group of players happened to come together all at once.

After Mick O'Dwyer took over as a manager in 1975, we were badly beaten by Meath in a National League quarter-final.

There was a mixture of the old and the young, and I'd say he decided at that stage he was going to put his faith in the young fellas. He did keep one or two of the older fellas. I had played with O'Dwyer in 1972 and '73 and he must have known that fellas were fading after being beaten by Offaly in the 1972 final.

A few of the younger lads were subs at that time... Jimmy Deenihan, Mickey Ned, myself and Ger Power. And then you'd John O'Keeffe and Paudie Lynch who were on the team.

There was so much enthusiasm within our minor team in 1970.

You always get that with minors anyway, but we got the smell of success and we realised how close we were to winning an All-Ireland minor title.

A lot of our fellas then, at that stage, went to college and played Sigerson with UCC, UCD, Maynooth, and UCG. It was continuous football then for that period which kind of hardened fellas up so they'd be capable of soon playing senior football.

The universities competition at that time was very strong, and it was very popular. There were a lot of inter-county lads playing with the colleges and also with the Combined Universities. It was a transition stage and we were getting battle-hardened from all the competitive games that we had played since turning 18.

My goal played a huge part in getting the replay against Galway in the final – it was very close to the end. But we were unlucky. It was a desperate, miserable day for the replay. We were probably unlucky to lose it.

It was a highly competitive game and it was good open football. The Galway players were very competitive and they looked very good, but the extraordinary thing about it was they never translated their minor success of 1970 or their under-21 success of '72 into senior success afterwards.

I was used to success at an early age… winning the Hogan Cup, winning the Minor Championship in Kerry. But, then suddenly, we lost a minor final, lost an under-21 final in 1972, lost the senior All-Ireland in '72… lost Munster Championships in 1973 and '74, so there was an awful lot of losses in a few short years.

I think for young fellas at that stage, trying to develop in our careers, it was a blessing in disguise because it kept our feet on the ground. You think you're good, but maybe you aren't *that good!* It is down to the individual really.

It is down to attitude, and I think a pile of our fellas just lived football at that time. We used to have some tremendous training sessions. When we trained at that time, we didn't train like the athletes of today at seventy-five percent. We trained at one hundred and ten percent the whole time, and the training was competitive…the full-back line would have competitions amongst themselves to see who was the fastest.

We had an unbelievable competitive spirit in all the players.

We had won the Hogan Cup in 1969 and we had won Frewen Cups and under-15 Munster Championships on the way up.

Paudie Lynch, Paudie O'Mahoney and myself… we played together for The Sem for a good few years. John O'Keeffe and my brother Tony were a year ahead of us but we were all part of the team that won the Hogan Cup in '69. And of course, that also helped in our development. That was a tremendous achievement because that was the first time St Brendan's College had won it.

The impact that Mícheál Hayes had… a primary schoolteacher in Tralee, and when he got involved in the Stacks club, it was massive. He nurtured a pile of quality players down through the years. He gave us the *grá* for football. He came from Kilkenny.

One incident remained with me forever.

The Stacks' team were going on a trip to Kilkenny and Mícheál told me I was too young. Some of the lads were two years older than me, but I was absolutely distraught over the fact that I wasn't brought on the trip. It gelled in me that I was never going to end up being an also-ran in the future.

That event, of all events, was the thing that really pushed me on to believe… *I'm as good as these fellas. I can do as well as these fellas irrespective of my age.*

We were 12 or 13 at the time, but I was desperately disappointed that I didn't get on the trip. That attitude kind of permeated through the whole group of players that played together. There was this kind of 'do or die' attitude that we never wanted to be second.

The biggest problem then is that, when you win, you believe you can't be beaten by anybody… but in 1976 and '77 we were found wanting against Dublin.

The friendships we made are great.

There is a good crew living in Tralee… Mikey Sheehy, Ger Power, Johno, myself, 'Bomber' Liston… and you've 'Ogie Moran and Seán Walsh… and Jimmy Deenihan is just out in Finuge… and we'd be very friendly, the whole lot of us still.

Medals are something to show that you did it, but it is *how* you did it and the *fellas* you played with and *how* you got on together and the *friendships* you have together… that's what is absolutely fantastic.

We had a great life for many, many years.

We were lucky in that a lot of our players were able to get jobs in Kerry or around, whereas a lot of my engineering classmates in Galway had to go abroad for work. Playing football helped the teachers to get jobs in Kerry, and for other fellas to get jobs here and there. We were lucky that we didn't lose too many people along the way, which happened a lot, particularly for university students who would often go their own way and follow their careers.

I worked with Kerry County Council as a student engineer for the summers, and I was effectively told that if I passed my final exams that there was a job there for me. That was like manna from heaven at that time, but I mean I wouldn't have been offered a job if I wasn't playing football for Kerry.

About seventy-five percent of our players were living locally. You had a couple of fellas, like Jacko and Mick Spillane living in Dublin, but generally most of the players were local, which was a big help. You didn't have this massive strain of having to travel to training and all that sort of thing.

When you are a young fella, you forget so much or fail to see things, because you are living in the moment more than when you get older.

But I can never forget Mick O'Connell.

I remember back in 1973 we were playing Cork down in Páirc Uí Chaoimh.

Mick O'Connell was still playing.

A few of the younger players were playing… Johno, Paudie Lynch, Ger Power… myself.

O'Connell preferred to come straight to the stadium.

He wouldn't meet beforehand – at that time we travelled in cars together and met someplace for a sandwich before the match. O'Connell arrived on his own and your man at the turnstiles didn't recognise him, so he turned around and walked away.

He just disappeared.

I also remember being in a hotel when the Kerry minors and Kerry seniors were playing in the All-Ireland final in 1970, and heard Micko telling the waitress to ensure that she put four raw eggs into a cup… and that I drank it.

I drank it. *I'd no choice!* I later trained with Mick O'Connell while he was doing a skipper's course in Galway. We used to train in Pearse Stadium. Afterwards we'd eat in the Warwick Hotel in Galway and O'Connell made sure that I had a good steak.

Even though he might be giving out to me during the training and things like that, it was all forgotten about when we sat down together and he recognised that I was a student and I needed a bit of meat on me.

Every night after training, Mick O'Connell and I ate T-bone steaks!

GER POWER

AUSTIN STACKS 2-8 NA HAGHASAIGH 1-6
Kerry SFC Final
Austin Stack Park, Tralee
OCTOBER 21, 1973

Winning the Kerry Senior Championship in 1973, on a team managed by his father Jackie (a month after the legendary Limerick star had led his county to the All-Ireland hurling title) is a game that lives with Ger Power.

★ **AUSTIN STACKS:** T Brick; G Scollard, M McCarthy, J Barry; N Kelter, A O'Keeffe, G O'Keeffe; J O' Keeffe, T Sheehan; M Sheehy (0-7), **G Power (1-0)**, T Kennington; B Curtin, JJ Barrett (0-1), T O'Regan (1-0). Sub: F Dillon for Sheehan.

★ **NA HAGHASAIGH:** J Bambury; R Devane, P Scanlon, S MacGearailt (0-1); S Long, M Ó Sé, R Casey; J Long, M Slattery; J O'Sullivan, T McDonnell (0-1), P Ó Sé (1-1); S Casey, L Higgins (0-1), G Dillon (0-2). Subs: T MacGearailt for S Long, G O'Connor for McDonnell.

THE ACTION

GOOD THINGS COME to those who wait and that was certainly the case when Austin Stacks became the kingpins of Kerry for the first time in 37 years, thanks to a convincing five-point victory over West Kerry divisional side Na hAghasaigh which secured their sixth ever Kerry SFC title.

In summer-like conditions, 12,000 were packed into Austin Stack Park in Tralee long before the match got underway. Managed by the legendary Limerick hurler and coach Jackie Power, who was fresh from leading his native county to All-Ireland success a month previously, Austin Stacks got off to the perfect start.

The game was won and lost in the 12th minute when Jackie's son Ger Power careered clean through the West Kerry defence to score the first of his side's two goals.

Eight minutes later, Tommy 'Bracker' O'Regan delivered the killer-blow, diving low to fist home the second goal following lovely build-up play by Tommy Kennington, Power, and Mikey Sheehy. The early goals gave the Rock Street men the confidence and the authority that breeds champions. At half-time Stacks went in with a seven-point lead, 2-3 to 0-2.

Na hAghasaigh, the original name of West Kerry's divisional team, who were in search of their first ever senior county title, had more than their fair share of chances in the opening half-hour. However, they frittered away some fine scoring chances and with the battle at midfield going steadily against them they were under constant pressure.

But, hoping to cause a fright 10 days before Halloween, the West Kerry boys gave their best in the second-half, reducing the Stacks' lead to four points at one stage when a certain Páidí Ó Sé scored his side's only goal.

On the day, Ger Power proved to be the match-winner. His memorable goal – a gem of opportunism – sent supporters into raptures after the impressive centre-forward cut through the West Kerry defence like a knife through butter. The result kick-started a golden era for the Tralee club, who went on to lift the county title again in 1975, '76, and '79.

★★★★★

66

I GREW UP on Ashe Street beside the old Dingle Railway. My father was working with CIÉ and he was transferred from Limerick in 1952... down to Tralee.

CIÉ had houses there on Ashe Street, where Hogan's funeral parlour and a flower shop are now... we lived in one of the houses along there. At the back, there was a fine big yard, a huge yard, and all the neighbours' kids played there. The Kennellys from *Kerry's Eye* were there and Willie O'Connor, the former secretary of the County Board, was just down the road.

I had two brothers... David who is still alive and Jackie, who died the year before last. We used to knock lumps out of each other there between hurling and football... and we'd have a nice few of the neighbours' kids coming into the yard. We broke windows everywhere... all the windows of the railway offices were beside us. Luckily enough, my father was the manager there.

Because we were breaking windows... *Left, right and centre!*

That's where it all started for me. It really was a great start in life!

I was born in Annacotty, in Limerick. We moved to Tralee in 1952 when I was only 10 days old.

They've put up a beautiful statue of my father Jackie... a fantastic statue in Annacotty, looking down over the village. It is a hurling statue.

He was a huge influence in my life.

He was involved with the hurling here in Kerry as well. He used to referee, and he trained the Kerry team – they won the junior All-Ireland in the 60s. He was also manager of the Limerick team in 1973 when they won the All-Ireland hurling title... the same year as he was manager of the Stacks team that won the county football championship. It all came together for him.

There are a few games in my career that stand out.

What started it all was the county championship win in 1973.

Austin Stacks hadn't won it in 37 years. That was the start of it because we had a good team at that time. We had five players who ended up on the Kerry team. You had John O'Keeffe, Ger O'Keeffe, Mikey Sheehy, Tony O'Keeffe and myself.

And then you had Dinny Long coming after us as well.

There was a huge crop of players who went on to represent their county. But our careers more or less started after winning that championship in 1973.

I used to play centre-forward for the Stacks but ended up playing wing-back for Kerry. They changed me back after a few games in the late-70s. I was put back to wing-back for a while, and then I ended up playing wing-forward and corner-forward.

The win in 1973 was the result of work done for many years. There was a chap called Micheál Hayes. Micheál was from Kilkenny and he came to the national school down there – the boys national school in Cloonalour, and he organised hurling, football… and a basketball blitz in the school. That was the start of it. He was then also involved with the Stacks club. Himself and James Hobbert were involved in the underage set-up. They really got it together. They brought us everywhere. As young kids we'd go to Cork… we'd go to Dublin to play matches.

Kerry also won the under-21 All-Ireland in 1973. But when we beat the Dubs in 1975, that was the start of everything. We were all young fellas… Jimmy Deenihan, John Egan, Mikey, Ger O'Keeffe… all that group came up from the under-21s in '73.

There were about four or five of us on the Kerry team at the time they were beaten by Offaly in 1972… the late goal that hopped up into the net. And then Mick O'Dwyer came on in, and he nearly cleaned out everything. There were only three players left – Donie O'Sullivan, Brendan Lynch and John O'Keeffe.

Everyone else was gone… retired. The under-21s from '73 came in and, I suppose, it went to our heads… straight out, to win the All-Ireland in '75. It was a great win. It was a great start to a career.

It was the beginning of Mick O'Dwyer. The fitness levels going into that match in '75 were something else. John O'Keeffe and Brendan Lynch at that time were the two oldest… everybody else was in their early-twenties.

I remember that game well. I was marking Bobby Doyle… I was playing wing-back at that stage. It was a semi-wet day. We were well fired up going into that game. Kerry hadn't won an All-Ireland since 1970.

I was captain when we won the All-Ireland in 1980. I had been captain of the Kerry minor team in 1970 when we were beaten by a point by Galway. And then

KERRY'S GREATEST FOOTBALLERS

10 years later when I was captain of the senior team, we were lucky enough to win against Roscommon.

I played with Mick O'Connell.

I played with Mick O'Dwyer.

I played with all the old team.

I also played with Donie O'Sullivan and Liam Higgins. Johnny Culloty was trainer at that time. They all more or less disappeared at the start of the National League in 1974.

In our time, we wanted to be Mick O'Connell. No matter what sport, you have to have your heroes.

Mick O'Dwyer was coming to the end of his career when I was playing with him. I think Micko just had a good look at what Kevin Heffernan was doing in Dublin and thought... *Look if we want to win it we have to do this.*

It's as simple as that!

He then changed the whole type of training we did. It went totally physical fitness. We could play football from May, but up to that we were more or less running the field... *Morning, noon and night.*

But it paid off!

The game is going that exact same way at the moment. If you go back to Dublin's six in-a row, the Dubs were fitter than anybody else. They were physically stronger, physically fitter than any other team, and they could bring on subs just as strong as anyone else on the pitch.

I think they were more professional than everybody else. They had the facilities, they had the personnel – they had all the right people in the right positions to help build a professional team.

Under Micko, a lot of players would try and sneak off and play with the club because, at the end of the day, we were going back to the club – you were under pressure from all angles.

Micko was before his time really. The best thing about Micko is... forget about Kerry! He went to other counties afterwards, and he did it there as well. He did it with Kildare; he brought them to an All-Ireland final. He did it in Laois and Wicklow.

I don't think any other manager has done as much as he did. Others stuck with their own county and when they were finished there, they gave it up.

But Micko lived for football!

He knew everybody. He knew the club scene, he knew all the young fellas coming up… he had one hundred percent interest in everybody.

The success in 1975 came a bit quick, but it was a good thing because we lost in 1976 and '77, but we came back then and won. At that stage we were young enough to keep going.

Micko was still there, and he knew exactly how to get the best out of everybody. His man-management was excellent. There was always a line you didn't cross. He was the boss and you knew he was *the boss*.

It was good that there was a distance between Micko and the team that came on afterwards… because there were only about two or three of us who had played with him.

Ninety percent of the team never played with Mick O'Dwyer, so they didn't know him.

I played with Micko for one season in 1973.

We were beaten by Cork in '73… they hammered us. After the 1974 Munster final then, a lot of players were gone by the time the National League started… the league at that time started in October after the championship.

Winning four All-Irelands in-a-row was special… especially after being beaten in 1976 and '77… and to come back then and win in '78! Then to lose in 1982 and to come back in '84 and win three more… that was some achievement too.

But football has changed now – the whole scene has changed.

The National League didn't mean much to us at all.

Well, if Kerry won it… it was more money for the County Board. But in our day, if you were going away to some places, fellas would be out the Saturday night having a few jars before the match on the Sunday and stuff like that.

They don't do that anymore. It is a different game.

You'd be wondering… *Is the talent there now that was there in the old days?* It is a more structured game. They are more or less told how to play. In our years, no forward was told how to play football… *If he didn't do it off-the-cuff, he shouldn't be up there.*

I look back at the whole thing with pride. The friendships I made are great.

There is a big golf tournament every year in Beaufort for John Egan – the John Egan Memorial Cup. There are always a huge amount of players there, even players from different counties there!

I think that's the good thing about the GAA – afterwards, you have friendships with all the other county players, and they come together and help out.

Sport in general, helps you with your life because you can be sure that you'll get the highs and the lows. *And you might have more lows than highs*!

It prepares you for life, because you are not going to be winning all of the time. When you leave football, you are going to have ups and downs in your normal everyday life. Sport prepares you for things like that!

I was involved with the Stacks afterwards, with the late Paul Lucey. We managed to win the county championship in 1994.

Then I did two years with the Stacks under-10s about three years ago. Some of them were brilliant footballers… *Absolutely brilliant footballers!*

I wouldn't be the best person on the sideline to stay nice and calm… so I gave it up! I would be a prime case of either getting into a row on the sideline or getting a heart attack. I enjoyed it though. I was amazed at how good some young fellas were. I'd be really surprised if they don't make it to senior… *They were just brilliant!*

The underage in the Austin Stacks club in the 60s and 70s was also absolutely brilliant. We had hurling, we had basketball, and we had football… all those three things were going on at the same time.

Fair dues to the people that organised it, because each one helps out the other game – basketball helps with football and hurling. The underage at that stage in the Stacks club was fantastic.

Absolutely fantastic! And it paid off. It is the only way to go… *Look after the young boys and girls.*

99

MICKEY NED O'SULLIVAN

KENMARE DISTRICT 2-12 SHANNON RANGERS 1-5
Kerry SFC Final
Austin Stack Park, Tralee
NOVEMBER 3, 1974

Kenmare District's victory in 1974 afforded Mickey Ned O'Sullivan the honour of leading his county the following year which ended with a glorious All-Ireland win over reigning champions Dublin (above, Mickey Ned does the honours with Dublin captain Seán Doherty before the game).

★ **KENMARE:** D O'Mahony; T Sheehan, J O'Sullivan, P Kelliher; M Murphy (1-0), D O'Neill, M Spillane; F O'Sullivan, D O'Sullivan (0-1); P Spillane (0-4), **M O'Sullivan (0-3)**, P O'Neill; P Finnegan, P O'Sullivan (1-0), PJ McIntyre (0-4). Subs: N McCarthy for O'Neill, D Finnegan for F O'Sullivan, T O'Connor for P Finnegan.

★ **SHANNON RANGERS:** P O'Hanlon; P O'Connell, P O'Donoghue, J Wrenn; D Mulvihill, M McEllistrim, D 'Ogie' Moran (0-1); T O'Donnell, P O'Connell; J Walsh (0-3), B Walsh, E O'Donoghue; B McCarthy (1-0), R Bamburv (0-1), M Carrig.

THE ACTION

HISTORY WAS CREATED at a windswept Austin Stack Park as Kenmare District won their first-ever county senior football title. The hot favourites Shannon Rangers were expected to dominate at midfield but instead found themselves playing second fiddle in the area, with the attacking Kenmare half-backs causing all sorts of problems for the North Kerry side.

The game was only two minutes old when Kenmare landed their first goal, when full-forward Paul O'Sullivan did well to connect with a ground ball that had broken loose off a Rangers' defender and his kick ended up in the back of the net.

Kenmare quickly added a further point when former Offaly inter-county player PJ McIntyre punched over a point in dashing style, and Pat Spillane added to Rangers' woes after a pass from Mickey Ned O'Sullivan. McIntyre then grabbed his second to make it 1-3 to 0-1 after only nine minutes of play.

Kenmare added their second goal when wing back and captain Michael Murphy went on a solo run before shooting home.

And after Brian McCarthy's penalty miss just shy of the half-hour mark, it certainly proved to be an uphill battle for Shannon Rangers. The divisional side, made up of Templenoe, Tuosist, Kenmare Shamrocks and Kilgarvan, had the game wrapped up by half-time when they led by 2-8 to 0-2.

Rangers' McCarthy made up for his first-half penalty miss with an early second-half goal after a cross by Eamon O'Donoghue. After this short-lived comeback by the North Kerry side, points by McIntyre and Pat Spillane (two) put Kenmare ahead by 2-11 to 1-4 entering the last quarter.

Crucially, it was Kenmare's forwards who really stole the show. Mickey Ned O'Sullivan was truly superb and Pat Spillane, PJ McIntyre and Paul O'Sullivan also excelled, treating the large crowd to a delightful exhibition.

★★★★★

66

I GREW UP in the town of Kenmare and there were two factors that had a major influence on me.

One, there was a garda transferred to Kenmare in the mid-60s called PJ McIntyre. He had played with Offaly and he played with Kerry in hurling and football. And boy... was he passionate about football! He got a lot of my age-group together and he set up a team and he took us training.

And at the same time, I went to boarding school in Coláiste Íosagáin in Ballyvourney, which was a hot-bed of football – mainly lads from Kerry and Cork.

There was great rivalry in the school, but football was kind of a religion and during my years there I had the privilege of playing in six Corn Uí Mhuirí finals, including two draws.

I also played in three Frewen Cup finals, and believe it or not I lost them all. But the experience was invaluable. We were playing at a very high standard and we were playing against St Brendan's, who had John O'Keeffe, Paudie Lynch... Ger O'Keeffe.

And then we were playing against Tralee who had Mikey Sheehy and Ger Power. We were playing at the highest level from 14 to 18... which was very important.

My father Edward – known as Neddy Ned – had a great interest in football and my uncle Mike Ned had won a county championship in 1942 hurling with Kenmare.

And going back three or four generations, they would have all played with Kenmare, but mainly hurling. So, there was a tradition there as well.

The game I enjoyed most in my career was with Kenmare – the 1974 county final. It was the first time that the Kenmare District won a county championship. It was breaking new ground; it was the fact that the whole area had come together, and decided that we had the talent and that we'd go the whole way. There was a great sense of satisfaction because there was a great team morale and a great time spirit.

The sense of group achievement was very important. It gave us an awful lot of satisfaction, especially for the supporters who followed football in the area down through the years – their ambitions were realised, as well as the players and the management.

What stood out on that day was that we scored nothing from frees – all the scores were from play. Shannon Rangers had a very good team at the time, but every score came from play which was unique in any county final.

It was all down to work-rate. That is the one thing I enjoy and remember most about the game.

Going back to the town with the cup and to see everybody was part of it – and they all came out to celebrate – was a reflection of the purpose of the GAA in terms of identification with place.

It goes back to what Canon Sheehan said long ago. He wrote an article... *The honour of the little village.* The GAA club is the one constant in Kenmare – the town and the population composition will change, but the GAA club is constant and it has the strongest roots.

I learned a lot from that year.

You could see what it took to achieve success; that there were no shortcuts and everything had to be covered. It was all about work-rate and attitude, and getting a cohesive group together, one with a good morale... and doing the right things.

Because we won, I was appointed captain the following year with Kerry. For some people, it would have affected their game, but it enhanced my game because of the sense of responsibility that you had to the team – you had to dig deep, much deeper than you ever dug before.

The one Kerry game that stands out for me is the one I remember the least – the 1975 All-Ireland final.

When you get an opportunity to captain a team in an All-Ireland final, it is probably the pinnacle of any inter-county player's career. To be representing such an amazing team that subsequently went on to win eight All-Irelands – it was such a great honour just to be part of that group.

But, to be the first captain of that group was something that I look back on with pride. Just to be associated with so many great players... I wouldn't say I was as good as them, but I was associated with them, and I was part of the team.

There was a great culture of excellence. There were no barriers – they kept pushing back the barriers all of the time and they stayed hungry. They were always trying to improve. No matter what they had achieved, it was put aside until the next game... *Which was the most important game.*

They felt they had to get to a higher level in their preparation for the next year if they were going to achieve. It was that sheer effort of pushing back barriers and that hunger that never dissipated, until they physically dissipated.

It is all about creating the environment and, I suppose, Mick O'Dwyer was instrumental in creating that environment where egos didn't exist. It was about the team. He was instrumental in getting players to compete against each other for positions. Nobody was handed a position.

Year after year, they had to fight for their positions, and that kept the hunger because there was pressure on us all of the time.

Everyone had to fight for it... year after year. That was the secret.

It was unlike Dublin in the last decade.

Dublin achieved by succession. They brought in three or four new players every year.

Kerry didn't have that luxury.

Dublin had the luxury of bringing in 10 or 15 percent of new players every year and getting rid of the top few age-wise. But O'Dwyer didn't have many coming through at the time because they all were of a similar age-group.

Instead, he used a lot of psychology to put lads under pressure. He'd create situations. He'd say... *Oh so-and-so is playing well now...* and he'd whisper in their ear that they were under pressure for their position. That kept the hunger.

I brought a lot of what I learned under Mick O'Dwyer into management myself. You obviously would have learned because nobody had achieved then what he had achieved as a manager, and you would see what he was doing and observe his man-management skills.

But, obviously, time moves on and you have to bring your own stamp, and your own managerial attributes so you can succeed as well.

My best friends were part of that Kerry team and we are still in close contact. I was probably lucky in that I played with the old Kerry team and the new Kerry team.

I went into the senior panel at 18 when the 1969 and '70 team was finishing up, which included the great Mick O'Connell, Mick O'Dwyer and Donie

O'Sullivan… all that age group.

They were exceptional players.

And, then, I was on the team during the transition from 1971 to '75, so I had the opportunity of playing with the older guys and moulding in with the new guys, across two generations of two great teams.

It is a great privilege to have played with the likes of Mick O'Connell, who was a complete perfectionist in everything he did. Just to watch him… aesthetically he was so graceful. It was pure economy of effort. He could tip a ball over the bar from 60 metres off the ground – total economy of effort and aesthetically so pleasing.

Despite all the medals and All-Ireland finals, the friendships stand out for me. You go through a similar education, you go through a similar 10-year training process, and you're in a bubble with a group of players where nobody can hide… you have so much in common.

And you know everyone inside out, warts and all. You are accepted as a group.

In the end, everybody suppresses the ego in the interests of the team. We socialised a lot together, we travelled a lot together on trips, we roomed a lot together, and those were the closest people in our lives for a long period of time.

It is a journey, it is not a destination.

The journey is far more rewarding than the destination… *The destination is transient.*

JOHN O'KEEFFE
(& PAUDIE O'MAHONEY)

KERRY 1-14 CORK 0-7
Munster SFC Final
Fitzgerald Stadium, Killarney
JULY 13, 1975

John O'Keeffe (in action against Dublin's Jimmy Keaveney in the 1976 All-Ireland final) never expected that his career would land him in the middle of an illustrious Kerry full-back line.

★ **KERRY: P. O'Mahoney**; G O'Keeffe, **J O'Keeffe**, J Deenihan; P Ó Sé; T Kennelly, G Power; P Lynch, P McCarthy (0-1); B Lynch (0-4); M Sheehy (0-3), M O'Sullivan (0-1); J Egan (0-2), J Bunyan, P Spillane (1-1). Subs: D 'Ogie' Moran (0-1) for Lynch, G O'Driscoll (0-1) for B Lynch.

★ **CORK:** B Morgan; B Murphy, H Kelleher, M O'Doherty; KJ O'Sullivan, K Kehilly, C Hartnett; D Long, D McCarthy; D Allen (0-3), S Coughlan, A Murphy (0-1); JB Murphy, D Barron (0-1), R Cummins (0-2). Subs: D Hunt for O'Doherty, J Coleman for O'Sullivan, J Barrett for A Murphy.

THE ACTION

CORK WERE LOOKING for their first-ever three in-a-row in Munster but were denied by a rejuvenated Kerry team that released their power under newly appointed manager Mick O'Dwyer. It was in with the new and out with the old, as O'Dwyer handed championship debuts to Tim Kennelly, Denis 'Ogie' Moran and Pat Spillane in Kerry's 3-14 to 0-9 semi-final defeat of Tipperary a month previously.

By this stage, Kerry icons Paud O'Donoghue, Donie O'Sullivan and Mick O'Connell had played their final game in the green and gold – in the Munster final defeat against Cork in 1974.

In 1975, Kerry led by 1-7 to 0-3 at the break, and awaited Cork's response.

However, the second-half saw the kind of performance Kerry supporters had grown accustomed to, having dominated Munster in the 50s and the 60s... winning 16 titles in that 20-year period.

In the opening minutes of the game Cork had completely commanded the play but, with both sides level at 0-2 each, the defining moment came in the 13th minute when a Pat Spillane shot deflected off Martin O'Doherty and went over the goal-line.

Kerry goalkeeper Paudie O'Mahoney became one of the heroes of the afternoon when he brilliantly saved a Jimmy Barry-Murphy penalty, pushing the ball out for a '50'. Both sides exchanged points in the early stages of the second-half but Kerry began to pull away midway through as points from Mikey Sheehy and 'Ogie' Moran put 10 points between the two sides – 1-12 to 0-5.

Later, a powerful shot on goal by Seamus Coughlan was assertively dealt with by O'Mahoney as Cork only managed six points from play against a formidable Kerry side. As referee Brendan Cross blew for full-time, Kerry's football pride was restored and Sligo awaited the Kingdom in Croke Park.

★★★★★

66

THE 1975 MUNSTER final was 'the start' and it also led to the realisation that this was a fairly special Kerry team, especially with so many young players. We mainly had an under-21 squad as the spine of the team, and then Brendan Lynch and myself were the two elder statesmen… I was 24 at the time, Brendan was 26.

From my own point of view, it was my first day out at full-back as such. It was kind of going into the unknown a little bit, particularly against such a good Cork team at the time. Cork had won the 1973 All-Ireland and probably underachieved with that particular team, so it was a pretty daunting task … especially in Killarney which was always high pressure; we were really under the microscope.

I was marking Ray Cummins. He was 'the director' of the way they operated… he was issuing, he was *calling* and making space…a real threat. It was a real test for us to see could we manage that task.

Jimmy Deenihan and myself were in the full-back line for the long-haul. There was a little bit of movement in the other corner now and again.

Why does this game stand out? There are always memories of Munster finals in Killarney; there's something special about all of those days.

You must deliver. Killarney is pretty daunting.

The supporters are great to clap your back before the game, but you better get the right result if you are walking back down towards the town afterwards. But *walking up* to the stadium made the whole thing so real… in amongst the local support. I often found the Munster final, pressure-wise, an occasion that was even more daunting than an All-Ireland final. It is *local*, there is no escape, and you had to deliver. *This was it!*

In fairness to Mick O'Dwyer, he prepared accordingly. There was no such thing as Micko leaving a little bit in reserve for further games… it was like Russian roulette… it was all-or-nothing. The preparation was geared towards a final… *Winner takes all.* We had to be at our prime.

There was some indication back in the early-70s that I might play full-back.

We had played Cork in an under-21 Munster final. At that time, I played all my football at either centre-back or midfield, and all of a sudden the team was announced in the dressing-room and I was full-back. This was the first indication… I had no idea that was going to happen.

I felt my career was over.

This is it.

I was being dumped back to the full-back line. It was Gerald McKenna – he often tells the story, and we laugh about it – who suggested the switch.

I was marking an outstanding player in Declan Barron. We had a great tussle. There were numerous aerial duels between the two of us.

Now, Cork won the game alright, but I think I showed something. And I think that was in the memory bank for O'Dwyer and the selectors. So it wasn't as if I just jumped into the No 3 jersey on the day of the Munster final in 1975. There was a good bit of preparation and O'Dwyer and the selectors would have seen it in training.

That's where you *really* see it, when you are training and marking the Kerry forwards. That's where you show that you are able for the job. There is no way you'd be in there otherwise.

After that under-21 game I went back with my club, and UCD in the Sigerson Cup, playing midfield. With Austin Stacks we won the county championship in 1973 for the first time in about 40 years and I was playing midfield.

I really enjoyed midfield, even with the Sem before that… it was centre-back or midfield, and playing full-back was just something I hadn't planned for really.

However, I was always kind of defensively minded. Even as a midfielder, I always had a feeling to mind the house, and stay goal-side of my man; that type of thinking. So there was always a defensive type of mentality there.

I didn't really fancy myself going forward that much, especially when we had forwards at the club like Ger Power and Mikey Sheehy. They could do the finishing.

Going on to have the career that I had at full-back seemed a million miles away to me at that time. It never dawned on me.

When you are in *the moment* and playing with Kerry – and particularly as we had lost the last number of years to Cork – there was no guarantee. In the 60s there was a bit of a drought in Kerry as well, so there was no guarantee that you were going to be playing on a winning Kerry team.

It is one thing to get on a Kerry team, but to be on a winning Kerry team was never guaranteed. We had no idea that these young lads coming up from the under-21 team were actually going to be so good, or that they would gel together and make such a formidable team.

We were lucky to have O'Dwyer at the time because he kept the whole thing going and he kept our feet on the ground. The mantra with O'Dwyer was that if we worked hard enough, we'd get the rewards. He could see that the skill levels were high… and that is always the criteria to play with Kerry; your skill level must be exceptionally high.

Top that up with really good fitness! O'Dwyer really had a brilliant concept of what was needed, because having played himself he knew what it was like in a high-tempo game for 60 and 70 minutes, even 80 minutes sometimes.

He was ahead of his time with regards to fitness. He saw Kevin Heffernan in Dublin at the same thing. The old tradition of training on a Tuesday and a Thursday, and playing a game at the weekend… he totally got rid of that.

He thought… *Why can't we train three nights a week or four nights a week?*

That was the start of the new era regarding fitness. If you wanted to live with the Dubs in particular, you had to do the extra work, or else you wouldn't be able to stay with them physically.

I don't remember an awful lot of that Cork game in 1975, except that it turned out to be a lot easier than I expected.

At that time, the real emphasis was on man-to-man marking; that was it. If you beat your man, you were doing a good job for your team. There was an energy about the team that day, and it was a *team* full of running. Even though Cork were more experienced, and stronger physically, we had terrific athletic ability throughout the team and we had an awful lot of real pace that Cork eventually couldn't live with.

The way I look at it – and we all felt the same way – was that we had no real baggage. We knew we could play and there was a team ethic there at the time that we played for one another.

The player in the better position would always get the ball; there was that type of mentality. That worked well for us and everything just seemed to fall into place. Even during the game, we weren't hit with the juggernaut we expected. I do remember my battle with Ray Cummins and, in fairness, I knew early on that

I could stay with him.

It is all about pace in a full-back line, and it is all about anticipation and being first to the ball. That happened with one or two of the early balls… that builds confidence as well.

We weren't expected to win that game and we went on afterwards to win the All-Ireland and, again, we weren't expected to beat the Dubs in the final.

When I look at the full-back line, I look at it as a kind of defensive unit within the team, and particularly with our goalie. Paudie O'Mahoney, who I considered to be exceedingly good, was in goals that day… he went through the whole championship without conceding a goal which is such a terrific achievement. Paudie was a really good goalie and had a really accurate kick-out. I always had supreme confidence in the ball going over my head if Paudie called, because you'd know it was secure. Our two corner-backs that day were Jimmy Deenihan and Ger O'Keeffe… we had to have an understanding as a unit, as we were coming up against a formidable opposition who were continuously switching and moving.

My father Frank played for Kerry in the 40s… and he was a great influence on me. There is no doubt about that.

We had a little bit of space in front of the house – a garden, a bit of a lawn. He spent a lot of time trying to get me to catch the ball over my head. I remember that as a young lad.

He then used to bring me to club games when his own club John Mitchels were playing. They were very successful during my youth.

My father was a past pupil of St Brendan's in Killarney… the Sem, and he sent me to boarding school there. That was a nursery for gaelic games. I have to admit that whatever kind of player I turned out to be, I have to give a lot of credit to that school. I was very fortunate to captain the team that won the Hogan Cup for the first time in 1969. Looking back on it, that was a great achievement under Fr Linnane, who was our coach.

I also have to give credit to my club Austin Stacks. I didn't play an awful lot of underage football. I think under-16 was the first time we played underage at competitive level, which would be unheard of nowadays.

I remember clearly playing basketball under a coach called James Hobbert and… that helped me learn to play defensively and how to mark without fouling. I'd put that down, without a shadow of a doubt, to how I was coached to defend playing basketball. In particular, man-to-man, where it's 'five fouls' and you're out of the game. You had to be clinical in the way you dispossessed someone.

Your focus was totally on the ball in basketball.

I played for a number of years under James. I also learned how to 'zonal defend' which was never coached to such an extent in gaelic games.

Micheál Hayes was a teacher in primary school in my time as well. He was a great Stacks man, and he kept an eye on us. He was terrific at organising leagues in the school.

I think that teams have to realise that you are roughly fifty percent of the game without the ball, and you have to have a strategy of how you are going to get the ball back. Even here in Kerry, most of the emphasis is on… *What do you do with the ball?…* and not nearly enough emphasis is on… *What you do without it.*

The art of man-to-man defending is nearly gone from the game, which is an awful pity. There are a lot of players not responsible for marking a man. There is a lot of loose marking, covering space, and players opting out of responsibilities.

You have to be very proud of what happened here in Kerry with our team.

But you also have to realise that we were all lucky to be part of the right team at the right time. You'll only be successful with a team, with an actual panel with everybody contributing.

I was very fortunate to be brought up in that era, and to get to play in those particular years with such outstanding players, and an outstanding manager. I was very privileged to be part of that and very lucky to avoid injury until it all came crashing down in 1984, when my hip gave up and I had no choice but to retire. I would have loved to have played on. I was 33 and I was still in very good shape, apart from the hip.

I was involved with Kerry for 15 years at that stage. I came in during 1969 as a sub on the senior team, so I was very, *very* privileged to have had such a long career with different teams.

99

PAUDIE O'MAHONEY

Defeating Cork in the 1975 Munster final was the breakthrough win for Kerry, when Paudie O'Mahoney (pictured with his daughter Roisin at the GPA Legends launch in Croke Park in 2019) made one of the saves of his life from a Jimmy Barry-Murphy penalty.

66

I WAS INTERESTED in football from the moment the radio was turned on, on a Sunday. My father always listened to the matches, and I would go out the back afterwards – we didn't haven't the price of a football so we kicked a Quix bottle around, a washing-up liquid bottle.

Funnily enough, in the long-term, that was a help to me because I had a powerful leg for kicking out the ball from kicking that Quix bottle. You couldn't kick it too far but I used to try and kick it as far as I could.

I'm from Woodlawn which is only a mile and a half away from Killarney town centre, so I was sent to school in town. But my mother thought I was a bit of a 'boyo' so she sent me out to Lissivigeen school. The headmaster was Tadhg

O'Sullivan, who was a big man up in Spa GAA Club. It was Tadhg who pushed me into football.

I had a good pair of hands, and I'd a fierce long kick off the ground. Tadhg felt it was very important that you'd a good goalkeeper underage. So, he put me back into goal for the long kicks. It was a relief to the team to get the ball up to the other half.

I went boarding then in St Brendan's College in Killarney. My mother put me in there because I got a scholarship, even though I was only living 15 minutes from the place.

We proceeded to win Munster under-15 championships, and then under-16 and under-17. We went on and won the All-Ireland Colleges in 1969 – the first time St Brendan's ever won it.

The thing about that is, I had played midfield for Spa in the 1968 under-16 East Kerry Championship, and I had been one of the star players. We won the whole thing easily.

The trainer of the St Brendan's team wanted me to play centre-forward then on the senior team. So, I started off centre-forward on the team. It was only as the season went on that he realised my pace wasn't what he'd thought, and he brought me in for trials for goalkeeping when we were on holidays – even though it was a clubmate of mine who was goalkeeper on the Brendan's team.

He left him in goals, but I was there as a sub for the forwards... and for the goalkeeping position.

I had several trials then for the Kerry minors.

At that time they had 15 selectors... *Would you believe that?* It was a gas set-up altogether. A fella called Dan Kiely from North Kerry, who ended becoming a senator, was our trainer. He was very good. He got us to the All-Ireland final and we almost won it. We drew the first game, but Galway beat us by a point in the replay.

That's where the whole thing began really. We went on to win the All-Ireland under-21 Championship in 1973.

Mick O'Dwyer saw that there was a team coming through!

In October 1973, Spa came back from a tour of America. We were after having a great time. I was a young fella, 21 years of age. All of my clubmates, who had never been outside of Kerry before, had gone wild in New York and Boston.

We arrived home with hangovers, and we were quickly looking for a pint of Guinness as a cure. As we were walking through Shannon Airport, going to the bus to get back to Killarney, someone said to me, 'Kerry are playing on Sunday, Paud… do you know that?'

I replied, 'I've no idea… and I don't want to know either!'

'Oh,' he says. 'You're playing… in GOAL!'

No one had told me anything about playing in goal for Kerry! It was a huge shock to me. I went straight to bed instead of drinking Guinness… I stayed in bed for 48 hours.

We came home on a Thursday, and I started with Kerry on the Sunday, against Roscommon in my first game. They weren't great… *I was lucky.* I got away with it. But that's how I started with Kerry.

I had my first home league game then, above in Fitzgerald Stadium. We played Cork who were All-Ireland champions. That was a big day out. It was a wet day too, but there was a huge crowd there. We lost by a point.

But we actually went on and won the league in 1974.

And then we played Cork in the Munster final in 1974… my first Munster final in Fitzgerald Stadium. I was proud to be playing with Kerry, but we'd a terrible team. Would you believe, there were players smoking in the dressing-room before the match that day.

In training, fellas used to go for a cigarette after a round of the field… they'd run into the dressing-room.

Now, it wasn't the trainer's fault because the players were all his age, and he found it difficult. Johnny Culloty was training the team. But I thought it was gas altogether, the whole set-up, because I'd been training Spa teams outside in Spa.

Cork were way ahead of us altogether.

We were caught for pace at the back. We were beaten… 1-11 to 0-7.

Even though I only let in one goal that day, Cork were all over us. They should have won by a lot more.

In the National League in 1975 Meath beat us in the quarter-final. There was a big team meeting after that. It was said that things would have to change, that this wasn't good enough anymore. It wasn't our fault… *The under-21 team coming through.* We were all dead keen to move forward.

That's when Ger McKenna, the chairman of the County Board, finally got Mick O'Dwyer in.

O'Dwyer brought us in for 27 training sessions in-a-row.

In the meantime, my goalkeeping skills had been well-known because of playing minor up to under-21, and if Spa were playing a serious team in the league or in the East Kerry Championship, I was thrown back into goal, even though I preferred playing midfield.

I was the first goalkeeper in Ireland to kick out the ball.

Until I came on the scene, all inter-county teams had one of the full-back line kicking out the ball... the goalie placed it for him.

I started kicking it out, so all goalies then had to learn to kick out the ball.

After we had the 27 training sessions in 1975, we knew we were *getting* there. It was all young fellas in the dressing-room – all young bachelors. Brendan Lynch was the oldest. He was 26... I was 23.

We went up to Tipperary for the Munster semi-final. That was our toughest game of the year. We beat them, and you could feel that there was something *happening*. John Egan took over that day, came out centre-forward and played very well.

My biggest game of all time was the Munster final that summer.

We were playing Cork. They were All-Ireland champions in 1973 and I thought they would go on to win four or five All-Irelands... they were *that* good.

In 1974 they had beaten us well in the Munster final. Dublin caught them in the semi-final that year because Cork thought all they had to do was turn up to Croke Park. Cork were still a very good team in '75.

We were very, very worried going out on the field that day. O'Dwyer was very worried as well. We were half-sick going into the dressing-room.

My big memory of it was... my father and mother were there, which was very unusual... to have them in the local stadium in Killarney.

There were about 40,000 people at the game, but there was a man standing behind the goal, Jimmy O'Brien... he had a famous GAA pub in Killarney.

I could hear him shouting at me.

He went behind the goals because we were good friends.

Cork started well, but then we got on top of them with a few points. And then, all of a sudden, Martin O'Doherty, the corner-back for Cork, had a mix-up with Billy Morgan. The ball went into the net.

John Egan cut through then, and he was fouled… and we got a penalty. Mikey Sheehy took it. Morgan saved it. It was a fairly good save.

We were up three or four points, when Jimmy Barry-Murphy broke through and got a penalty. Jimmy Barry-Murphy had the *name*, the *reputation*, he'd been so good in the 1973 All-Ireland final.

He lined up the ball.

And didn't I say a prayer to myself on the line.

I dived to the right and the ball hit off me. It was a very good save… the prayer definitely helped.

We played some great football after that… there was no turning back. Pat McCarthy and Paudie Lynch took over in the middle of the field. Mikey Sheehy started kicking points… and so did Mickey O'Sullivan.

I think Cork would have gone on to win the game had that penalty not been saved, and more than likely they'd have gone on to win the All-Ireland as well. We'd have been struggling then the following year to beat them up in Cork – we struggled to beat them anyway in 1976, but we'd have been complete underdogs if we hadn't made the breakthrough against them in '75.

I think Cork would have gone on to win three All-Irelands in-a-row. They won in 1973, but they lost out in '74 because of their own mistakes. Part of that was that Billy Morgan wasn't kicking out the ball. Donal Hunt was kicking out the ball in the semi-final against Dublin and his man went out and played as a third midfielder. Dublin won the game easily because of that.

I reckon that penalty save made a huge difference to Kerry, especially in front of the home crowd.

I remember fellas above in St Finan's Hospital looking out at the game through the windows. That's where my dad worked… and they used to look down at the field when they were working. My dad was off that day, but you'd know there was a squad of maybe 100 patients… maybe 100 nurses looking down from above.

GAME OF MY LIFE

Patients had participated in the construction of the stadium in the 30s, so that was always nice to see.

I was playing in my favourite football ground in the country that day. I played in most of them in the country, but I never came across a playing surface as good as Killarney.

Croke Park had a slope on it when I was playing. Kicking out the ball from the Hill 16 end… you were running up at least a foot of a hill.

The interesting thing about that Munster final is, after it was all over and we went down the town, my father and myself went into Jimmy O'Brien's to have a drink together.

And we met Jimmy Barry-Murphy and his dad… and we spent the evening together – the fella who had taken the penalty, and the goalkeeper who'd saved it. No doubt, it was one of the greatest days of my life.

We won the match, and I won my first Munster medal.

I beat Cork for the first time in a big match, and I felt I was better than the best goalkeeper in Ireland on the day, the man who was on the other side of the field… Billy Morgan.

That day epitomises what the GAA is all about in Kerry. It is all about camaraderie, friendship and the coming-together of people from South Kerry and North Kerry in Fitzgerald Stadium… meeting them afterwards, walking down from the ground into the town.

I have to say, the GAA followers in Kerry can be critical, but they are very genuine and they know their stuff.

That is what epitomises gaelic football for me. I loved playing for Kerry… I loved the camaraderie of the lads.

I don't think there was ever a nicer bunch of players.

That win against Cork gave us huge confidence.

We went on to play Sligo in the All-Ireland semi-final in 1975 – it was only their second time ever in Croke Park. They beat Mayo in the Connacht final… their second time winning it.

They got a penalty after 12 minutes. The game was very touch-and-go at the time, and I made a better save that day than I did against Jimmy Barry-Murphy. Mickey Kearins took the penalty.

In the final against Dublin I played well again, and we won without conceding any goal. It was the first time, I believe, that a goalkeeper went through the whole championship without conceding a goal.

We had no fear in the world going out against Dublin, because we felt Cork were a better team than them. It was tough on Dublin because the papers had them about three-to-one on.

We noticed going around in the parade before the match that they were all chewing gum, and shaking. We were smiling away... laughing. There wasn't anything expected of us.

Whereas, the wheel turned in 1976, and it was the other way around.

We went on to win four All-Irelands in-a-row. I retired after losing to Offaly in 1982, because I got tired of Mick O'Dwyer telling me I'd be on for the next game.

The only reason I stayed on for so long was because we played every second game in the National League... myself and Charlie Nelligan. But then when it came to the Championship, it was left up to the selectors.

Charlie and myself are good friends, but I got tired of being on the bench.

I never got on that well with O'Dwyer. I was working in Dublin – I moved to Dublin in 1978, and every time we had a trial game in Killarney I'd say to him... 'Tell me now before the team is picked, am I going to get on or not?'

When I got injured during the All-Ireland final in 1976 I'd to go off on a stretcher, and Charlie came on. It was tough on him that day too, because Dublin beat us.

It was difficult to come back. I came back from injury too fast really. It was a very bad injury... my Achilles tendon had snapped.

One of the things that stands out in my life is that I became a 'boozer'.

As a minor I never drank, but there is a lot of drink around sport, really. It became a burden for me over time, and maybe for some more people as well, not just in Kerry. It was part of the whole structure of the GAA at that time – you went drinking for the winter and went playing football for the summer.

I haven't had a drink now for three years. It taught me a lot of lessons.

I'd to go back to Dublin in my car after training for the weekend with O'Dwyer and the lads, and then I'd get the paper and find I wasn't picked on the team.

I'd be back down in Killarney then, walking down the street, and someone might hit me on the back and say, 'Oh Paudie… you should be on that team. You are a better goalkeeper than your man!'

It got to me. It really got into my head.

I couldn't handle it, so I drank away with the people tapping me on the back.

It cost me a lot both privately and publicly. But the wheel has turned finally, thank God!

My marriage broke up over sport. I trained Spa, I trained East Kerry, I trained Killarney, I trained the Kerry juniors… and I wasn't coming home.

Whether it was an excuse to go out and have a drink? Or whether it was the fact I was just one of the boys? It was a bit of both.

So, from that point of view, I have regrets. If I'd to go back and do it all again, I don't think I'd drink. And maybe I'd have been tougher with O'Dwyer too.

O'Dwyer was good, and a lot of the players loved him. I like O'Dwyer, but Billy Morgan or someone like that would have been just as good a manager.

He did very well, but he had the services of 40 outstanding players.

There were some fascinating players back then – a crossover of two excellent teams. Mick O'Connell came on in the Munster final in 1974. I knew Micko well. When I was in college in Galway, he came up to do a navigation course for trawlers.

He arrived up and he was looking for fellas to train with him. Myself and Ger O'Keeffe, who'd be playing with the under-21s, were there. We trained… because it was O'Connell, and because we got a free steak from the County Board afterwards. We'd be starving going to college.

But Micko was gas to train with.

We'd do a bit of passing first – training at that time wasn't that serious. If you passed the ball even one foot sideways, he wouldn't go near the ball. He'd make you run after it yourself.

Also, I remember he used to put on a pair of wellington boots. They were cut down low, the same as football boots, but there was lead in them.

He used to run around the field in them– he was as fit as a fiddle.

I was thumbing to the National League final in 1972, coming from college. You'd have no money in those days. I'd my best clothes on, going up to Dublin with £5 in my pocket.

I was thumbing in Oranmore and Jack Mahon picked me up, and Mick O'Connell was in the passenger seat. He made us stop and go into Maynooth College… he wanted me to go into goals for a few practice shots.

The goal was full of mud, and I'd my best clothes on me. I told him to go get stuffed, but he insisted I go over to a green area, where he kicked the ball to me.

When we arrived in Dublin, the team was staying in the old Jurys hotel which was up near Trinity College. But Micko made sure we got dropped down by the canal and he said, 'Take out a football there, Paudie!' He'd two more footballs with him. I ended up carrying two footballs and walking with this hero beside me, and all the buses stopping… everyone waving.

He used to love that. He is a character. I was disappointed that I didn't get a chance to play more with him… but at least I got to know him well.

SEÁN WALSH

KERRY 3-20 CORK 2-19
Munster SFC Final Replay
Páirc Uí Chaoimh
JULY 25, 1976

Winning his first All-Ireland with Kerry in 1978, Seán Walsh (above, second from right in the back row) had no idea that the team would dominate the game into the middle of the next decade.

★ **KERRY:** P O'Mahoney; T Kennelly, J O'Keeffe, J Deenihan; P Ó Sé, G O'Keeffe, G Power; P Lynch, P McCarthy; D 'Ogie' Moran, M O'Sullivan (1-2), P Spillane (1-3); B Lynch, M Sheehy (0-11), J Egan (0-1). Sub: **S Walsh (1-3)** for O'Sullivan.

★ **CORK:** B Morgan; S O'Sullivan, B Murphy, D O'Driscoll; J Coleman, T Creedon, K Kehilly; D Long (0-1), D McCarthy (0-1); C O'Rourke (0-4), S Coughlan (1-0), S Murphy (0-5); J Barry-Murphy (1-3), D Barron (0-3), D Allen (0-1). Subs: K Collins for O'Sullivan, B Field (0-1) for O'Rourke, S O'Sullivan for Coleman, C O'Rourke for Coughlan, C Murphy for Field, K Murphy for Creedon.

THE ACTION

IT TOOK A replay and then extra time, but Kerry were eventually crowned 1976 Munster champions in front of a crowd of 45,000 packed into a newly redeveloped Páirc Uí Chaoimh.

The Munster final became the first major game to be played in the new grounds, when Kerry and Cork drew 0-10 each

An opportunist goal from Mickey Ned O'Sullivan with just five minutes gone gave Kerry an early lead in the replay. But, by half-time, Cork were in front. On the resumption Paudie Lynch sent Pat Spillane through on goal and the Templenoe man cut inside Barry Murphy before finding the back of the net, despite Billy Morgan getting a hand to the pile-driver.

A Jimmy Barry-Murphy goal sent Cork into the lead once more and opened the sluice-gates for a torrent of Cork scores in an impressive four-minute spell of attacking football. The home team led by seven, 2-14 to 2-7, and with Cork remaining six points clear coming into the last 10 minutes Mick O'Dwyer introduced Seán 'Supersub' Walsh, who scored in controversial circumstances with two minutes remaining.

Walsh took a ball from Mikey Sheehy and whipped a terrific shot goalwards from the right-hand side. Morgan was beaten, but full-back Brian Murphy cut across to clutch the ball. However, the adjacent umpire almost immediately reached for the green flag to signal the ball had crossed the line.

The reaction of the Cork supporters to Walsh's goal was intensified when Declan Barron planted the ball in the Kerry net in injury time, only for his effort to be disallowed – the Cork full-forward was adjudged to have been inside the square before the ball.

After Pat Spillane bagged an equalising point for Kerry in the 70th minute, there was a further twist to the tale when a long-range effort from Sheehy landed on the roof of the Cork net – the score didn't count with the referee signalling that he had blown full-time immediately after the ball left the Austin Stacks man's boot.

In the opening 15 minutes of extra time there was only one team in it. Kerry had a four-point lead at the interval, which they held to the end.

★★★★★

66

THE 1976 MUNSTER final replay really stands out for me. It was a very controversial game. Near the end, Mikey Sheehy took a free that was 14 yards out. I was standing inside.

He passed me the ball.

I took my shot, but Brian Murphy saved it on the goal-line.

The umpires adjudicated that he had stepped back over the line, so there was a lot of argument over it. The ball went down the field… and Declan Barron ended up palming a goal. But that was disallowed.

The referee John Moloney got laced, but in fairness he was acting on what the umpires did; it was their decision.

There was a lot of talk about it… people still talk about it.

It was a game that defined my career because I was a sub all that year. I had played minor in 1975, so all of '76 I used to come on as a sub. I scored 1-3 that day and that certainly established me, and I made the team the following year.

Until then, I was known as 'Supersub'.

Everyone wants to get on the starting team.

It just so happened that year, that any time I did come on, things went right for me… I think it was convenient to leave me in the subs and bring me on.

It got a lot of publicity, because there was a footballer called David Fairclough, who was playing with Liverpool at the time, and he was known as 'Supersub'… so the media started calling me that too.

In the first game, it was Brendan Lynch I came on for, and in the second game I came on for Mickey O'Sullivan. The three of us were more or less rotating at that time.

There was a fierce atmosphere at those games. During the first game in Páirc Uí Chaoimh, the crowd broke onto the sideline, and I remember a scuffle between Kevin Kehilly and Brendan Lynch… anything could have happened with the crowd on the field.

Both games were on in Cork because there was work being done in Fitzgerald Stadium at the time. Kerry had given a commitment because it was the opening of Páirc Uí Chaoimh, so we went there for the two games.

That was the breakthrough for me.

I knew I was going to come on in the replay. I was looking at the selectors the whole time wondering when I would be called… but I knew I'd be put on with about 20 minutes left.

I won my first All-Ireland in 1978.

I was one of the youngest lads coming into that team in 1976. Then the following year in '77 I ended up playing full-forward. 'Bomber' Liston was coming through that year, so I was moved back out to midfield… and the 'Bomber' was put in full-forward.

As the youngest on the '76 squad, it was a huge thing to be playing with lads who had won an All-Ireland the previous September.

I never thought, breaking into the Kerry team, that we'd go on and win seven All-Irelands. On the law of averages, if you were lucky enough to win two or three that would be fantastic over a 10- or 12-year career… we never expected what happened.

But it was great playing with established household names… John O'Keeffe, Paudie Lynch, Brendan Lynch, Ger O'Keeffe… Ger Power and Mike Sheehy. They were playing with the seniors for a few years. I was 13 or 14 watching them when they started, and here I was four or five years later playing with them.

We were very lucky to come together… and then we had Mick O'Dwyer as well, of course… such a fantastic manager. He was a great motivator. We were just *lucky*. While it was a very skilful team, O'Dwyer made us work extra hard. Our fitness level… we even went beyond Dublin.

Kevin Heffernan brought Dublin to a level… Cork had a level too, but I think O'Dwyer brought us to *another* level.

He had an attitude that there were good footballers in Kerry, but he wanted to have us the fittest. That Cork team that won in 1973, that was a seriously talented team, but for some reason they didn't stay together.

There was way more in that Cork squad, looking back on it.

Mick O'Dwyer went for all-youth, and that was a *very* young Kerry team that won in 1975 – that set the scene. After winning one or two All-Irelands, it was very hard to try and keep a lid on it, as young fellas. You might win one or two, but trying to maintain it is difficult. O'Dwyer was able to do that. He kept us together. He never got too close to us. That was his secret. He got on with every fella, no problem, but he kept his distance. He wasn't a drinker himself which helped, because even though he'd be on holidays with the team and everything, he wasn't exactly sitting down at the table if lads were having a few drinks.

I think that was a huge advantage for him. He was able to keep that discipline… and keep a distance. He was like a schoolmaster… that was the way we looked at him. It was like being in national school and he was our teacher.

He had *that* control.

A big influence for me growing up was John Dowling in our club. When I started playing with Kerins O'Rahillys, we weren't very strong, but he kept the scene going there. I would have known John outside of football as well, but he was just so committed. I wouldn't call him a coach… he was old-style, but there was a whole pile of respect for him. He'd been there and done it, and he knew what he was talking about. You always need people that youngsters can look up to. When I was growing up, John was certainly one of those.

My father played colleges, but my mother… Noreen Kavanagh, her brother won an All-Ireland with Kerry. Dan Kavanagh played with Kerry, and his son Donal Kavanagh also went on to play with Kerry. It was in the family from my mother's side.

We actually lived on the Austin Stacks side of town. My father and mother were renting a house there, before they bought a house on the Strand Road side. I was 12 when we moved. At that time you were inclined to play with whoever you hung around with on whichever side of town, so I ended up playing with O'Rahillys. My father got involved in Strand Road – he was chairman, so that certainly influenced things as well.

It's great that my sons Tommy and Barry John have continued that tradition, and won two All-Irelands. Tommy was playing in 2009, and Barry John was a sub… and it was a great day for the whole family to see your own lads involved. I've another son Seán and he's on the Strand Road seniors. He's a good footballer and he's doing well too, and my daughter Claire is secretary of the juvenile club… so they are all involved.

Our Kerry team was a very close team. It is only looking back on it, that you realise there is a fierce bond there. There is a great understanding.

It is a kind of family.

There is a sense of pride having represented Kerry, but at the same time there is a very healthy attitude in the county towards Kerry footballers. You are not put up there as a superstar. It's really more a... *You played football, you did well...* and that's where it stops!

There are a lot of footballers who have played with Kerry and, no matter where you go, you'll bump into lads who've played. I think that is a big help. I think in other counties it can be a problem that they are put way up there, whereas in Kerry you are left alone. There is nobody genuflecting in front of anyone.

Okay, you played football... Grand... We'll move on!

Funnily enough, Mick O'Dwyer often said that very good Kerry teams have ironically come out of losing All-Ireland minor teams. Sometimes, it can be a good thing just to get to that level. And if you lose a minor or an under-21, it makes you hungrier.

When you are playing sport underage it is nearly as important to know *how* to lose as it is to know *how* to win, there is no doubt about that.

A very young Kerry team won in 1975 and then we lost in '76 and '77, and I think that was a good thing because lads were *very* young. We suddenly realised... *If we don't work hard enough, we lose!*

Football for me was a hobby.

It has gone very serious now. I'm just amazed how some of the modern players keep at it, even at club level. A club player now in Kerry at the moment is putting in the work that we were putting in as county players 40 years ago. It has gone to another level and you just wonder... *Where is the fun?*

Something has to give, because there is more to life than just sport. We didn't take it seriously in the winter. We did a bit of training, played National League, but it wasn't a priority. But then, come the first of May... *That was it.*

EOIN LISTON

BEALE 1-11 BALLYLONGFORD 0-7
North Kerry SFC Final
Ballylongford
NOVEMBER 27, 1977

Eoin 'Bomber' Liston tussles with the late Mick Holden of Dublin in the 1979 All-Ireland final.

★ **BEALE:** Tony Griffin: T Hayes, M Joyce, L Browne; Tom Griffin, D 'Ogie' Moran (0-3), T Allen; P Liston, G Griffin; T McMahon, **E Liston (0-2)**, D Liston (0-1); Tim Griffin, M Shanahan (0-4), Joe Casey (1-1). Subs: J King for McMahon, J Casey for Tim Griffin.

★ **BALLYLONGFORD:** J McCarthy; K Kennelly, P O'Donoghue, B McCarthy; C Heaphy, M McEllistrim, D Mulvihill; J Walsh (0-3), B O'Connor; B Walsh (0-2), M Keane, T O'Connor; T McEllistrim, E O'Donoghue, B Bambury (0-2). Sub: S Boyle for T McEllistrim.

THE ACTION

UNDERDOGS BEALE, CAPTAINED by Kerry star Denis 'Ogie' Moran, claimed their first-ever North Kerry SFC title before a very large attendance in Ballylongford.

Beale were also contesting their first North Kerry Senior Championship final, whereas a star-studded Ballylongford were playing in their 11th final in 13 years.

Bernie O'Callaghan's charges laid down an early marker when Moran pointed a '50' with just two minutes gone. And talk of an upset was certainly on the cards as early as the ninth minute when Beale led by 0-5 to 0-1. At this stage, Pádraig Liston and Gearóid Griffin had the better of the midfield exchanges over Jackie Walsh and Barry O'Connor, and to make matters worse, the Ballylongford half-back line was being completely overrun.

Moran closed the scoring in the opening 30 minutes when he pointed a free in the last minute – Beale's first score since the ninth minute, which left it 0-6 to 0-3 in their favour.

The game's decisive moment came in the 39th minute, when Ballylongford, trailing by five points, were awarded a penalty after Barry Walsh was fouled inside the square. Up stepped Walsh. But to the dismay of the home support, he put the ball over the bar.

They say momentum is everything in football, and four minutes later the result of the game looked to be put beyond any doubt when Beale corner-forward Joe Casey hit a rasping shot off the underside of the crossbar. Despite protests from the Ballylongford camp, referee Joe Langan determined that the ball had gone over the line as it bounced down after striking the bar. Beale were definitely in the driving seat at this stage and had an eight-point advantage, 1-9 to 0-4.

When Eoin 'Bomber' Liston closed the scoring with a superb point in the last minute, Beale cruised into a comfortable seven-point lead.

On the day, there was no doubting Beale's superiority. The win was the first of Beale's famous three in-a-row North Kerry SFC title-winning run, which also resulted in the Ballybunion club winning six of the next eight finals between 1977 and '84.

★★★★★

66

WE HAD PLAYED together with Ballylongford as part of the Shannon Rangers Divisional team, winning the county championship, and then we had to play against Ballylongford in the final of the North Kerry Championship.

Our chairman John Francis Ahern offered to play in Ballylongford.

It was our first North Kerry Championship final, while they had a huge team and had won five of the last 10 titles.

It was a huge match for us, and our win decided that 'Ogie' would be captain of Kerry in 1978. Shannon Rangers were to provide the captain as county champions and if Ballylongford had beaten us Barry Walsh or Jackie Walsh, who were on the county panel at that time, would have been Kerry captain the following year.

Donie Mulvihill for Ballylongford was a serious, *serious* footballer and he'd stay running all day. Bernie O'Callaghan, who was in charge of Beale, put Tom McMahon on him. They had a great battle, but it was a tactical move that worked in our favour.

Myself and my two brothers Donal and Pádraig, along with a first cousin of mine, Tom Allen, were playing with Beale. It was just so special for us to actually win a North Kerry Championship, and it was the start of a good run for our club.

There was some row in Shannon Rangers at the time, and Tarbert, Ballydonoghue and Ballyduff left Shannon Rangers. That left two clubs – Ballylongford and Beale.

The others came back years later, but at that time we were left with just the two clubs, and Jackie Walsh and 'Ogie' were involved in picking the team for the county championship.

That was great… it was the only county championship medal that I ever won.

There was a great bond between Ballylongford and Beale because of that; we even went on tour afterwards together to America.

But that final was a huge match for us, because Ballylongford were used to winning North Kerry Championships. We hadn't won one and here we were in the final, and going over to their backyard. They had Paudie O'Donoghue, Éamonn O'Donoghue, Brian McCarthy… and Conor Heaphy, God rest him – he was a super player.

At the time, the tradition of winning North Kerry Championships wasn't there. We were Novice in 1976.

We won the Kerry Novice Championship that year as well, in '77, but to go on and win the North Kerry Championship was special. Those matches, they were like our All-Irelands, and we were playing with all our friends, the fellas we'd grown up with.

At the time they made a special banner.

SUPER BEALE.

And the whole parish travelled to Ballylongford.

It was good, friendly rivalry with them, but very competitive.

We would have been underdogs, definitely.

But, in fairness, Bernie O'Callaghan got our fitness levels up to what was required. He had played with Kerry and he drove our lads hard.

'Ogie' and myself were training with Mick O'Dwyer, but the rest of the lads really trained hard under Bernie. We had a lot of good footballers too. We were very united and very focused, and things just went well for us on the day.

Niall Horgan had trained us from under-14s up.

I would have been about 19 or 20 at the time of the win against Ballylongford, and a good few of the team had come up through the ranks together. 'Ogie' and Liam Browne, who was a colossal player for the club for many years. Mike Joyce was another great player and a brilliant servant to the club.

John Francis Ahern was related to a lot of the Bally crowd and I'd say it was a bit of bravado or whatever, but he offered to play the final over in their own backyard.

You wouldn't see that happening too often.

The win gave us confidence as a team, and suddenly we won three in-a-row. We lost one then, before we won two back-to-back… we lost another one, and we won another one. We went on to win six out of the next eight years from a team that had never won one, and we had so much fun, especially with that first one.

We went to Ballylongford and we sang with the Bally lads, and then they came over to Ballybunion and celebrated with us.

That was kind of a tradition at that time. Whoever won…the loser would go to their town and celebrate with them, which was a lovely concept because you really got to know all the players.

It was a real turning point for the club. We built on that confidence and we came from being novice up to the Junior Championship, became intermediate champions, and we played senior – we got to two county semi-finals during that time. We feel we should have won a county championship in 1989, but I don't know if we really believed we could do it at the time.

Looking back on it, it all stemmed from that match against Ballylongford in 1977.

I have such fond memories of going on to play with Kerry.

First of all, if we hadn't been getting success at club level we wouldn't have been picked to get on the Shannon Rangers team. And by being picked on the Shannon Rangers team, it propelled the two of us, myself and my brother Pádraig – 'Ogie' was there already – to get our first games for Kerry on the same day.

He was on the '40' and I was full-forward against Offaly in Tralee.

That would have been late in '77. That is a great memory of togging out for my first game with Kerry.

My own nickname… 'Bomber' came from the early-70s, playing soccer on the beach in Ballybunion. The West German striker Gerd Müller was known as 'The Bomber'. We would have different nicknames for each other playing soccer on the beach every Saturday.

It never bothered me what people called me. I'd be still known as 'Bomber' to an awful lot of my friends. I've no issues with it.

We were over at David Moran's stag over in Cheltenham a few years ago. We had great craic. There were about 16 of us there together, and we were coming back on the plane flying into Cork and there was a fella – I won't name him – whom I had got to know on the trip.

He was charging his phone on top of the food tray.

He was back two seats – Kieran Donaghy and myself were at the front – and he called out my name… 'Bomber?'

I didn't hear him so he shouts… 'BOMBER!'

The air-hostess was passing and she heard this fella shouting 'Bomber' and she got an awful fright… especially when she saw the charger up on the tray. He realised then what was after happening and was saying to her… 'NO… NO!'

But she wasn't having any of it.

She reported him to the pilot, and we were both told to wait on. I waited just so that I could back-up his story… so they knew he was no blaggard.

He just said, 'Google Eoin Liston there'.

And they Googled it and they saw that my name was… 'Bomber'.

Mick O'Dwyer was a hero of mine growing up.

Mick O'Dwyer and Mick O'Connell were the two huge heroes of that generation. My first time going to an All-Ireland final was in 1972 when I was a 14-year-old.

I was called into the Kerry under-21s in April 1977, and that year we went on to win the All-Ireland.

My first time meeting Mick O'Dwyer was in April '77. We played Clare and we then went on and played Cork, before going on to play Leitrim and then Down in an All-Ireland final that year to win the under-21s.

That was my first time seeing O'Dwyer in the dressing-room. That day I was playing corner-forward and he moved me out to midfield. I linked up well with Jack O'Shea that same day. It helped, as I was called into the senior training that year.

While I didn't make the team until October of that year, I had trained with the Kerry team through the summer of '77. When Dublin beat Kerry in the All-Ireland semi-final that year, I was No 24 in the subs.

Mick O'Dwyer was a fella you looked up to, and then to have the pleasure of training under him and seeing how passionate he was…. he was there *first*, he was there *last*; he gave everything at every session, and we would have done anything for him. Then, I was lucky enough to get a teaching job down in Waterville that following September. That would have been September of '78.

Not only was I going up and down with him for the next eight years in the car to training sessions, we used to train together down in Waterville too… it was like having my own personal trainer.

I had a great eight years down there with my own *personal trainer*.

MIKEY SHEEHY

KERRY 3-13 DUBLIN 1-8
All-Ireland SFC Final
Croke Park
SEPTEMBER 16, 1979

Mikey Sheehy in classic style as he takes on the late Christy Ryan in the 1981 Munster final against Cork.

★ **KERRY:** C Nelligan; J Deenihan, J O'Keeffe, M Spillane; P Ó Sé, T Kennelly, P Lynch; J O'Shea (0-1), S Walsh; T Doyle, D Moran, P Spillane (0-4); **M Sheedy (2-6)**, E Liston (0-1), J Egan (1-1). Sub: V O'Connor for O'Keeffe.

★ **DUBLIN:** P Cullen; M Kennedy, M Holden, D Foran; T Drumm, F Ryder, P O' Neill; B Mullins, B Brogan; A O'Toole (0-1), T Hanahoe (0-2), D Hickey (0-2); M Hickey, B Doyle (0-3), J McCarthy. Subs: J Ronayne (1-0) for M Hickey, G O'Driscoll for J McCarthy, B Pocock for O' Toole.

THE ACTION

WATCHED ON BY a crowd of 72,185 in glorious sunshine, Kerry won the All-Ireland for the 25th time, securing their second victory in the Kingdom's famous four in-a-row.

Defeating Clare, Cork and Monaghan along the way, Mick O'Dwyer's side came into the 1979 final as strong favourites having scored 5-11 against Dublin in the final 12 months earlier.

Starting without Ger Power, losing John O'Keeffe to injury, and having Páidí Ó Sé sent off did not deter Kerry, who crushed Dublin with a shattering Mikey Sheehy goal after 11 minutes, a Sheehy penalty after 56 minutes and a John Egan goal eight minutes from the end.

The opening goal came after Mick Kennedy conceded a free which was taken by Ó Sé. His kick found 'Ogie' Moran and when the elegant centre-forward flicked a peach of a pass out to Sheehy on the right, the Austin Stacks man took the gift with open arms and blasted the ball past Paddy Cullen.

Despite facing a stiff breeze in the opening 35 minutes, Kerry comfortably led 1-7 to 0-3 at half-time.

Sheehy's second goal – a penalty just shy of the hour mark – gave the Kingdom a double score lead of 2-10 to 1-5 and put the result beyond any doubt.

Armagh referee Hugh Duggan had no hesitation pointing to the penalty spot after John Egan was brought to the ground after receiving an Eoin 'Bomber' Liston hand-pass that split the Dublin defence. Sheehy coolly stepped up and gave Cullen no chance as the ball thundered into the top left corner of the net.

Kerry put the seal on victory when Egan was involved yet again and finished off a brilliantly worked goal in front of a sea of blue on Hill 16. The Sneem man linked up well with Jack O'Shea before side-stepping Tommy Drumm, and then Fran Ryder, before bundling the ball over the line past Cullen.

A tally of 2-6 resulted in Sheehy finishing the championship as top scorer with 6-18.

★★★★★

"

IN CERTAIN GAMES you could be playing and the ball wouldn't break for you very kindly but on that particular day in the 1979 All-Ireland final against Dublin, any time the ball broke… it broke my way.

I had one of those days… and it was in Croke Park, so it was kind of a day you'd dream about.

You have to get the breaks and I got the *breaks* that day. It would be top of the list with regards to the games I've played.

The first and last All-Ireland finals I played in – 1975 and '86 – were very special days too, because the *first* one is always going to be memorable and with the *last* one in '86 I had a fair idea it was going to be my final All-Ireland. But in terms of performance, the 'game of games' for me was certainly the 1979 All-Ireland final.

It was a good day for me personally, and we won the game impressively too. We had beaten Dublin in 1978, after losing against them in the final in '76 and the semi-final in '77. Things went well on the day. Sometimes in a game like that, when you are preparing for it you are kind of saying to yourself… *I want to have a good start.*

Luckily enough, I'd say I got a point after about 25 or 30 seconds. A ball came into Pat Spillane and he passed it on to me. It came in from the Cusack Stand side and I nailed it over the bar.

Straight away, my marker was under pressure and I was on the front foot. It's amazing how it works. I know it might sound silly and very simple, but it does actually make a difference.

I got a goal midway through the half after Ogie Moran passed me the ball – he could have nearly gone for it himself.

People said, 'Oh, ye worked on that in training!'

I suppose, you do at certain times… but some things just end up happening on the day. When the ball broke from 'Bomber' – Mick Holden was the Dublin full-back – it went to Ogie and I was coming off Ogie's shoulder. He could have gone himself but he gave it to me and I scored. At that stage, you just *know*. I ended up scoring 2-6 and I could have scored more but the game was probably over in the last 20 minutes.

People were saying to me weeks afterwards… 'Oh, you could have broken records!'… but you don't ever think of records in the middle of a match. And it never bothered me that I didn't break any records.

It was just one of those days that I was getting chances and, as I've said, it wasn't all about preparation… *The ball was breaking for me.*

David Foran was corner-back, and he was a very good footballer. He actually played a lot of his football at centre-back. He was a good tight marker, a fine athlete, and an outstanding footballer. Because he was such a good footballer, I was saying to myself… *I can't let him get on top of me early on… I can't let him beat me for the first two or three balls.* That might have let him take control straight away.

Sometimes, you can be rushing at things, and you can be trying too hard. But that particular day, I needed to start well… *And I started well.*

Foran actually got caught for the first goal because he jumped for the ball with Mick Holden and the 'Bomber', when he probably should have waited. It was possibly his centre-back instincts – a centre-back was not as tight a man-marker as a specialised corner-back in those times. They'd nearly follow you to the jacks at half-time… they were quite happy not to touch the ball… once you didn't touch the ball.

Funnily enough, I got the two goals, but they don't really stand out for me. The thing that really sticks out for me was the start of the game.

I felt good going into the game. I felt very, very fit. I was only 25 years of age… and 25, 26, 27, 28… they are probably your peak years. I felt strong, I hadn't any injury all year.

I was playing good club football.

Austin Stacks were going well at the time too.

Again, so much comes down to confidence… and the thing that certainly stands out was the first minute of the game. I don't think there was even a minute gone… there were only 30 seconds gone when I got the first score, and that actually stands out to me more than the goals and the other points I got.

I felt… *Jesus, you're on here now.* And I knew straight away because my marker had his head down a little bit.

It was very early in the game, and he gave me too much room. He was trying to sweep with somebody. There was somebody coming in on the other side as well – I think it was John Egan that he was watching with one eye.

That moment stands out very, *very* clearly.

The noise of the crowd when you score... particularly if you score a goal, it is just an amazing feeling. It is an incredible emotion.

You get a sense of the crowd when you run onto the pitch at the start of the game, but when you get a score, it's different. *Very different.* You don't even think about the crowd at the game most of the time, and really you are playing on instinct... off-the-cuff. When I got a chance I'd always think... *I've got to nail this!*

You'd know you mightn't get another one in the game.

That's when all the practice comes in, from all the years... when you were young down in the Stacks' field, or in training with Kerry. When you get your chance, you've got to take it. Sometimes we do and sometimes we don't, but when you do... the feeling, the emotion is just incredible.

And the roar of the crowd in Croke Park is something else.

I found the net twice that day, thank God.

And got to experience that joy twice.

Football has had a huge, *huge* influence on my life.

All the lads of our era, and even the lads of the present era, particularly when you are from a county like Kerry... we all know that when we put on the county jersey we are expected to produce the goods.

We are judged really on All-Irelands. And our performance in All-Ireland finals.

Football has had a huge influence on me, and my life in general.

We make massive friends out of it. We make friends for life. I just see myself as so lucky to have been part of that squad, and to have been coached and managed by the best in my eyes, the best manager in gaelic football of all time... Mick O'Dwyer.

I find it a privilege still.

I feel really honoured to have been part of that set-up.

That team was obviously full of brilliant footballers, but they were also great lads. We gelled very well as a team. There were no egos on the team either, and I felt

Micko was responsible for that. He kept it competitive, though he was very loyal to his players and that was certainly part of the jigsaw as well.

Nobody comes near him as a manager.

I know Jim Gavin's record with Dublin in the last decade might look that little bit better than Micko's on paper, but ours was a different generation. It was a different type of football.

It was a different game back then.

When you have a backroom teams nowadays there might be 10 or 12 individuals helping out in important ways, but Micko did everything himself. He might have had four selectors with him, but he did *everything*. Now the selectors were very good, and they were very sharp on the line, but Micko was the coach and he was the physical trainer… and he was the tactician… and he was the psychologist.

By psychologist I mean, he was a fantastic man-manager. He knew if you were going well, or if you needed a bit of a break… and he knew if you needed to be pushed that little extra bit. He was way ahead of his time.

JIMMY DEENIHAN

KERRY 1-12 OFFALY 0-8
All-Ireland SFC Final
Croke Park
SEPTEMBER 20, 1981

Kerry captain Jimmy Deenihan lifts the Sam Maguire Cup after defeating Offaly in the 1981
All-Ireland final and completing a famous four in-a-row of championship victories.

★ **KERRY:** C Nelligan; **J Deenihan**, J O'Keeffe, P Lynch; P Ó Sé (0-1), T Kennelly, M Spillane; J O'Shea (1-0), S Walsh (0-1); G Power (0-1), D Moran (0-2), T Doyle (0-1); M Sheehy (0-5), E Liston, J Egan (0-1). Subs: P Spillane for Egan, G O'Keeffe for M Spillane.

★ **OFFALY:** M Furlong; M Fitzgerald, L Connor, C Conroy; P Fitzgerald, R Connor, L Currams; T Connor (0-1), P Dunne; V Henry, G Carroll, A O'Halloran; M Connor (0-4), S Lowry (0-2), B Lowry (0-1). Subs: J Mooney for T Connor, J Moran for Henry.

THE ACTION

JIMMY DEENIHAN CAPTAINED Kerry to a famous four-in-a-row, as a brilliant Jack O'Shea goal in the dying moments sealed a celebrated victory against a resilient Offaly side in front of a crowd of 61,489 at Croke Park.

By the time the Cahersiveen man rattled the back of the Offaly net, Kerry were five points clear, thanks to a lovely point from the boot of Mikey Sheehy three minutes from time.

Offaly, in search of revenge after defeat to Kerry in the 1980 All-Ireland semi-final, shaped very well in the early stages as Matt Connor had the Faithful County two points up within five minutes. By the 18th minute, however, Mick O'Dwyer's side led by three as scores from Páidí Ó Sé, Denis 'Ogie' Moran, Ger Power and further points from Sheehy made it 0-5 to 0-2.

Offaly managed to get back on level terms – 0-5 apiece – by half-time, with points by Seán Lowry, Brendan Lowry and Tomás Connor. Gerry Carroll rattled the crossbar after the restart, but that was as good as it got for Eugene McGee's side, who only managed to add a further three points after the interval.

Kerry took the lead when Seán Walsh kicked over a well-worked point, and further scores followed from John Egan and the in-form Sheehy. Offaly did finally open their second-half account when Seán Lowry slotted over his second point of the afternoon on the hour mark, but Kerry responded immediately as efforts from Sheehy and Tommy Doyle put five points between the two sides. Kerry looked comfortable at this stage and after Sheehy cancelled out a Matt Connor point, it was time for Jack O'Shea's glorious goal.

Eoin 'Bomber' Liston tore up the field to find Egan before the Sneem corner-forward delivered a long pass to Sheehy. The Austin Stacks star quickly laid the ball off to the in-rushing O'Shea. He took possession 25 yards out from goal, close to the Cusack Stand, before unleashing an unstoppable shot into the far corner to the surprise of Offaly goalkeeper Martin Furlong.

★★★★★

66

THE FIRST TOY I got as a kid was a football. My mother bought it for me at the Puck Fair when I was about three years of age. She used to go there every year for a few days with her parents Mick and Hannie Horgan.

From that time on, my life was all about football until I started teaching in Tarbert Comprehensive School in 1975. My time was then divided between teaching and football. When I was attending Dromclough National School, St Michael's College Listowel, St Mary's College in Strawberry Hill in London, and then the National College of Physical Education in Limerick, football dominated my life... and everything else was secondary.

As my late father Mikey Deenihan was a Kerry football fanatic, the topic of conversation in our house as I grew up was usually about great Kerry players of the past and present, such as Con Brosnan, Bob Stack, Johnny Walsh... and current players at the time like Mick O'Connell and Mick O'Dwyer.

I was inspired by these stories. He took me to Croke Park for the first time to see the 1959 All-Ireland semi-final between Kerry and Dublin in which O'Connell gave a memorable performance. Leaving the stadium that day my father remarked, 'I hope to see you play on this pitch someday.'

His wish came through in 1970 when I played there with the Kerry minors.

Finuge was a hurling club first, back in the 20s. My father and others started the football club in 1937. The club was thriving until the introduction of the parish rule in 1954. As Finuge village spans both Lixnaw and Listowel parishes it was prevented from having players from both parishes on its teams and had to disband.

The club was revived in 1961 when the County Board introduced a by-law stating that the Listowel parish side of Finuge would be regarded as being in Lixnaw parish for football purposes. So we regrouped again in '61 and the club has been hugely successful since, winning the inaugural All-Ireland Junior Championship in 2004.

I still play an active part in the club.

Over the years, I played in several important matches where a lot was at stake. On reflection now, however, the All-Ireland final against Offaly in 1981 was probably the most important game of my career.

Another game that immediately comes to mind was the Munster minor final in 1970 when Kerry beat Cork.

Cork had dominated Munster minor football for the previous five years and were the All Ireland champions in 1967, '68 and '69. The core of our 1975 All-Ireland winning team came from that minor team.

Defeating Cork in the 1973 Munster under-21 final was another important step for Kerry as Cork had given us a hammering in the Munster senior final that year.

Of course, beating Cork in the Munster final of 1975 in Killarney was special as they were Munster champions the previous two years and were hot favourites. We had a very young squad of players. The average age of our defence was 22 years, and we were up against a very seasoned Cork forward line… Ray Cummins, Declan Barron, Dinny Allen and Jimmy Barry Murphy. They were the top forwards in Ireland at that time. We emerged as winners, and that was the start really of the Kerry revival in the 70s.

In 1975, winning the All-Ireland final for the first time was also brilliant… beating a Dublin team that had emerged the previous year as All-Ireland champions. Like Cork in Munster, Dublin were also hot favourites. The commentators felt that we were too young, and that Dublin would be too strong for us. We were easy winners on the day.

There are other games too that are so memorable. One of them was in Gaelic Park in New York in 1978 against the Dubs! We had lost the All-Ireland final in 1976 and the All-Ireland semi-final in '77… and the so-called experts had written us off. There were demands within the county for major changes, including getting rid of Mick O'Dwyer as manager and Gerard McKenna as chairperson of the County Board.

It was generally felt the team was underachieving… but fortunately for the team, both men survived.

We knew that was a game in New York where we had to demonstrate that we could match Dublin physically. Whereas Dublin were after winning two All-Irelands and were in New York to have a good time, we went there with a different attitude… to prove to them, and to our many detractors, that the Kerry team was not finished.

It was a mud bath that day in Gaelic Park because of heavy rainfall, but we did prove a point, that we weren't physically in any way intimidated by Dublin. We went on and hammered them that year in the All Ireland final... but our campaign in '78 started in New York.

Other games that bring back fond memories are defeating Austin Stacks in the county final in 1980, which resulted in me becoming captain of the Kerry team in 1981, and winning my only North Kerry Championship with Finuge in 1987.

The fact that I was the trainer of both teams made the games even more satisfying for me personally.

However, the game that I would have to remember most at this stage of my life was captaining Kerry to win the All-Ireland final in 1981. Captaining Kerry to win an All-Ireland is a singular honour... but to be captain of the four in-row team made it even more special.

The previous year we played Offaly in the All-Ireland semi-final in a very high scoring game... 4-15 to 4-10. Offaly felt that they had the opportunities that day to win that match.

So, in 1981, they believed that they had a very good chance of winning the All-Ireland. It was very close.

There were only four points between the sides coming into the last five minutes, and then Jack O'Shea got that celebrated goal.

The move leading to the score started with me in the full-back line.

I collected the ball on the end-line. I spotted Tim Kennelly over my left shoulder and delivered a 40-yard pass to him. He kicked what was a perfectly placed 60-yard pass to Tommy Doyle, who passed the ball to John Egan. John played a one-two with Eoin Liston and then punted the ball to Mike Sheehy, who hand-passed the ball to Jack O'Shea. Jacko hit an unstoppable shot to the roof of the net. As the late Michael O'Hehir said in his commentary during the course of the passing movement... *They are really rolling now.*

The Kerry defence played particularly well that day. We were playing against a very good Offaly forward line and we held them to a very low score... just eight points. But the match could have gone either way. Gerry Carroll hit the crossbar early in the second-half and if Offaly had scored that goal, it could have been a different result.

Offaly had some really top class forwards at the time, including Matt Connor, Johnny Mooney, Brendan Lowry, Seán Lowry and Carroll. The fact that we kept them to just eight points was a remarkable achievement.

It was really important that we won, as we were equalling the record set by a previous Kerry team in winning four All-Irelands in-a-row, and we had arranged to go to Australia on an around the world trip that November… definitely, going as runners-up in the All-Ireland final would have been an anti-climax. It was so important that we went as All-Ireland champions.

On the day itself, there was a swirling wind that didn't help either team. We were unfortunate that Pat Spillane got injured a couple of weeks before the game… he was a huge loss. Mike Sheehy got injured three weeks before the game in a county championship game and he couldn't participate in a lot of the training. He went out with an injured foot that particular day… he had to get an injection in his ankle to enable him to play.

By then, we had developed a very good understanding amongst our six defenders, especially our full-back line.

Our defence probably never got the credit and recognition that it deserved in winning the four-a-row. As Mick O Dwyer often emphasised, there was no point in scoring goals at one end and haemorrhaging them at the other end.

In that particular year, Clare scored just six points against us in the first round of the Munster Championship. Then… and this was an *amazing* achievement… in Killarney in the Munster final Cork only scored three points over 70 minutes… a Cork forward line that included Dinny Allen, Declan Barron and Dave Barry.

Mayo in the All-Ireland semi-final only scored a goal and six points. Against all those teams we played in the championship in '81, we just conceded 1-23. We had a very tight, disciplined defence. While our half-back line was a bit more adventurous and took more chances, we were always very tight in the full-back line.

We tried to legitimately close down our opponents and we worked well together. There was very good communication between myself and John O'Keeffe in particular, because we had played together in all the All-Irelands from 1975 to '81. The other corner-backs at different times that played with us were Ger O'Keeffe, Mickey Spillane and Paudie Lynch… all excellent and unselfish defenders.

But we ensured that even when our forwards found it hard to get scores, our opponents weren't getting scores at the other end.

In the All-Ireland final against Roscommon in 1980, for example, we were missing 'Bomber' Liston in that game… it was definitely the defence that helped win that game for Kerry. They got a goal and two points in the first 10 minutes, and only scored four points for the rest of the game. It was a remarkable performance because they had some really great forwards… Dermot Earley, John O'Connor, John O'Gara, Michael Finneran and the McManus brothers. It was unquestionably the greatest Roscommon team ever. They deserved to win an All-Ireland with that team.

The Kerry four in-a-row team was built from the back. Micko always said the full-back line, to him, was the most important line on the team. To him, it was like the front row on a rugby team.

At that time the full-forward line were the strikers of modern day soccer. Most of the scores came through them. If they were neutralised, your team had a better chance of winning.

Winning the four in-a-row really didn't sink in at the time.

We were on a journey to win five in-a-row, and it was just part of that journey. I was conscious of equalling history… my acceptance speech afterwards in 1981 referred to that… that we were very much on *the journey* to win five in-a-row and be recognised as the greatest Kerry team ever.

Unfortunately, from my own point of view, I got injured in June 1982. We were after winning the National League and we were just getting ready for the championship. We won the National League without putting much effort into it. I broke my leg in training the first evening we were back training for the championship… that was the end of my season.

And then Pat Spillane aggravated a knee injury. The absence of both of us definitely hurt the team. Pat came on in the final against Offaly, but he wasn't right.

Brendan Lowry, for example, got three points that day in '82. I had marked him in three games and he only scored one point in those three games. If I was playing that day I doubt if he would have scored three points from play, but who knows!

As I get older, I look back and I just feel privileged to have been part of a team that played an exciting brand of football, and that people still recall our team with admiration.

We went out on the field without any set plans. We did things spontaneously. Our game was basically just running off the ball, supporting each other, and doing things spontaneously rather than having them thought through too much beforehand.

We were very fortunate as well to have had such an exceptional coach and manager in Mick O'Dwyer. He was just totally committed to the team and to Kerry football.

He will go down in history as the most successful manager ever in gaelic football. Kerry owe him a huge debt of gratitude and so do all the players who played under him over that period of time. I had a very close friendship with Micko, which had developed over the years when we both played for Kerry from 1972 to his retirement in '74... and during our visits to New York to play for Kerry in the New York Championship. That friendship still continues to this day.

Unfortunately, three of that great team have now left this world... Tim Kennelly, John Egan and Páidí Ó Sé. The rest of us meet annually at the John Egan Golf Classic organised by Vincent O'Connor.

I just feel very fortunate to have known and played with those three great men, and to have been part of what many people feel, with some justification, was the greatest Kerry team ever.

AMBROSE O'DONOVAN

KERRY 3-14 CORK 2-10
Munster SFC Final
Fitzgerald Stadium
JULY 1, 1984

Ambrose O'Donovan leads the Kerry team in the parade before the Munster final against Cork in 1984.

★ **KERRY:** C Nelligan; P Ó Sé, S Walsh, M Spillane; T Doyle, T Spillane (0-1), G Lynch; J O'Shea (0-1), **A O'Donovan**; J Kennedy (0-4), G Power (0-2), P Spillane (2-1); M Sheehy (0-3), E Liston (0-1), W Maher (1-0). Subs: D Moran (0-1) for Power, J Egan for Maher.

★ **CORK:** J Kerins; M Lynch, M Healy, J Evans; N Cahalane, C Ryan, J Kerrigan (0-1); D Creedon, C Corrigan (0-1); T Nation, M Burns (0-2), D Barry (1-4); D Allen (0-1), J Allen (0-1), T Murphy. Subs: K Kehilly for Healy, B Coffey (1-0) for Corrigan, C O'Neill for Burns.

THE ACTION

IN TAKING THEIR 61st Munster title, Kerry blended youth with age and the captain, Ambrose O'Donovan, a 22-year-old newcomer to the side, was the toast of Killarney and his native Gneeveguilla, where celebrations continued into the early hours.

Two goals from Pat Spillane either side of the half-time break proved the difference against the defending champions. In his 10th season as Kerry manager, Mick O'Dwyer was in search of his sixth All-Ireland title.

Kerry struck the first hammer blow just 20 minutes into the game; 'Bomber' Liston linked up well with Spillane on the right wing and, after he regained possession, the big Ballybunion full-forward selflessly laid the ball off to the in-rushing Willie Maher, who delightfully took the honour of finding the back of the net.

Seven minutes later, Kerry struck for goal number two. A superb long Jack O'Shea ball was excellently controlled by Mikey Sheehy, who put it on a plate for Spillane and the Templenoe man coolly left-footed to raise the green flag. Kerry led 2-9 to 0-7 at half time.

On resumption, Kerry seemed to put the result beyond any doubt when, four minutes after the break, Liston and Spillane linked up well again, with the latter sliding the ball into the net for Kerry's third goal.

A well-taken point by 'Ogie' Moran six minutes into the second-half gave the hosts an 11-point lead, 3-10 to 0-8. However, Cork fought back and the Rebels gave their supporters a rare opportunity to raise the roof when Dom Creedon carved out an opening for substitute Barry Coffey to burst through the Kerry defence for a well-struck goal.

Kerry's lead had slipped to five points with only eight minutes left on the clock. A second Cork goal came 27 minutes into the second-half when Dave Barry blasted the ball past Charlie Nelligan. That was Cork's last contribution to the scoreboard, however.

When Tipperary's John Moloney blew for full-time there was a release of pent-up emotion after the bitter disappointment of the previous two years. After Seamus Darby snatched victory for Offaly in 1982 and Cork defeated Kerry by a point in '83, a sense of a new dawn was felt in the stands as supporters, bursting with excitement, stormed the field.

★ ★ ★ ★ ★

66

THE BIG MATCH for me would have to be the 1984 Munster final.

The fact it was the Centenary final was one thing, but there was so much more! Kerry had lost their bid for five in-a-row in 1982, and I was a sub in Páirc Uí Chaoimh in '83 when we were caught by a sucker punch, when a last-minute goal went in.

In 1984 then, a lot of the so-called experts were saying that this Kerry team was gone over the top; saying we were old, and all the rest of it. The GAA Centenary was a real big deal that year, and it wasn't lost on Mick O'Dwyer.

O'Dwyer, being the shrewd manager that he is, he wouldn't make a big deal about it but he said, 'Now, this is a special year in the GAA's history... the Centenary, and whoever wins this will be remembered!'

I suppose, in a way, he was kind of saying... *Look, we lost the five-in-row, we were unlucky in '83... This will be a great way to make up for all those years.* Because they were heartbreaks, there is doubt about that!

1984 was a special year for me too, because I'd broken onto the Kerry team. I was a young fella coming on to the team, and I had the captaincy trust on me, but to be honest about it the last thing on my mind that year was the captaincy. I just wanted to fight my way onto the team. I knew I was close enough, and there was always going to be injuries...I felt that would be the year that might define me.

Breaking onto the team and becoming captain in my first year was very unusual, but was due to the misfortune of Diarmuid O'Donoghue... which has been well documented.

Diarmuid should have been the captain. We were actually travelling together the night he got injured – I had to drop him home to his mum and dad, Lilly and Jamesy... God rest the both of them.

He broke his wrist and Killarney Legion didn't have a captain, but Gneeveguilla had won the East Kerry Championship. The Killarney team came together and said an East Kerry man should be captain. That's how I got the captaincy, but the captaincy was the last thing on my mind at the start of 1984.

I got injured then in a club game, before we played Tipperary.

I had to fight my way back.

We had challenge games at that time, As vs Bs, and they were tough matches… everybody was fighting for places. After one trial game, Micko came up to me afterwards and said, 'You keep going the way you're going. You are in touching distance to make the starting team.'

I knew I was close.

There was another two or three weeks until we had the final trial game before the Munster final. It was on in Beaufort.

And Micko said to me when we were coming in after…'Get yourself right now and focus on the Munster final!' I was put onto the A team that day, so I knew how close I was. Little things like.

There was definitely pressure on us going into the Munster final that year… there is no point saying there wasn't.

The game was on in Killarney. The *atmosphere*… there was a fabulous, *fabulous* atmosphere in Killarney. It was a full house. It was a beautiful Sunday… you could cut the tension.

A Munster final against Cork in Killarney is the nearest thing you'll get to the biggest game of the year in Croke Park.

Cork were Munster champions, they were coming to Killarney as champions – with the best support in the country. The Cork supporters love coming to Killarney… they'd nearly prefer coming to Killarney, than going to Páirc Uí Chaoimh.

That day, they weren't found wanting. It was a beautiful day. The sun was splitting the stones… something that sticks in my memory.

The likes of Páidí Ó Sé, God rest his soul, and all those boys, they didn't like losing games at home. They'd suffer if they lost a game in Killarney. Even in the league, they didn't want to lose games at home in front of their own crowd. Whatever about away – it was bad to lose any place – but it was especially bad to lose at home.

Mick O'Dwyer was of the same mind all year… *We're playing in our own backyard and we don't want to be beaten in our own backyard.*

That was the message that whole year. From the time we started pre-season that was a point that O'Dwyer kept making… *We're going to be in a Munster final, and we'll be playing Cork at home in... Centenary year.*

Things fell right for us!

The heat that day, as I've said, was almost unbearable. There was a big intake of water that day. There were bottles of water everywhere… and more bottles in buckets full of ice.

But it was a beautiful day for football… a little bit too hot, but beautiful.

The game itself started frantically enough. I remember… always with Kerry and Cork, especially in our time, in the first 10 or 15 minutes there would be a bit of sorting out done. You'd be laying down a marker, and there would be a couple of big hits going in. Myself and Jimmy Kerrigan met early on, and that kind of set the tone.

We all knew it was a game we could not afford to lose.

There was an incredible tension, even with the more experienced fellas.

I found Seánie Walsh brilliant… he'd talk to us. Páidí Ó Sé was brilliant… 'Bomber', 'Ogie', Mikey and Ger Power… all these fellas would talk to us.

But there was no big chat before the match that day… every fella was clued in. We just sat down and just focused ourselves on the game… *What kind of a game we were going to play.*

Normally there might be a bit of banter, but that day against Cork you could cut the tension inside in the dressing-room. Fellas were keyed up.

Mick O'Dwyer said at one stage… 'Lads, what's gone is gone!

'What we've won, we've won… and what we've lost, we've lost.

'Forget about it! This is 1984… this is a totally different year.'

And he said, 'Think of what ye want to be remembered for!'

We had a fantastic team through the 70s. We lost in 1982, and we lost in '83, and now O'Dwyer told us there were two ways we could go… *We can be looking back at ourselves and saying… Ah we did this… and Ah we did that… or… We can look forward and forget the past. Forget the wins, forget the defeats… This is the one we want to win… 1984.*

1984 was a very special year but, being honest about it, every year you put on a Kerry jersey is a special year. There is a big deal with putting on a Kerry jersey, because you are representing your family, your club… and your county, and there is a lot expected of you. It is a special thing.

Anyone who has worn the county jersey and played for Kerry, or any other county team, will tell you it is a big deal.

There were a lot of players that year, the likes of 'Bomber', 'Ogie' and Seánie Walsh, all these boys… they still had a lot left in the tank.

The boys at that time had real tunnel vision. We were asked to do a lot of training. We trained very hard and there were never any complaints. We were told to come in for extra nights, myself included, and we just did it. Even though we were tired and sore, we'd do another three or four nights on the spin.

We might be in on a Saturday morning at nine or 10, and do an hour and a half. If O'Dwyer felt we needed to do it, that it wasn't going as good as he felt it should be in training, he'd do that… get us in. But I never heard anybody complaining. It was just… *All for training*… and we'd say… *That's fine. Grand… Nine o'clock.*

I didn't realise what fitness was until 1984, even though I trained in '83 with them. We knuckled down and we knuckled down early.

We started in January, which the boys were saying wasn't normal for them… it's normally February or March that we'd come back. But we started training at the end of January in Kerins O'Rahillys.

There were two big things I found with O'Dwyer, and with the Kerry team.

There was a belief in O'Dwyer, and a trust in O'Dwyer.

If O'Dwyer told us to go through the wall, we went through the wall. That was the level of trust and belief he instilled in players. When he stood up and he said something… everyone took it on board.

The other great thing about O'Dwyer was that if you had a weakness, or if there was something wrong with your play, he would never blaggard you in front of 30 fellas. He'd call you aside.

He'd bend the finger over to you, and you'd walk up the field. You might walk 10 or 15 yards with him and he'd chat with you… *You need to do this, you need to tackle more… Or you need to fall back more, you need to break the ball… Or you need to put it in first time… All the rest of it.* But it was never done in front of a crowd. It was always done one-on-one.

And that was to everybody. There was no roaring and shouting in front of a whole panel of players. He'd go up nice and politely to you and say, 'I'm going to bring you in now for an extra week of training. We're going to train Monday, Wednesday, Friday… and you'll do Saturday and Sunday morning.'

And that would be it, there would be no more about it.

That's the way it went.

It was amazing. That was the first thing that impressed me as a young fella! Seeing all these fellas… legends… the likes of 'Bomber', John O'Keeffe and Páidí… and they still had a belief and a trust in O'Dwyer.

It was frightening, and second-to-none what he did.

Going into Croke Park for the All-Ireland final against Dublin in 1984, this woman came up to me. Now the crowd was full and I was tensed up and everything else, but this woman – whether she was a nun, I cannot say – pressed a miraculous medal into my hand, and she told me, 'Clip that onto your togs… that'll see you through!'

Now, at the time I wouldn't have been a very religious man, but I wouldn't say I was a total pagan or anything, so I knew what she handed to me.

I never met the woman afterwards, but I would have loved to. She just pushed it into the palm of my hand when I was going in and she says, 'The best of good luck today, she'll look after you… the Blessed Virgin.'

That just stood out to me because of the faith she had number one, but can you imagine going to an All-Ireland final with a miraculous medal… you are mixing religion and GAA… the whole lot together.

When I started playing, Gneeveguilla was a young club but we had a couple of great men involved in underage football.

We had Brendan Cronin, God rest him, and John Kelleher, the principal and teacher in Boherbue was very good… and my namesake 'Ambrose Don' and the McCarthys. They were all very good football men. The club was only formed in 1960.

There was always someone with us at matches and there was a great effort put in. We were lucky enough; I won a good bit underage with Gneeveguilla.

I joined a good crop of players in Gneeveguilla, and I played senior very young. I was maybe 14 and a half when I started playing senior, and I played championship when I was 15.

We boxed above our weight. We won a couple of O'Donoghue Cups in East Kerry, and East Kerry was strong at that time. Spa were very strong, Crokes were strong, Legion were strong… and Rathmore were strong, but we could hold our own with the likes of Dr Crokes. We won three O'Donoghue Cups and we won the county championship in 1980. We had very good footballers at that time.

I remember playing a league match in Moyvane. 'Big Paddy' was centre-back for Moyvane. I was only a young fella and I had to go down to meet the chairman before the game because they wanted to ask me if I was comfortable playing. First of all they asked my parents, and then they brought me down to the chairman and, of course, I said I was happy.

I had two brothers on either side of me, Nellie and Mossie… and that was our half-forward line. On 'Big Paddy' that day… he won't mind me saying this… I knew well I had the legs on him. But it was still a baptism of fire… if you come out of Moyvane, you will come out of most places!

Club is very important.

The GAA family is a fantastic family, be it club or county.

I'd still be very good friends with 'Nudie' Hughes and Eamon Murphy in Monaghan. The same can be said of the Cork fellas, and the same with the Dublin boys. It's nice to meet them.

It's a big family and it is a family that looks after itself as well. The friends I've made from gaelic football, I've made for life.

Before the 1985 Munster final, I had a shoulder injury and I was strapped – it was kept very quiet. Conor Counihan was centre-back for Cork. Now, myself and Conor are very good friends, but I remember I was going through and Conor left his position… and Conor didn't leave centre back that often. He was always a kind of stay home centre-back.

He came and he took me with a belt of a shoulder.

I looked at him and I said, 'Conor, you went for the wrong one!'

I won't say what he answered back to me, but we spoke about it afterwards. Someone had leaked to Cork that I was heavily strapped. He said himself that he just wanted to test it out so that I'd be happy in the knowledge that I'd be able to continue.

Of course, it wasn't the wrong shoulder, but I said, 'Wrong shoulder Conor… WRONG SHOULDER!

I look back at my footballing career with huge pride, but I feel lucky in a way because it was a great time to be there.

I saw both sides of the coin with Kerry. I was there in the good times and then in the latter years from 1988 up along, we struggled a bit. We had good teams, but we struggled.

I always felt there was a fierce respect for the Kerry jersey and any man who made it will know what I'm talking about – there is a fierce sense of achievement when you pull the jersey over your head.

But it always comes back to the club! Every footballer who makes the Kerry team must thank his club, and I'm no different. It is what the club instils in you from a young age, and what you inherit from people who are training you and managing, that will shape you for your future.

A good club, and the rest will look after itself!

TOMMY DOYLE

KERRY 0-14 DUBLIN 1-6
All-Ireland SFC Final
Croke Park
SEPTEMBER 23, 1984

Tommy Doyle celebrates with Mick O'Dwyer after he captained Kerry to victory over Tyrone in the 1986 All-Ireland final, but it is the first of the Kingdom's three in-a-row in the 80s, defeating Dublin in '84, that lives with him.

★ **KERRY:** C Nelligan; P Ó Sé, S Walsh, M Spillane; **T Doyle**, T Spillane, G Lynch; J O'Shea (0-1), A O'Donovan; J Kennedy (0-5), D Moran (0-1), P Spillane (0-4); G Power, E Liston (0-3), J Egan. Sub: T O'Dowd for Egan.

★ **DUBLIN:** J O'Leary; M Holden, G Hargan, M Kennedy; P Canavan, T Drumm, PJ Buckley; J Ronayne, B Mullins; B Rock (1-5), T Conroy (0-1), K Duff; J Kearns, A O'Toole. J McNally. Subs: M O'Callaghan for McNally, C Sutton for Ronayne.

THE ACTION

THE RICHNESS OF Kerry's play, complemented by a positive approach, produced a contest which saw Dublin struggle from the very start and only momentarily looked like All-Ireland champions when Barney Rock found the net eight minutes into the second-half. Like any good structure, the foundations of Kerry's surprise victory were undoubtedly laid at the back as the Dublin forwards continually met a brick wall as they so desperately went in search of their second title in succession. Only two Dublin forwards scored in the game.

Dublin won the toss and played with the wind into the Canal goal, but it was the Kingdom who got off to a flying start – three points up within nine minutes thanks to an Eoin 'Bomber' Liston effort and two well taken scores from John Kennedy, the first of which was a free. Barney Rock opened Dublin's account with a point from a '45' midway through the opening half.

Both sides exchanged points before Pat Spillane left Brian Mullins sprawling and whipped over a great point to send Kerry in leading at half-time by 0-7 to 0-3. Dublin's first and only point from play in the opening half had come in the 27th minute, when Tommy Conroy, aided by the strong breeze, raised the white flag to narrow the deficit to two.

That Rock goal came in the 43rd minute as he rounded Mick Spillane before avoiding a tackle from Charlie Nelligan to stick it into the back of the net, giving Dublin a much-needed, albeit temporary, boost. The margin was reduced to just three points, and doubts were starting to surface amongst Kerry supporters.

However, just as Kerry looked like they had lost their rhythm, 'Ogie' Moran, who, upped his game after being restored to centre-forward, linked up well with Spillane to score an excellent point. When Kennedy tapped over a close-range free two minutes later to reclaim his side's five-point lead, Kerry's confidence was restored. Two Rock frees were cancelled out by another Spillane effort and a Jack O'Shea point, before Rock and Liston exchanged further points.

Kerry were unrelenting in their quest for football glory.

★ ★ ★ ★ ★

"

I CAME HERE when I was about seven… we came back in about 1963.

My father had emigrated to America in 1947 when he was 17 or 18. We came back to Camp, and my father and mother bought a farm.

I really got into football when I went to secondary school in Tralee where I came across Donie O'Sullivan.

Donie was a great player at the time… he captained Kerry in 1970. And Donie was teaching us. There were three very important people in my time, when I was young… Donie O'Sullivan, Liam Sayers… Liam was a Curaheen man… and Seán Óg Sheehy.

Seán Óg had played with and captained Kerry as well in 1962.

I became enraptured by the GAA.

I had no boots and I remember going into Tralee with £2.50 in my pocket, in old shillings.

I went in with my brother John. We said we'd go into John Dowling's to buy boots. So, in we go anyway, and we were looking in the window at Dowling's sports shop, and all of a sudden out comes John Dowling. He was like a God to us.

We were looking at the boots and John, who became a great friend of mine afterwards, says, 'What are you looking for?'

He was showing us all the boots and then he said… 'These are the boots the Mickos wear!'

Of course, the 'Mickos' at the time were Mick O'Dwyer and Mick O'Connell. So they were *big boots* at the time.

I remember… they were £14.

We were gazing at them.

But in fairness to John, he said, 'Come in, come in… come in!'

He didn't know us from Adam. He sat us down, and between this, that, and the other thing, when we walked out of the shop I'd say we had given him £5. It wasn't even half the price of the boots we got. He gave us boots, and he gave us green and gold socks… and out the road with us, thumbing home back to Camp… and immediately down the field we went kicking ball.

That's how that craic started… God rest John Dowling.

There was a fierce affiliation with the Strand Road and Annascaul at the time because Dinny O'Shea, who played midfield for Kerry with John Dowling in 1955 and '56, is from Camp. And you had Dinny Falvey in Annascaul, who played as well for Kerins O'Rahillys with John Dowling.

At the time rural clubs had no pitches… there was nothing.

John Dowling was a fantastic clubman.

Afterwards… *I'll never forget it.*

In 1986, when my son Kevin was born, I was living in Tralee at the time. I was living in Laurel Court, and John Dowling landed up late one night… about half eight or nine. Kevin must have been only a couple of weeks old.

I said, 'Come in, and sit down'… and, of course, this craic started.

'Your young fella has to play with The Narries.'

I said, 'No, my young fella will play with Annascaul… He's going back west, where my father came from'.

A friendly argument started, of course.

He pulled out a box, and opened it, and there was a pair of little boots inside… blue boots. I don't know where he got the boots from, but he *shocked* me. He actually shocked me.

'I gave you your first pair of boots,' he reminded me.

'How could you have remembered that?'

He said, 'I happened to come across you afterwards'.

John Dowling was a serious man at the time for going into the schools. 'I got to see you in the school, and Donie O'Sullivan was telling me about you,' he continued.

'I gave you your first pair of boots, and I've watched you all along up since'.

He still shocked me.

'I'm here, now!' he said. 'And these are a pair of boots for your young fella, but he has to play with The Narries'.

We were there all night!

I didn't play much under-14s with Annascaul, because at the end of the day I wasn't affiliated with any club.

There were two other very good people at that time.

There was a man by the name of Conn Sherry from Derrymore… and Pat

Healy. Pat and Conn used to cart a gang of us around playing under-14 matches… we were playing under the so-called name of Derrymore. We were 12 and 13 years old, playing away and we actually got to the semi-final of a rural under-14 Bord na nÓg competition.

We were drawn against Templenoe… we didn't even know where Templenoe was at the time… us, just a bunch of young fellas back in the 70s.

Off over to Killarney with us, and into the small pitch. It used to be in front of Fitzgerald Stadium. And we played Templenoe in an under-14 rural semi-final which was a huge thing because at the time we didn't even have a pitch.

We drew with them, and we had to play them again a week or two after.

They hammered us the second night. The second night was the first time… and we often talk about it, that Pat Spillane, myself and Mick Spillane encountered one another.

Pat and Mick at the time were going to the Sem in Killarney. There was some reason why they didn't get out for the first match, but they certainly got out for the second match!

I just stood back… *Pat… was amazing.*

It was the first time that I saw a lad of our age… Mick Spillane… standing over a 50-yard free… the old pigskin football. And at 14, he stuck it over the bar.

Off the ground.

A different level.

I looked at him and I thought… *Holy Christ, is this the level these fellas are at?*

They were awesome, the two of them. Pat… just forget it, he was out on his own. Little did I know how close we'd become afterwards.

I got up to under-16 level and we had to affiliate with a club at that stage. Annascaul came shouting and roaring, and sure I had to play with Annascaul, really, with my father from Annascaul.

I was an average player. I was just lucky that I always had a good focus and a passion. I wouldn't lace some of the players' boots.

I was lucky that Micko had good time for me. I was lucky that he saw in the likes of myself, Páidí Ó Sé, and Tim Kennelly, fellas who would go the whole hog. I'd never have the skills of a Pat Spillane, a Jacko… or a Mike Sheehy.

But I played in a lot of games.

Of course, the 1982 final is one you'd want to forget.

I'd a lot of good days with the club. Getting to a senior county final with Annascaul in 1993, considering where we came from, was some achievement. I'd begun togging out with Annascaul at senior level when I was 15 and a half… going out to Lyracrumpane and playing a team called Clounmacon.

No showers… nothing.

Afterwards, washing ourselves down with water from the side of a ditch, drying ourselves with a towel… and home.

That's how I started, but for me, there were so many milestones in my football career… from the first time I put on a Kerry minor jersey to the first time I togged out for Kerry seniors. I togged out in a Munster final in 1978 against Cork in Páirc Uí Chaoimh. I was lucky enough to be picked. I was marking Tom Creedon. We had a tough tussle, and I kicked two or three points off him. I did quite well. I didn't end up finishing the match because the two of us ended up throwing left hooks and we were put off by Seán O'Connor.

But at that time, it was fine; there was no big deal made about it.

Then to captain Kerry was a *big deal*. You can talk about all the matches, but for me there were so many milestones like that along the way.

I got injured in 1976. I was above in the Curragh in the army at the time. I had half a chance of making the Kerry team. I was playing in the Medical Services Cup with the Curragh Command when I got injured.

I hurt my leg. But, of course, when I was picked by Kerry to go up and play a challenge game against Louth, of course I was going. Whatever way it happened… the ground was very hard, I came down on the same ankle again.

A couple of buddies of mine in the army… they saw that I wasn't making any kind of improvement. So they brought me to this gentleman, God rest him, by the name of Michael O'Neill in a place called Myshall, in Carlow. He was a famous bone-setter.

In I went to this big old house, and this massive man was inside. He looked at me and he said, 'What's your problem?'

I told him, 'I've an awful pain in my ankle… I can't run'. I'd been out at this stage for three or four weeks.

Hands on… a big powerful pair of hands. And he says to me, 'Ah, you've a problem alright, you've a bone out of place in your ankle'.

He kept talking. 'Do you know you've about 54 or 55 small bones in that ankle?

'You've had this bone out for a long time, there is a lot of fluid in it… if we don't sort it out, you won't play again.'

I'll never forget it. I was inside in this big room, and there was nothing inside in the room but a huge grandfather clock, a chair and a desk. That's all, there wasn't a picture… *Nothing.*

I was sitting in the chair and he said, 'Put your leg up there to me'.

Then he asked, 'What time is it?'

I looked at the clock. He nearly knocked me out… whatever he did. A dart of pain hit me and it nearly knocked me off the chair. He twisted my ankle, and he says, 'I've put the bone back in'.

It was like I had broken my leg. The dart of pain that hit me brought a cold sweat clean out through me.

'Take this!' he said. 'And wrap this around your leg… and rub this onto it. Don't train or do a thing on that for three weeks… and you'll be fine'.

I kept rubbing in this lotion he gave to me and, fair play to the man, three weeks later I was out running and training again. I became very friendly with the man afterwards because I had to visit him on more than one occasion over the years.

In the famous All-Ireland semi-final against Dublin in 1977 I was tucked in corner-forward for about 20 minutes. In '78 then, I got on the Kerry team. I played in that Munster final I mentioned, and did quite well. But my season ended quickly enough after that.

In the All-Ireland semi-final against Roscommon, I was playing centre-forward. About 20 or 25 minutes into the game there was a tangle, and I broke my arm. I didn't know I'd broken it, kept playing… it was pouring rain at the time. I looked at my arm… and there was blood all over it.

Brendan Lynch came running and said, 'Christ, get off the pitch… your arm is broken!'

Before I knew it, I was in the Richmond Hospital getting it operated on.

It knocked the s**t out of me at the time. *How am I going to get back from this?* It gave me fierce trouble and still, to this day, 40 years later, there's an eight-inch plate and nine screws in my arm. I did that much damage.

I was out for eight months.

There were no phones at that time, but one night Mick O'Dwyer arrived at the house in the white Merc. I had got word that he was coming. Joe Keohane tipped me off and said that Micko was coming to see me.

He took me down the field, and we had a great chat.

'Are you going to be back?'

'Look Micko, I don't know... I've no power in this arm any more. I don't know what's wrong'.

'Stick with it!' he told me. 'Come into training!'

I went training, and I did a bit of running... but when I tried to play ball, it didn't come right for me. But the fact that O'Dwyer drove from Waterville up, and spent about an hour with me... that was a defining moment. He had more to be doing if he wanted. It gave me the lift I badly needed.

In 1974, I'd been selected to represent Kerry in an under-21 trial game.

I was saving a field of hay with my father when a letter came to the house. A challenge game... North vs South. I was picked as a half-back. I was a young fella at the time, 19... just finished minor.

I got the boots... down to the cross, and thumbed in from Camp to the old Austin Stack Park. It was a long drive up. It is totally different today.

I played left half-back. Ger O'Driscoll was playing midfield. I played very, very well, considering that I was saving a field of hay up until about two o'clock that day.

After it, I thumbed home.

Before I left, I was asked if I wanted to play with Kerry the following day. Kerry were playing a challenge match against Cork in Kiskeam. It was the opening of a pitch.

I hadn't a clue where Kiskeam was!

'I will,' I had told them. 'No problem!'

I thought it was the best thing in the world, but looking back... they probably couldn't get anyone else to go. I didn't care... *I was going...* if I had to walk to Kiskeam I was going.

I was collected the following day, a Sunday.

Off I went, and who did I draw in the challenge match... only Dinny Allen.

He had played with Cork before that, but he was suspended at the time and was coming back. Dinny had a fair reputation. He was a great forward. I was playing right half-back and Dinny was No 12, and I did alright on him.

Normally, challenge games at that time were just a bit of craic, but Dinny was trying hard… he was trying to make an impression. Billy Morgan was in goals that day. Cork had a good team out.

That was my first senior match with Kerry… the opening of Kiskeam pitch.

Annascaul were in Division 2 and we were hanging in there.

I'd always be a good clubman.

We were in Division 2, which was good for us, but I was now playing with Kerry at the time.

The County Board fixed county league matches and O'Dwyer and the boys… they said they didn't want us playing. In fairness to O'Dwyer, he was always a great clubman, but two to three weeks before a championship match he'd say… 'No more club games!'

It was two weeks before the Munster final.

I knew going home that I was going to be under pressure, because if we lost our game against Lispole, we could have gone back down to Division 3.

Liam Higgins was a selector with Kerry at the time, but Liam was still playing with Lispole.

What am I going to do? I was asking myself.

It was a Saturday evening match… I'll never forget it.

I went and togged out. I knew that I was going to be in fierce trouble.

He'll drop me for the Munster final.

I played anyway, and we won well. We won by eight or nine points in Lispole. There were no mobiles, and I said to myself… *I won't be home five minutes and he'll ring me.* And sure enough, I wasn't in the door and I heard the phone.

I answered it and all I got was… 'Well…you togged?'

'I did.'

'We'll deal with it Tuesday night,' he continued.

'Alright,' and I hung up. At that time myself, Mikey Sheehy, Johno and Ger Power were going to training in the same car. Over we went, and there wasn't a word said.

We went through a two-hour grueller on the field.

The craic at the time was… *Quarter past seven for half.* Micko didn't care what you were doing… you were on that pitch by quarter past seven. Micko came out and blew the whistle at half past.

If he was in a good mood we'd usually finish up at a quarter to nine, but if he was in a bad mood with us he could keep going until nine… or a quarter past.

Out with the whistle and the stopwatch… that's how he trained us!

The session was going on a bit and the boys were blaming me.

Next thing, Micko shouts, 'Right lads… Private come over here'. There were a good few people watching. In those days you could have a few thousand people watching, particularly in the summer.

He took me down to the corner of Fitzgerald Stadium, as you come into the stadium… down into the corner. I'd say I put down the roughest half an hour of my life.

I crawled off the pitch.

I don't know how I actually made it back to the dressing-room. The boys, of course, were breaking their arses laughing… they had finished their showers and all.

In I stood, under the cold shower… seeing stars all over the place. I could hardly stand up. I sat in the car, and drove home. I wasn't even able to go down and eat. It took me weeks to get over it

But that was the end of it. There were no more words about it. I was lucky enough that I togged out for the Munster final… that he didn't drop me.

We often talked about it together afterwards, and Micko really appreciated the effort I made for the club.

But Christ, did I pay for it!

I had great success with the club

In 1988, we won our first West Kerry Championship in 31 years. We went senior in 1993… we'd won a couple of intermediate titles before that.

But, for me, one of the proudest days playing club football was when we drew Mid-Kerry, who were county champions. They had beaten St Brendan's in the senior final, and we had beaten St Mary's in the intermediate final. At the time, if you won three intermediate titles you were allowed to go senior. We decided we'd go, because we'd never again get the chance.

A small club like Annascaul… we'd have had nothing if it wasn't for Fr Curtin, who gave us a pitch, and Tommy McCarthy and these fellas, who for years put fierce work into the club… so we said we'd go senior.

In the county championship at the time… if you lost, you were out! We drew the champions of Kerry in Annascaul.

We put a massive effort into it. I travelled from Tralee four and five nights a week, and we trained Saturdays. I took over training myself. We beat Mid-Kerry in Annascaul that night by 10 points… *And us making our senior championship debut.*

For us, that was unbelievable. I came up with the club from Division 5. We couldn't even put out an under-16 team in my time. We had to join up with Lispole when I played minor and we won a Minor Championship.

There was never an under-21 team.

We used to tog off in Annascaul at the back of the national school, where the lads used to put their bicycles. In 1984 we opened a pitch, and Dublin came down to play us, but before that we had nothing. Lispole had nothing. The only pitches in West Kerry were in Dingle and Castlegregory.

That drive, that hunger, that loyalty… pride and commitment, that is what got us there. But every club had it. Anywhere you went – and I played for Annascaul all over the county – fellas would be coming at you. They didn't care if you had ever put a Kerry jersey on or not… *They came for you.*

You went up to places like Tarbert; you went up to Castleisland; you went down into Ballinskelligs, down into Reenard… down into Kenmare… back to the Gaeltacht… *And they came at you.* You got a football education fast, you learned what the game was all about. You learnt how to be a leader, and you learnt how to be a winner.

Fellas in Knocknagoshel…. they came at you and they didn't care who you were. But that was it then! We'd have a pint and the craic, and they'd be the first fellas shouting for you in a Munster final, or above in Croke Park.

The 1984 All-Ireland final would be the *Game of My Life.*

In 1983, Dublin won the All-Ireland with just 12 players on the field at the end when they beat Galway in the final. Kieran Duff, a good buddy of mine, was wronged in that game.

We had been beaten by Cork that summer. I thought it was a huge shock, but let's face it, we'd been going constantly for nine or 10 years. We all went our way... maybe everybody needed a little bit of space.

Around November of 1983, O'Dwyer rang... contacted us all to tell us he wanted to meet us all in Bernie O'Callaghan's, outside in the Cliff House in Ballybunion.

Out we go this Saturday in the middle of November, in the pouring rain, and we had a training session on the pitch. Then we went down to Bernie O'Callaghan's, but we didn't know what to expect, or what was going to happen.

We all sat down.

Micko started and his first words were, 'Lads, Dublin can win an All-Ireland with 12 men... I'm quite happy to go and try to win another one with what I have in the room here!'

He laid out his plans... it was Centenary year. He wanted a Centenary All-Ireland. That's all he wanted. *We all wanted it.* We went training that following Tuesday night, and we didn't stop playing football of any description until September 23 the following year, when we beat Dublin in the Centenary All-Ireland.

We won the League, which was something we never really did, but he wanted to win that as well.

Micko had said... 'I want a clean sweep in '84'.

JACK O'SHEA

KERRY 2-12 DUBLIN 2-8
All-Ireland SFC Final
Croke Park
SEPTEMBER 22, 1985

Jack O'Shea breaks past Robbie Kelleher (above) and shoots over the head of Pat O'Neill in the 1978 All-Ireland final against Dublin, and seven years later in '85 he was still in brilliant form against Dublin's greatest opponents on the biggest day of the year, when he shot 1-3 in the opening half.

★ **KERRY:** C Nelligan; P Ó Sé, S Walsh, M Spillane; T Doyle (0-1), T Spillane, G Lynch; **J O'Shea (1-3)**, A O'Donovan; T O'Dowd (1-1), D Moran (0-1), P Spillane (0-2); M Sheehy (0-3), E Liston, G Power. Sub: J Kennedy (0-1) for Power.

★ **DUBLIN:** J O'Leary; M Kennedy, G Hargan, R Hazley; P Canavan, N McCaffrey, D Synottt; J Ronayne, B Mullins; B Rock (0-3), T Conroy (0-2), C Redmond; J Kearns (0-2), J McNally (2-0), C Duff. Subs: T Carr (0-1) for Redmond, PJ Buckley for Mullins.

THE ACTION

A JACK O'SHEA point after just 11 seconds set Kerry on their merry way as the Kingdom put in a marvellous performance to put Dublin to the sword and retain the All-Ireland title. The winners completely dominated the first-half with Eoin 'Bomber' Liston, yet again, causing nightmares for the Dubs.

Kerry led by nine points at half-time, 1-8 to 0-2. However, the men in blue stormed back in the second-half reducing Kerry's lead to a single point with just five minutes remaining. Two Joe McNally goals in a 10-minute period brought a spirited Dublin side agonisingly close to snatching victory. When Barney Rock pointed to make it a one-point game, Dublin had all the momentum.

The week after the game would be dominated by the controversial decision by Mick O'Dwyer's and his players to feature in an advertisement for Bendix washing machines, with the line... *Only Bendix could wash this lot.* The advertisement appeared in several newspapers on the morning of the game.

Barney Rock got Dublin's first score with a second-minute free, but they had to wait another 26 minutes for their next. By that stage, Kerry had a goal and seven points to their name and a significant stranglehold on the game. Kerry's goal came in the 11th minute, after Pat Canavan was adjudged to have fouled Ger Power as he bore down on goal. O'Shea blasted the resulting penalty into the top left corner giving keeper John O'Leary no chance.

Dublin re-emerged after the interval a completely different team and, aided by the wind, brought the game to Kerry. However, Dublin's resurgence seemed short-lived when O'Dowd went through for a fine goal in the 49th minute – Kerry's second. Dublin did however fight back again and had the ball in the net three minutes later when McNally got his first of two.

Remarkably, that Kerry goal proved to be their only second half score until five minutes from time, when they upped the tempo again to play like real champions. The game hung delicately in balance for the final few minutes before two vital breaks, at a time when Dublin went in search of an equaliser, resulted in Pat Spillane kicking over a great point from 45 yards out. O'Dowd and substitute John Kennedy added two more.

★★★★★

66

MY DREAM EVERY year was to walk behind the Artane Boys Band, as it was called back then, in September… *That was it!*

There was nowhere else I'd rather be.

There are only 30 people who can walk behind the band on All-Ireland final day and to be one of those is a unique experience. It is something any young person will cherish if they do get the chance.

To be one of those 30 is amazing.

I just took the game by its stride. I never got nervous about matches. I was always mentally well-prepared going into games and I put a lot of that down to Mícheál Ó Muircheartaigh, who trained me for 17 years up in Dublin.

As a psychiatrist, I think there is no better person. He always had me convinced that I was in superb shape, that I couldn't be any better, and that I was perfect and ready to go.

We played Monaghan in the semi-final in 1985; it was a draw, and it went to a replay.

As a team, at that stage, we were probably coming to the end as such. But that was an outstanding semi-final.

The drawn match was a real, *real* bad day. Eamonn McEneaney kicked an unbelievable point from about 47 metres out at the end of the game to draw it. Prior to that, Mikey Sheehy had kicked a great free as well to put us in front. It was a real tough battle, but it was one of those days when the weather nullified a lot of skill and pace.

We got the chance the second day to recover. The second day, it was a much better day… it was a brilliant game. What I remember most about that semi-final was that I ended up playing centre-back for more or less most of the second-half because Seán Walsh went off injured.

Then we had Dublin in the final.

It is one of the games that stands out because, when you are growing up, you always dream of scoring a goal in the All-Ireland final. You go through all of these things in your head when you are young and what you'd love to do on an All-Ireland final day.

In the first 10 or 15 minutes we got a penalty. I was the nominated penalty-taker for a couple of years after Mikey Sheehy missed a penalty in the 1982 All-Ireland final. I stood up to take the penalty, and then I kicked three points, all within 15 minutes of the start of the game… all from more or less the same spot.

When you talk about All-Irelands and playing in All-Ireland finals, you dream about scoring a goal and you dream about kicking points, so that is one of the games that stands out to me in that respect.

We had a fantastic first-half performance. We were nine points ahead at half-time and then in the second-half Dublin came back at us in a big way. Joe McNally got two goals and it was down to a point or two but Ger Lynch set up Timmy O'Dowd for a great goal in the second-half and that brought us back to four or five points in front again.

It was nip and tuck then for the rest of the game. Dublin were coming at us, but we were hanging in there. We restored our hold in the game again towards the last 15 to 20 minutes and held on.

It is a huge confidence boost when you start well in a game, when everything is right, and you're happy with how everything is going.

But when you get a penalty, you don't really think about it. You know you have to go up and take it, but you don't feel any extra pressure to be honest… *If I score… Brilliant… If I miss it, it's not the end of the world.*

I took another one in the first two minutes of the All-Ireland final in 1986, and I hit the crossbar. But you just have to stand up. You are nominated to take the penalty so you just have to stand up and take it. It's tough getting a penalty that early in a match, but you've plenty of time to recover if you don't score it.

John O'Leary was a great goalkeeper, but as you are walking up to the ball your main focus is… *Hit this ball perfectly!* You have to make up your mind and stick with it… you have to be positive.

I got a real good strike on it … it was going to take a good goalkeeper to save it.

I was at a good stage of my career. I was well established and I was confident going into that game.

Brian Mullins was marking me that day and I always felt that if I got moving, Brian would struggle with my movement all over the pitch. More or less, the three points I scored in the first-half came nearly from the same spot, and I kicked them more or less the same way. It's just one of those things… I had four shots at goal in the first 20 minutes and I got four scores. I was on a high from there on.

The good thing about our team was all our players were very good ball-winners in their own right… they could all win their own ball.

All those players had great vision and we always had this belief to give the ball to the man in the best position. 'Bomber' kicked one out to me… if not two of them out to me, for those points.

From playing with these lads, you knew that if you got into a space that they'd see you and they'd find you. We had a theory as a team… *Hit the space with the ball, rather than hitting the man… Let the player use his pace to get into that space.*

We had phenomenal forwards. As forwards they were phenomenal players but they were always great ball-winners.

The work rate of that team was also great. Mick O'Dwyer always instilled in us that our defence began with No 15 John Egan… then all the way back. When we lost possession we worked as 15 defenders, and when we won possession we were 15 attackers. That was always the frame of mind we carried into games.

I played midfield with Ambrose O'Donovan in 1984, '85 and '86, and we had a good understanding. Ambrose was a tough player. He got in there and got in about them… whereas I was more mobile around the pitch and it suited me.

Likewise with Seánie Walsh back in 1979, '80, '81 and '82… through those years, Seánie and myself had a brilliant understanding. He held the midfield too… and I did more roaming.

That's just something that falls into place with a team.

But it was all about work-rate at that time. Our training at that time was *so competitive*. Micko made training so competitive and it brought every player on… every player developed. Nobody was irreplaceable. There was always somebody on the sideline waiting to jump in.

It was unique, and the other thing unique about that team back then was that in all the games, Kerry only used one sub in most matches.

If you weren't in the first 15, or 16, you weren't going to get a game.

When we won the four in-a-row in 1981 he only used one sub in any game. It was the same in 1984 and '85. There was only ever one sub, maximum two, used at any time.

That team had gone through eight-to-10 years with only two defeats, and the players always had huge belief.

When you get to a final especially, you just need to leave it all there. You can't come away with regrets, and we didn't have too many regrets back at that time.

I was very fortunate to come up in 1975 as a minor, and come into the senior team in late-'76. You have to be lucky to come into a team at the right time with a group of dedicated people.

Micko wanted total dedication, or he just wasn't interested in you. Our training sessions were unreal to be part of. You looked forward to going in to them.

Even when it came down to sprinting in training, fellas were challenged and wanted to beat one another. That built up a huge comradeship. No one ever looked over their shoulder because they knew the next fella was working just as hard.

There was no certainty. We knew we had to keep working.

We never wanted it to end… and we never thought it would end.

I think Micko's biggest asset was his man-management skills.

He was able to man-manage *everybody*. He didn't train me the same way he trained the 'Bomber'. He didn't train the 'Bomber' the same way he trained Mikey Sheehy.

He knew exactly what everybody needed and he knew exactly how to get to people. Now he mightn't get at you directly himself… he might send somebody else the message, but he knew you'd get the message. He just had that power to get the best out of everybody.

Tactically, there was nothing any different and nothing really changed, no matter who the opposition were; he had everybody thinking and tuned in the right way. He had no doubt that we could pull out the results.

Micko started from the roots up. He got the players in that he wanted in.

He had a huge emphasis on speed, strength, training hard… being physically in great shape, that's the kind of players he wanted. If you couldn't or didn't want to be part of that, he didn't want you. There were a lot of great players in our time that didn't get a chance because they wouldn't give the commitment that he required.

Unknown to all of us, he knew exactly what I was doing, and what I was capable of; he knew exactly what everybody was capable of and that was probably his greatest asset.

When I was very young, I used to watch Mick O'Connell and Mick O'Dwyer train in Cahersiveen… they used to come together a couple of times.

And then I saw Mick O'Dwyer play at club level for Waterville down in Cahersiveen. He was such a determined player himself. He was such a forceful player, and the driving force in the Waterville team all through the early 70s, when they had a fantastic team. He even convinced Mick O'Connell to come play with them.

Watching the two Mickos playing from a very young age was a huge influence on me growing up. Living opposite the football field was also a huge plus, because, when I was between four and 10 years of age, there wasn't a game played in Cahersiveen that I wasn't at.

I was behind the goals kicking the ball back.

And it wasn't *just* to kick the ball back, it was to kick the ball back over the bar.

We used to have a contest…a gang of us, to try and get the ball, and kick it back. I've many great memories and years of happy times growing up in Cahersiveen.

We'd a very, very strong underage group at that time in our town. We won the under-14, under-16 and minor championships, which was huge. We also won the Dunloe Cup with the school. At that time, we'd a great crop of lads coming together.

There was a man in Cahersiveen at that time called Paddy Murphy and he looked after all of the underage at St Mary's. It wasn't a case of five or six fellas looking after an underage team, it was just one man who took it upon himself to take on the team, and Paddy led us through under-14, under-16 and then minor. He brought us all the way through himself.

I was fortunate enough to have a fantastic career.

You dream about things when you are young, but you never feel it is going to happen. But I think you have to be lucky to come at the right time, and you have to be lucky to get the breakthroughs.

I remember playing minor in 1974 for Kerry. I scored 1-3 in the first round and then I was dropped for the Munster final. That was a shock to me, but I hung in there and got back in the team in '75.

I had success nearly every year then in my career, and it wasn't just me. I just came at the right time and it was about being with the right lads.

We'd fierce friendships.

I transferred from St Mary's in Cahersiveen to Leixlip in 1985 but I was still playing with Kerry until '92. I went through 17 fantastic years with Kerry and with fantastic people.

It is such a privilege to meet them at any time.

I ended up playing club football until I was 42.

I never picked up an injury really – that was a huge plus for me all through my career. I was playing at all times and I missed very, very few games.

I look back on that and think… *What a career to have…* it's something you couldn't even sit down and dream about really, that it would all go so well.

BILLY O'SHEA

LAUNE RANGERS 1-10 SHANNON RANGERS 0-11
Kerry SFC First Round
Killorglin
JULY 10, 1995

Laune Rangers' brilliant run through the mid-90s, when they won the All-Ireland club title, were the best of times for Billy O'Shea (seen in action above against South Kerry in the 2004 county final).

★ **LAUNE RANGERS:** P Lyons; A Hassett, P Sheehan, M O'Connor; M Hassett, T Burns, S O'Sullivan; P Prendiville, C Kearney (1-1); J Shannon, T Fleming (0-4), L Hassett (0-2); **B O'Shea (0-2)**, G Murphy, B O'Sullivan. Subs: J O'Shea for Murphy, P Griffin (0-1).

★ **SHANNON RANGERS:** N Moloney; M Scanlon, C O'Connor, Diarmuid Twomey; J Holmes, M Purtill, Don Twomey; L O'Flaherty (0-2), T Foley; L Weir (0-2), J O'Connell (0-1), K Culhane; G Costelloe, J Kennedy (0-5), E Hennessy (0-1). Subs: E Liston for Costelloe, S Dowling for Foley.

THE ACTION

THE START OF an All-Ireland winning campaign that sits most fondly in the hearts of many in Killorglin was this hard-fought win that set Laune Rangers on their way to glory in Croke Park on St Patrick's Day 1996.

For long periods it looked likely that the visitors might cause an upset, and had former Kerry star and Shannon Rangers player-manager Eoin 'Bomber' Liston played a part in the game earlier than his introduction as a half-time substitute the end result might have been an entirely different outcome.

Laune Rangers got the all-decisive goal when Conor Kearney found the net four minutes before the half-time break. Billy O'Shea's blistering run created space for Kearney, and the midfielder fisted past Ned Moloney to put the hosts a point ahead.

The in-form O'Shea and Liam Weir added further points for their respective sides, before a well-taken Fleming free gave the hosts a two-point advantage at the half-time break.

Laune Rangers had momentum on the restart, but John Evans' charges clocked up five wides inside the opening seven minutes. Shannon Rangers, now boosted by the introduction of Liston at the interval, took full advantage of the home side's misfiring and were level by the 42nd minute thanks to points from Eamonn Hennessy and John Kennedy.

It set the scene for a dramatic finish. The sides exchanged further points, before Weir and Kennedy put Shannon Rangers two in front with just nine minutes remaining.

Just as it looked like one of the championship favourites was going to make an early and unexpected exit, the impressive Billy O'Shea stepped up to the plate when it mattered the most. O'Shea slotted over the host's seventh point, and when Paul Griffin raised the white flag with four minutes left on the clock with the equalising point, the momentum swung back in Laune Rangers' direction.

In the dying moments, Liam Hassett gave the Killorglin side the narrowest of leads before a Tommy Fleming free on the hour mark clinched a two-point victory.

★★★★★

66

WE WERE RAGING hot favourites against Shannon Rangers, and we were one of the favourites for the county championship. We played our opening game in the track here, which is the JP O'Sullivan Park in Killorglin. It was a Monday evening… a perfect evening for football… no excuses or anything like that.

The 'Bomber' Liston was training Shannon Rangers, so we knew they'd be ready for us. We won by two points. I'll never forget it… it sticks out in my mind all of the time. I got a point near the end to put the balance back in our favour… and on my run I hopped the ball twice.

I still think… *If the ref had spotted that, and they turned around and got a point, we probably wouldn't have won the match… We'd never have got to the All-Ireland final.*

That happened with about four or five minutes to go in the game.

It changed the game.

I believe… *If the referee had ever pulled us back… That was the whole thing finished.*

It is that one incident that I will always remember, because in the rest of the championship after that, we went on and won it fairly handy. And then we went on to the All-Ireland and won it.

I'll always remember that night.

It was a real tough, physical battle. It had all the attributes of a good football game. But the 'Bomber' came on at half-time and changed the course of the game. Everyone asked, 'Had he started, would they have beaten us?'

They had Liam O'Flaherty playing midfield, and he was playing midfield with Kerry at the time. They had a few good Kerry junior players as well, so they weren't a bad side by any manner of means. They didn't have a great record in the championship. They only won it once, in the late-70s.

When a footballer looks back on a career he'll always think of the glory days of an All-Ireland club win… and what it meant to the town, and the craic afterwards. When I think about those celebrations, I also have to think about the small little things that happened in other games… *Had the referee pulled me on those two hops, what would have happened?*

It was straight knockout back then. There was no backdoor or anything like that. If we'd lost that day, we were out. It was a cracking game of football.

After that match, the route was fairly okay. We played Eoghan Rua in the next round, a combination of Spa and Gneeveguilla. Ambrose O'Donovan was playing in that match. Then we beat Kenmare District comfortably enough in the semi-final… and we had East Kerry in the final which was a boring auld game to be honest. We won that by four points. It wasn't a great county final, and the rest of the championship certainly wasn't memorable.

After that we were into the All-Ireland stages. We played Bantry Blues down in Bantry, and that was a cracking game. The Munster final was against Moyle Rovers and we beat them comfortably.

The All-Ireland semi-final was played on an unmercifully bad day, a rotten day for football. It was in Ennis… we beat Corofin 0-8 to 0-6. The final wasn't the greatest game of all time, either, but nobody around here really cares about that. It is all about the result. The final score against Éire Óg was 4-5 to 0-11.

It was a massive achievement. We were only the third club in the county to do it. Crokes had achieved it in 1992, and Castleisland Desmonds won it in the mid-80s.

The mid-90s were a great time. The club was going well, and I started to go well; we'd a lot of representation on the county side… the Hassetts, Mike and Liam, and Mike Frank Russell.

It was a successful era for the club. And it was a great time as well because we were really enjoying football, and the craic that comes with winning. It was a rollercoaster… a crazy time for the club and for the town. *Good times.*

Really, *really* enjoyable times, and they went on for about two or three years. We were lucky enough to contest a number of county finals. From 1993 to 2004, we were in six of them, which is a lot. I can remember all the homecomings… getting up on Quirke's lorry… being carried over the bridge, and up the hill.

How it made it up the hill I've no idea, with all the players up on top of it. It is things like that you'll always remember… the crazy stuff that health and safety wouldn't allow today.

How were we able to get away with those things… standing on top of a quarry truck holding a Laune Rangers coloured flag. Crazy, monumental times… and the truck going up a steep hill in Killorglin.

In Bantry, before the Munster first round game, myself and Tommy Burns decided to go for a walk… a quick walk before the team meeting in the Bantry Bay Hotel.

It was about 12 o'clock in the day, and we heard music going on below. We could hear this bit of banter outside in the carpark. We went to check and see what it was… it was a crowd from Falvey's Bar here in Killorglin who had organised a bus. Sure, wasn't there an all-merciful session going. There was music and craic, drinking and smoking… the whole shebang that would be associated with a good session was taking place at 12 o'clock in the day.

Myself and Tommy looked at each other as if to say… *We are missing out on all of this.*

But we weren't, not really. We had all of that after the match, but that was typical of the fun that was being had at the time. The bonding of the whole community was just fantastic to see.

The GAA club brought all that to the area, which is amazing. People still talk about those years, and the fun and enjoyment they had following us from 1995 to the end of '97. That was the run.

It all came to an end against Crossmaglen Rangers in the All-Ireland semi-final in Portlaoise. We really should have won. We were leading with a few minutes to go. They got the breaks at the end, and they went on to win the All-Ireland comfortably enough, beating Knockmore in the final.

I had been in with Kerry since 1991.

I went straight from the minors into the seniors. We had the same manager and Mickey Ned O'Sullivan was keen enough to bring us in quickly.

The success in winning the club championship in 1996 didn't really affect me in terms of getting on the Kerry team, as I was already in there, but it certainly didn't hurt to keep the profile up. When you are playing a high standard of football at that level it doesn't do you any harm.

We were lucky. There were four of us on that panel that ended up winning the All-Ireland with Kerry in 1997 as well.

I look back on my time with Kerry with huge pride.

I can remember all my time playing with Kerry because it was always an honour, always a pleasure and a privilege.

Because we won the club county championship in 1995, I had the honour of captaining Kerry the following year.

That was Páidí Ó Sé's first year as manager.

We did okay in the National League, which we weren't doing so well in over the previous years, and we got to the All-Ireland semi-final. Unfortunately our preparation wasn't great for that semi-final. We were a bit naive going in against Mayo in 1996, but thankfully we learned a costly lesson and it was a great effort in '97.

To win an All-Ireland in the second year for a management team is good going, even though Kerry would have been one of the favourites going into that year's championship. After '96, lessons were learned very, *very* quickly.

That was the end of the famine as well. It's hard to imagine that Kerry had gone 11 years without winning an All-Ireland.

That married into the same time as when Laune Rangers were going well. We'd won the All-Ireland club the previous year so you can imagine the excitement and the atmosphere around the place… it was really positive.

We flew home after the All-Ireland win with Kerry in 1997.

I didn't see the lads at all until they collected me at the hospital and brought me to the airport and onto the plane. I got off the plane and went back into the hospital inside in Tralee. I don't know what the whole thing was about to be honest with you.

That was the only time I got to see the boys.

I didn't even see them during the flight down because they were all doing their own thing. I was thrown into the corner beside Doctor Davy Geaney and told to stay quiet.

Within 24 hours of breaking my leg, I was straight on a plane heading down home and into another hospital.

Different times. There was a bit of madness about; you need that too.

They were crazy times.

99

DARA Ó CINNÉIDE

The loss to Mayo in the All-Ireland semi-final in 1996 created the hurt necessary for Kerry to win the title 12 months later, Dara O'Cinnéide believes (here is second from right in the front row in '97 on All-Ireland final day when Kerry regained revenge for that defeat).

★ **KERRY:** D O'Keeffe; K Burns (0-1), M Hassett, S Stack; C McCarthy, S Burke, E Breen (0-1); D Ó Sé, S Moynihan; B O'Driscoll (0-1), M Fitzgerald (0-5), B O'Shea (0-2); G Farrell, L Hassett (0-1), **D Ó'Cinneide (0-3)**. Subs: John Crowley for Burke, Donal Daly for Farrell, Seán Geaney for O'Driscoll.

★ **CORK:** K O'Dwyer; M O'Connor, B Corcoran, M Farr; C O'Sullivan, S O'Brien, M O'Donovan; L Honohan (0-1), N Cahalane (0-1); D Davis, J Kavanagh (0-3), J Buckley (0-1); M O'Sullivan, C Corkery (0-3), P McGrath (0-2). Subs: D Culloty for Cahalane, M Cronin for Buckley, A Dorgan for O'Sullivan.

THE ACTION

'BARBADOS HERE WE COME!' were the words bellowed by 30-year-old Stephen Stack as Billy O'Shea triumphantly returned to the Kerry dressing-room with the cup held high, signalling that a proud football county had once more found its voice. Five years of pain were wiped away in an instant when Clare referee Kevin Walsh put the whistle to his lips to end an emotionally-charged game.

How satisfying too for Listowel Emmets man Stack, the only remaining member of the Kerry team with an All-Ireland senior medal to his name, who had just put in a performance that challenged for the Man of the Match award. Not that the men in green and gold needed any extra incentive to end Cork's three-year reign as Munster champions, but the Kerry players were offered an end of season trip to Barbados by main sponsors Kerry Group if they overcame their arch-rivals.

In the end, Kerry's huge army of supporters were singing in the rain following this sub-standard Munster final, but they didn't care. The winning is all that matters.

It was what was expected, and more – a tremendous contest that went right down to the wire between two teams that were locked together on the scoreboard with four minutes of ordinary time left, before 'The Maurice Fitzgerald Show' went into overdrive.

It wasn't until the 33rd minute that Kerry took the lead for the first time when, after a man-to-man joust with Mark O'Connor, Dara Ó Cinnéide punched the ball over the bar to send the visitors in leading by 0-6 to 0-5 at half time.

Both sides were level four more times after the restart, before Fitzgerald stood up 60-plus yards from goal and lofted over an exceptional free-kick to put Kerry a point in front with just seven minutes remaining.

That was the kick that finally swung the game in the Kingdom's favour, and the hungry Kerry supporters tasted victory.

★★★★★

66

THE MUNSTER FINAL in 1996 was the turning point.

There are a number of reasons why that game stands out. It was Páidí Ó Sé's first year as manager of the Kerry team in the championship.

It was also the first year that we had beaten Cork in a Munster final in 10 years – Cork had the upper-hand since the fall of the great Kerry team of the 80s. They'd beaten Kerry in 1987, '88 and '89… and '90 was an awful heartbreak. 1991 was a blip from Cork's point of view, as was '92, but in '93 Cork beat us, '94 Cork beat us… and in '95 Cork beat us putting an end to 'Ogie' Moran's reign. I was involved in two of those years… 1994 and '95.

We had won the under-21 All-Ireland in 1995 so there was a sense in '96 that there was a good group coming. We would go on to win a second under-21 All-Ireland in '96, but we didn't know that at the time.

We got over Tipperary in the first round, but it took us a while, and we beat Waterford in Dungarvan. There was a bit of pressure on Páidí because Tipp had been ahead after an hour in Clonmel, a couple of weeks previously. Supporters weren't too sure if we were much good.

We went down to Cork on a wet day. It wasn't packed to the rafters; people in Kerry might have lost faith, but one thing that stuck with me to this day, 25 years later… there was a younger support there. It was a terrace-crowd; they were vocal.

It was around that time too that replica jerseys were becoming popular. Wexford won the All-Ireland hurling the same year and they were very vocal, very colourful supporters. It was the first time I noticed it; the terraces were getting noisy, and famously England were hosting the European Championships… and *Football's Coming Home* was the song of that tournament.

The Kerry supporters were singing that on the terraces that day. It is not a song I particularly like or anything like that, but I couldn't get over it. It was the first time I had seen Kerry supporters depart from the tradition of just observing a game, and *really* supporting the team… *really* getting behind the team before a ball was thrown in.

It lifted us.

It was the crossing of the Rubicon, really!

It was validation. *We are good enough to win a Munster Championship, we are good enough to beat a great Cork team, who had it over us for years, down in Páirc Uí Chaoimh on a wet day.*

It just had all of the ingredients, and I think crucially as well it gave us an indication that despite the commentary that might have been in the media about us being a wishy-washy team… *We actually were good enough.*

Famously, it was said at the time that the Kerry forwards wouldn't break eggs; I was one of those Kerry forwards. I think, crucially, we sensed that the younger breed of Kerry supporters were back to support us. They didn't care, they just wanted a day out and they wanted to roar their heads off for a Kerry team. It was new to us. *It was a new thing to me anyways.*

As a kid going to Kerry games, I hadn't seen that.

You might see cheering, and you might see the odd paper crepe cap or hat, but this was flag-carrying, jersey-wearing… chanting. I'm sure a lot of it was an Austin Stacks or Dr Crokes big club-based thing where they all knew each other on the terrace, but they backed us and it was the first time I had seen it as a Kerry player.

We really appreciated it at the time.

I've no doubt about it; that helped us get over the line down in Cork.

The point that Killian Burns got… *I'll never forget it. I'm emotional thinking about it!* The crowd just went bananas. It was amazing.

We won more afterwards, but it was just such a big day in Cork in 1996!

A figurehead in all of this breakthrough was probably the greatest player that ever played with Kerry… Maurice Fitzgerald. This was his 10th season and he still hadn't won an All-Ireland medal, and the talk was going to be… 'Was this fella ever going to win an All-Ireland medal?' Now, the following year of course, he went on to do it on his own; he lifted us all over the line.

Then, there was also Seamus Moynihan. His debut was losing to Clare in 1992.

There was a perception that a lot of that group were damaged goods. The older lads… those lads will say the younger lads who came on the scene in 1994, '95 and '96 and won the All-Ireland under-21s in 1994, '95 and '96… that we gave them the lift that they needed, but they also gave us the guidance that we needed. There was a lovely blend there.

Páidí himself had done a bit of pruning and weeding out of players. He had started to form his own group, his own identity. He was quite happy to have the likes of Maurice Fitzgerald, Éamonn Breen and Liam O' Flaherty as the experienced heads and to *have us...* the brash young lads that were winning All-Ireland under-21s with him before that.

There was something *happening*, but we needed that game to get there, and that's what happened that day. I think people presumed that we got over-confident after that game and that's why we lost the subsequent All-Ireland semi-final to Mayo, but it kind of does a bit of a disservice to the Mayo team at the time because that was a damn good team, who were in two All-Ireland finals in-a-row in 1996 and '97.

They were a big, strong, physical team, and they were better than us in 1996. But losing to Mayo was unacceptable, because the Kerry people felt that when we'd beaten Cork we'd go the whole way.

It was an awful land a couple of weeks later to lose an All-Ireland semi-final, but we did win a second under-21 All-Ireland a week or two after that again, and that was huge. So, you had two Kerry under-21 All-Ireland winning teams and then a year later you had two Kerry teams in a Sigerson final, pretty much.

You'd Tralee RTC and UL, who actually had more Kerry players on their team than Tralee RTC at the time.

The identity was being formed, and Páidí was at the centre of the storm all that time.

Cork were going for four Munster Championships in-a-row in 1996... it was so unusual.

People forget, it was a really, *really* dark period for Kerry football. To get over the line in '96 was a great feeling, and the one thing a lot of the players to this day say is... 'Thanks be to God there was no social media in those days!'

We wouldn't have been able to handle the pressure.

It was enough to have *Kerry's Eye, The Kerryman, The Kingdom,* and *Radio Kerry*; in fairness to them they were only reporting what they were seeing, but they were particularly vocal when it came to criticising us. In those days, we were very aware of that. There were respected columnists, respected people, criticising us all of the time. *Imagine a social media storm added to that!* We wouldn't have survived that. We wouldn't have been able for it.

As a journalist myself, I really regret and resent it, because the criticism did a lot of damage to good players. In the dressing-room we just developed a 'F**k the Begrudgers' attitude.

I don't think it was personal, but it was very hard to swim through the tide at that time.

Do you know what convinced me at the time that we were good enough? It was going to third-level college and looking around me and thinking... *Hold on a second here, I'm better than all these players... And the best players I see around me are Kerry lads.*

It is not the Meath lads, it is not the Cork lads... It's the Kerry lads!

For me, that was the validation I needed, externally. I knew we were good, but I needed to see it being tested at Sigerson level and stuff like that... that was a big thing.

That 1996 Munster final was when all the doubts disappeared.

Every one of my three points that day against Cork were precious but, to be honest with you, I didn't play that well.

Killian got his memorable point at the end of the game, and corner-backs weren't really scoring back then. He sallied up the field and we were looking... *Oh no Burnsy has the ball, he doesn't kick points!* But he kicked an unbelievable point, and then made a mad big dance back to our defence afterwards, because it was kind of an insurance point.

Again, it was just a big confidence boost. Maurice Fitzgerald kicked a monster of a free halfway through the second-half – a big, *big*, vital kick in a low scoring game. They were the big scores of that game.

There is a reason for everything, and we needed to lose that Mayo game afterwards to give us a bit of humility and to train like dogs into the winter of 1996. It gave us a hurt. It was humiliating and that carries you a long way; there is a lot to be said for it. With all the sports psychology out there, there is a lot to be said for a hurt, hungry team... and we trained like no team had ever trained that winter in 1996.

Páidí Ó Sé did not lose out.

He was so certain it was going to happen the following year. That was the big thing, he never doubted himself, and he never doubted us. *There was no doubt with Páidí.*

We won the League in 1997; there was just so much wind in the sails at that stage, and every game was a project. There were only four games to win that All-Ireland... Tipperary nearly caught us in Tralee, and Clare, who had a really decent side, gave a right battle in the Gaelic Grounds in July. Cavan then came through in Ulster, which was an unbelievable result, and unbelievable symmetry because it was 50 years since the famous game between the counties in the Polo Grounds in New York.

This was a new Cavan team that was young... we'd beaten them in the under-21 final in '96. It was only in injury time that we beat them, winning by four points. They were also coming with momentum.

After Cavan, we'd Mayo... our old friends from the previous year, so every game was a kind of a project in itself.

I don't know if it was because we were so young, some of us at the time, but we just hung on every single word that Páidí said in training sessions. You see what he was like in the documentary when he was at Westmeath; multiply that by 10, and that was what Páidí brought to the training ground in those years because there was such a hunger there.

He got the job as well under a bit of a cloud, because 'Ogie' Moran had three years and before that Mikey Ned had a number of years, and all the ex-Kerry players from the golden years were coming through now as managers. Páidí had put out huge pressure to get the job. He'd been very vocal when he didn't get the job previously so the pressure was on him straightaway. He had Séamus MacGearailt, another An Ghaeltacht man, in with him as a coach. They had a lovely set-up... a young Jack O'Connor was in there as a selector.

They had Johnny Culloty, Bernie O'Callaghan and Tom O'Connor... all good lads. They were really brilliant to us as young players back then. They were great Kerry men.

It was amazing. I look back on it now and I think... *Were we naive or were we soft?* But Páidí was exactly what we needed at the time just to remove the doubts.

He was so confident himself, and somehow he managed to create this spirit in the team where there was always a bit of craic... every training session, every game... and every post-match. The craic was unreal!

And I mean this with respect to managers who came before and after him, but the game just got more serious afterwards and the craic went out of it a bit. That was even happening towards the end of my own career, even though we were winning All-Irelands.

The craic wasn't the same.

It was so much fun under Páidí; I don't know if it was because we were innocent… but the game was innocent as well. You look at those old games, and they are very innocent… tactically, and in every way. You can see the belts coming a mile off. They are honest. There was no sneakiness.

There were no tactics, but Páidí was something else in those years.

I always say it, and I said it to Tomás Ó Sé when he retired. He had 15 years playing with Kerry and he won five All-Ireland medals.

Tomás was very much making the point for years that it is all about winning medals in Kerry, and I remember saying to him, 'Tomás, you only won five medals out of 15 years… so two-thirds of your career was a failure!' I hope it dawned on him. I played 12 years senior with Kerry and won three All-Ireland medals, so seventy-five percent of my career was a failure… if you judge it by All-Ireland medals, but it was a different time in football.

We are not a team that meets up, or hangs around or plays golf together. Next year we'll be 25 years out in Croke Park after winning the All-Ireland in 1997. We are not pally-pally, but we created great memories together so the respect is there between the likes of myself and the likes of Seamus Moynihan and these lads…. fellas that you'd go to war with any day of the week.

Every team has its identity, and Páidí definitely created a very strong identity with that group. I don't know how the modern player thinks, but for us it was about the unbelievable friendships we made. We travelled the world together.

Someday, somebody will write the story of An Ghaeltacht going from being a Junior B team – the Novice Championship, which we won in Kerry in 1992 – to being within a kick of a ball of winning an All-Ireland Senior Club Championship 12 years later with the same group.

It's a fairytale.

Thirty years ago we won a West Kerry Championship that gave us a belief;

I was 16 years of age. At 17, we won a novice title and I was playing midfield marking Liam O'Flaherty, who was an established Kerry senior; and then at 18 I was winning a county junior title. It took years to win an Intermediate title – it's the hardest one of all to win in Kerry – but we won that, and we won the senior fairly quickly afterwards.

But to get to Croke Park, then… we probably got there two years too late. We had reached our peak. We were on the downward curve, but still, it is a hell of a story. With the Ghaeltacht club, we were never going to be at the top table for too long. That was some group of players. The four Ó Sés… Fergal gave a huge contribution to the club in those years both as a manager and a player. It was a really strong core group of lads, who are still involved in coaching in the club and helping out in whatever way they can. They are men of character.

There was just a great group, and that was all happening parallel to Kerry's success in the mid-90s, late-90s, and into the 2000s.

But we were never going to be around for too long. We're not Nemo, we're not Corofin or Crossmaglen… these big clubs that people are used to seeing year-after-year. That was a once in a generation group. It is a pity we didn't win the All-Ireland, but we reconciled ourselves with that. It would have been a hell of a story to go from winning a novice to winning an All-Ireland Senior Club Championship.

We'd be very proud of what the lads did at that time, and we're very proud of our parts in it. The club will always come first for me ahead of Kerry. It will never again happen. It's hard enough to win a Bishop Moynihan Cup.

People say to us, and particularly when I finished up playing a lot of people used to say to me, 'Ye probably underachieved as a club'.

And I'd say, 'What the hell?'

We suffered so much as a club because we had five or six inter-county players missing all the time. We couldn't win a county league title, and we only won one the very last year I played for the club. It's impossible when you've six lads missing training every night, going in with Kerry. It is impossible to create game-plans, and create a team spirit, so I think we overachieved by winning the two senior titles that we did.

DARRAGH Ó SÉ

KERRY 0-13 MAYO 1-7
All-Ireland SFC Final
Croke Park
SEPTEMBER 28, 1997

Darragh Ó Sé with Marc and Tomás in 2007 when all three brothers were honoured with All Star awards

★ **KERRY:** D O'Keeffe; K Burns, Barry O'Shea, S Stack; S Moynihan, L O'Flaherty, E Breen; **D Ó Sé (0-1)**, W Kirby; P Laide (0-2), L Hassett, D O'Dwyer; Billy O'Shea, D Ó'Cinneide, M Fitzgerald (0-9). Subs: D Daly for Kirby, J Crowley (0-1) for Billy O'Shea, MF Russell for Ó'Cinneide.

★ **MAYO:** P Burke; K Mortimer, P Holmes, D Flanagan; F Costello, J Nallen, N Connelly; P Fallon, D Heaney; M Sheridan (0-3), C McManamon (0-1), J Casey; C McDonald (1-1), L McHale, D Nestor. Subs: J Horan (0-2) for D Flanagan, D Byrne for Sheridan, PJ Loftus for Nestor.

THE ACTION

THE WAIT IS over. Eleven years of pain were put to the sword as an awesome performance from Maurice Fitzgerald, who stood head and shoulders above the rest, inspired Páidí Ó Sé's troops to success.

Before the game, the survivors of the Cavan and Kerry teams, who contested the Polo Grounds final 50 years previously, were presented to the crowd.

Fast-forward 70 minutes later, and it was Liam Hassett from the Laune Rangers club in Killorglin who was presented with and lifted the Sam Maguire – the first Kerry man to do so since Tommy Doyle in 1986.

Kerry's perfect afternoon was blemished in the 22nd minute when Billy O'Shea had to be stretchered off with a broken leg after a collision with Fitzgerald. Credit to the Cahersiveen stalwart, he was left unaffected by the incident and was later an indisputable Man of the Match, Player of the Year... and the championship's top scorer.

Kerry were well-deserved winners, with the game won and lost in the opening 35 minutes as the Connacht champions gave a first-half performance of shocking incompetence, taking 23 minutes to register their first score.

However, a second-half fightback which exposed Kerry's nerves took Mayo to within a point of their previously cruising opposition. When Seamus Moynihan was penalised for fouling Diarmuid Byrne, and Ciarán McDonald slotted home the resulting penalty, it looked like a Mayo comeback was on the cards. Two points within a minute from James Horan followed, but despite scoring 1-2 in the space of two minutes, Mayo failed to alter the scoreboard for the final 20 minutes.

And cometh the hour, cometh the man. The 1997 final will be forever remembered for the exploits of Fitzgerald, who raised his game to a near celestial plane at the perfect time to send Kerry on their way.

Mayo's inability to close the one-point gap at 1-7 to 0-11 eventually proved fatal as Fitzgerald steadied Kerry's ship with a point 11 minutes from time. In truth, it wasn't a classic, but Kerry won't complain after closing the chapter on the longest period of footballing deprivation the county has suffered since the turn of the century.

★★★★★

66

LIKE ANY YOUNG Kerry footballer, winning a first All-Ireland is the pinnacle of your career. All my life, I wanted to play in an All-Ireland final for Kerry, and then this opportunity came. And it came early in my career as well, which was lucky.

We played Mayo in the final and the game is remembered for Maurice Fitzgerald's exploits that day... *How good he was.*

At the same time, it was just one of those games that I wanted to go on forever. I got a point early on, and that settled me down and gave me fierce confidence.

We kicked on from there. We took the game to them after that and, in fairness, there were some great performances from Kerry.

Liam O'Flaherty played very well. Pa Laide played very well. Denis O'Dwyer played well... Barry O'Shea played well at full-back.

There were performances all over the pitch.

I was happy with my own game because I was marking Pat Fallon the same day, and I was lucky enough to catch a couple of kick-outs.

At one stage, I kicked a free. I caught a ball from a kick-out and I took a quick free. It was within range for Maurice and I remember him giving me a hard time afterwards for not putting the ball down. He was kicking so well at the time, that he would have kicked it from anywhere. I could see it from his point of view... and I remember getting the b******ing from him at the time and thinking... *Jesus!*

I had given the ball to Liam Hassett, and he made a balls of it.

The game was in the old Croker.

It was in the old Hogan Stand where we got the cup. It was back in the day when the supporters would come on to the pitch after the game.

There were just so many big highlights. I remember Jack O'Shea lifting Maurice Fitzgerald off the pitch. For someone like Jacko to do it... we all looked up to Jacko all our lives and then for him to shake hands with us and congratulate us was just amazing. *And I didn't even think Jacko knew me!*

It was just all those things.

Meeting my father after the game and him shaking hands with me and stuff like that... there were just a range of emotions there that were going to be very hard to emulate afterwards in later games.

We were lucky enough to get to more All-Ireland finals regularly, but that first final for me was just unreal. The emotion of it; it was just one of those days where everything came together, and the fact Páidí was training the team as well meant there was a family connection. Tomás was on the panel too.

That win was after 11 years as well. People were waiting a long time to get that.

That's a long time not to get an All-Ireland in Kerry.

The celebrations in Kerry – and they don't overdo the celebrations in Kerry because they are lucky enough to have won a good few times – were particularly special because we hadn't won for so long.

The best feeling of all is when you are leaving Croke Park on the bus... and Sam Maguire is at the front of the bus.

It is where you want to be. *That is where you want to be!*

It was great to see Maurice Fitzgerald reach the promised land that year.

It would have been a shame for Maurice to end his career without an All-Ireland medal because of the quality of the player that he was.

He was an exceptional leader in the dressing-room as well, and even the display he gave after having the clash with Billy O'Shea, when Billy broke his leg... to effectively have the composure, the mental strength and fortitude to go on and play the way he did afterwards, was something else.

Some of the scores he got that day were unbelievable. People forget it, the free off the ground on the right-hand side... *Over the bar!*

Then the sideline kick at the end to win it.

And he was doing that every day.

It wasn't a classic game, but for me and a lot of the players it was just that day where boys became men then.

That was the turning point in my career.

When you have won an All-Ireland medal it gives you the confidence. You play with more belief in yourself, and you are not as cagey.

The highlight that sticks out was meeting my father after the game, where we were having the banquet.

He shook hands with me and said, 'Well done!'

It was like I was after winning the lotto, to get that. He wasn't a big man for giving you any compliments or anything like that, so that was huge for me.

I rarely got them, so I can assure you... *I certainly enjoyed that!*

He was old fashioned in that way. He was the kind of a dad who never said you played badly, or equally then if you played well he never said that you played well. It kept you on your toes.

It did us no harm.

You didn't get to think about it a lot, but it was such a huge source of pride that myself, Tomás, Marc... and Páidí were all able to represent Kerry.

There was the other side of it then as well... the fact that Páidí was manager meant there was always going to be a question of nepotism.

But to be fair to all of us, Tomás, Marc, and myself included, we were there on merit, and I think we proved that over the years.

We went out, we gave it our all for Kerry.

It was difficult afterwards, when we played Westmeath in Tralee one night and Páidí was in charge of them. I found that hard to play against Páidí, but at the end of the day it was Kerry we were playing for and that was it.

I had to train even harder and put it in on the pitch under Páidí, or else I would have been called out for it. I had to play that bit more physical; I always felt I had to prove myself twice as much as the next fella because of that.

It was no harm for me either because it kept me on my toes.

I am so lucky to have played in that era where Kerry were winning All-Irelands and there was a great quality across the board.

I was also lucky enough to play with some of the greatest players that ever played the game.

The best player that I ever played with was Seamus Moynihan, there is no doubt. He was by far and away the best. He was outstanding against Armagh in the semi-final in 2000 and he was outstanding in the final against Pádraic Joyce as well on the two days. Seamus was an exceptional player.

To get to play with these fellas was just so amazing.

Our success with An Ghaeltacht back then was very special as well. We are a small rural club and it was a big decision to go out on our own in the county championship.

Some of the members didn't want us to go out on our own in the championship; they didn't feel we were good enough. I always had huge belief that we were plenty good enough.

We proved it, and we won two county championships. That was a huge achievement for a small club. A lot of clubs have tried it and failed.

And then we went on another bit… won a Munster Championship, and played in an All-Ireland club final. We were blessed.

We got the most out of ourselves. We probably should have won more at club level. We had Marc, Tomás, myself, Aodán MacGearailt… and you'd Dara Ó Cinnéide; you are talking about a club team with your full-back, your centre-back, your midfielder, your centre-forward, and your full-forward… the core of the team playing with Kerry.

We were gone for Kerry games for a lot of that period, so it shows how good the club team was to be able to get us into those positions without us.

It was very hard on other teammates then, because we'd come back in and take their places.

I'd always a huge interest in football. The fact that Páidí played with Kerry… I saw that from a young age. I saw a lot of players coming back after Munster finals, and they were around the house.

Just to see these heroes in the flesh and so close to home, was just a huge privilege.

And then we'd a coach, who was with us all the way up and he was the main driving force between all our players… Liam Ó Rócháin. He was the main guy really in all that. He drove us all on to that level. He was at every training session from under-12s, 14s, 16s, and minors; he was with us all along.

Without him, we wouldn't have had the success at An Ghaeltacht that we did.

He brought us to games, he created training, he created a culture, and it was down to him… obviously there were other people along the way, but Liam was the constant.

TOMÁS Ó SÉ

KERRY 1-14 CORK 1-11
Munster SFC Semi-Final
Fitzgerald Stadium, Killarney
JULY 5, 1998

Tomás Ó Sé battles with Aidan Dorgan of Cork in the 1998 Munster semi-final in Killarney before been taken off at half-time, and ending a game that defined his brilliant football career.

★ **KERRY:** D O'Keeffe; **T Ó Sé**, B O'Shea, S Stack; S Moynihan, L O'Flaherty, E Breen; D Ó Sé, D Daly; P Laide, D Ó Cinnéide (0-1), D O'Dwyer; MF Russell (0-4), J Crowley (0-5), M Fitzgerald (1-4). Subs: E Fitzmaurice for T Ó Sé, L Brosnan for Laide, N Kennelly for Ó Cinnéide.

★ **CORK:** M Maguire; M O'Connor, B Corcoran, O Sexton; C O'Sullivan (0-1), S O'Brien, M Cronin; P Hegarty, D O'Neill, R McCarthy, L Tompkins (0-1), D Davis (0-1); A O'Regan (1-1), J Kavanagh (0-6), A Dorgan (0-1). Subs: N Murphy for O'Neill, D Wiseman for Sexton, F Murray for Dorgan.

THE ACTION

A NEWLY REDEVELOPED Fitzgerald Stadium provided the perfect backdrop as Cork came to the lion's den to try and dethrone the All-Ireland champions in their own backyard.

A Maurice Fitzgerald goal 12 minutes from time proved to be the difference as Páidí Ó Sé's charges stumbled over their arch-rivals to set up a novel Munster showdown against Tipperary – the first time the two sides met at the provincial final stage since 1944.

It was 11 years since Kerry trotted out as defending All-Ireland champions, and Killarney was bursting at the seams, with 43,994 lucky souls getting to witness both sides of this age-old rivalry do battle in a free-flowing game.

Aidan Dorgan proved a handful for a young Tomás Ó Sé, but Seamus Moynihan put a curb on the Corkman's activities when he was switched to right corner-back after half-time. Although his side won the game, it was a debut to forget for Ó Sé, who was taken off at half-time by the Kerry manager, his uncle Páidí Ó Sé.

As crowds filtered onto the sideline due to overcrowding, the first point of the second-half came in the 44th minute when Johnny Crowley slotted over for his first of five.

When Cork scored their goal 22 minutes into the second-half to go two points up after O'Regan won the tussle with Stephen Stack, it was the visitors first score from play in the closing 35 minutes. Two previous Kavanagh frees had kept Larry Tompkins' side in touching distance.

However, Fitzgerald's 58th minute goal killed off a brief Cork revival, as Dennis Bergkamp-esque-style, he beautifully put his chance away. After the Cahersiveen man's goal, Kerry scored three of the next four points to sink the Rebels and put the result beyond any doubt. The last point came from Crowley, who suitably capped off a Man of the Match performance.

★★★★★

66

MY FIRST GAME for Kerry was against Cork in 1998, and it was a game I played horribly in.

There was a lot of pressure because Kerry were All-Ireland champions, and it was knockout back then. I had just got in the door… I had been a squad player in 1997. I started at corner-back. Killarney was absolutely heaving. Cork had Larry Tompkins as their player-manager.

It was the biggest learning curve I ever had.

I got hammered into the ground really. I was destroyed by Aidan Dorgan, and it definitely helped define my career.

There are learning curves in any man's career, but to get hammered into the ground in your first game… *against Cork, in Killarney, knockout championship…* and I was gone at half-time.

It took me a few months to come around from it.

It was tough, but I had to figure it out by myself… play club, and come back the following year. There was also Kerry under-21s the following year, when we lost to Kildare in the All-Ireland semi-final. I didn't get back in to play senior that year again after that performance against Cork, so I had a long time to stew on it.

So, when I came in 1999, I came harder than I ever did. It was the start. Every year from then on, I never took anything for granted, and I never took my position for granted.

I was absolutely nervous. I needed to relax a bit more.

Get the work done, get the preparation done… have everything done in terms of fitness, months before, weeks before, days before… and then have the confidence to know that I'd the work done and I was going to be alright.

But it was still a big ask.

I was performing in training. There wasn't a question of me *not performing* inside in training… and our forwards were excellent in training. I was marking Maurice Fitzgerald for a lot of it.

I never again played corner-back for Kerry… *Ever again.* I was out in the half-back line. I just wasn't a corner-back. I wasn't a man-marking defender, and for the likes of Aidan Dorgan, who was a small fella, and was just full of energy, and full of running, and full of jinky runs... he wasn't a player that suited me.

At that time, in terms of analysis and preparation on opposition teams... there was *nothing*. I'd read a newspaper and they'd tell you whatever, but there was no fellas picking up certain players. You just went out and you picked up whoever came in your direction.

Times were different. I think the amount of work that goes in now with players in terms of preparation, in terms of analysis, is huge... and it helps them.

I just wasn't ready for that type of player, and I wasn't ready for the corner-back position. Had I been marking a small, busy forward like that for three weeks or a month before it, I would have been ready.

But I wasn't.

I didn't know what was on the cards.

I knew afterwards I just had to knuckle down and do the hard work again, and come back the following year.

You just knuckle down from Christmas. Winter time you come back in, and it's just like a new sheet, a new card... a new year, and I didn't really think about it after that.

The week after the Cork game, we played a county championship game against East Kerry and I marked Johnny Crowley. West Kerry put me in full-back... and I got another roasting inside there.

Johnny had a goal got within three minutes, and he won a penalty then after that... I fouled him for that penalty.

It was the one and only time where my confidence was totally shot, and I'm glad it happened at the very start because you learned from it. I was only 19 at the time. There are ups and downs. I was lucky that Darragh was inside there at that time, and I was lucky Páidí was inside there at that time too.

All I could do was focus on the next training session, and the next training session... and the next training session, and the following year just came along and I just ripped into it again.

I was out wing-back, and I didn't look back after that. It was a different kettle of fish out on the wing.

I now knew... *You've got to knuckle down here boy and be ready for all sorts.*

Be ready for any type of a player that comes at you... before the game be ready, and not to get too engrossed in occasion, but know what you're facing... *And be ready for it!*

Cork under Larry Tompkins were hardy.

They had no fear coming to Killarney. Tompkins himself wasn't ever going to have any fear coming to Killarney.

The atmosphere was electric. We were defending the All-Ireland, and it was against Cork... and it was in Killarney, so there was a huge build up to that day. The hype in the county was fabulous.

I was brought up with dreams of playing with Kerry. I was brought up watching Páidí, hearing the old stories of the great Kerry team... and then watching Darragh making the Kerry team.

I was sitting on the bench in 1997 so I saw what it meant for the people of Kerry to win it, and the players of Kerry to win it... it was huge. It was absolutely massive.

It was a sharp learning curve because inter-county senior football is tough. No matter who you play for or who you take on, or what players you're facing, it is a learning curve at the best of times.

It's not that I wouldn't have thought about that game afterwards... *I did.*

I thought about that game and it haunted me a small bit, but that's life as an inter-county footballer, you have to wait six or seven months before you get back in to right it.

You never know what is around the corner.

It is always a relief to win a first All-Ireland. I think we were good that way to be fair. We were competitive and we didn't lack hunger. We got to a lot of finals... we didn't win all of them, but we won five. We should have won some more, but you need that luck on the day as well.

We never took anything for granted and I think that was the biggest lesson that game taught me... *You just don't know.* Just because you play for Kerry doesn't mean you are going to have a great day every day you go out. It is a high pressure environment.

I thought I was ready that day against Cork, and I wasn't.

It took me a good few years when I retired to get over the buzz and not miss it. *I loved it.*

We had great days… brilliant days with the club, huge days with the club, and brilliant days with Kerry.

It was an unbelievable time. We didn't realise how special it was and how competitive we were, or the fact that we had a realistic chance every year of winning the All-Ireland. It was massive for everyone in the county, and the supporters. Every year we had trips… it was just brilliant. I've nothing but good, fond memories especially of the craic we had… the social side of it.

There's the fact that we were competitive with the club at the time as well, and the fact there were so many lads from An Ghaeltacht involved… the managers we had, and the relationships we had with the County Board… it was the perfect mix. It was the perfect storm for about 10 or 12 years.

The area of An Ghaeltacht is big, but the population is small. The numbers we have are small, so to be able to come out of the county with the clubs that are *in the county* and the history of some of the clubs, and the strength of some of the clubs… we beat Austin Stacks in one final… a massive achievement. *We beat them all.*

Gallaras was like a fortress for us. Nobody wanted to go there, and it was brilliant that a small little pocket of West Kerry was a strong hand in the county for six or seven years. We were very lucky. We were lucky enough to win county championships, and win Munster clubs, so it was a phenomenal journey with the club. But it was different. I'd never compare the success that you'd have with the county to the club. I think it is *different.* I wouldn't put one above the other; winning an All-Ireland or winning something with your club. I wouldn't… you couldn't say one was better than the other.

The fact that we got to the All-Ireland club final in 2004 and couldn't get over the line was very difficult. Whatever about Kerry getting back from an All-Ireland, to get to go back up to Croke Park with your club again would be very, *very* difficult.

I don't know what it is, but it is hard to appreciate it all while it is happening.

But it was great; I had mighty craic with the two lads there, Darragh and Marc. We had our ups and our downs, but we helped each other when we needed to. We maybe didn't realise how good we had it.

Páidí being there as well was special with him as manager. There weren't too many fellas that came from Micko's great Kerry team that had success as a manager, so to see him manage Kerry to win two All-Irelands was huge.

It was some journey.

There is this myth out there that you have to live like monks, which you do, but you can have a right good balance, and still perform at the highest level.

And because you lose a game, it isn't because of being out and about a few weeks before *that* game. We had a great balance and managers respected that. We respected training, we respected opposition, we respected matches... and then when we had time to have a bit of fun, we did that too. We'd have the craic, we'd have the fun, and we'd have the laughs.

We got to 10 finals... so we had 10 trips abroad.

And we enjoyed every one of them. We did very well and we were very appreciative of the County Board. We got on very well with the board. I don't think that can be underestimated in any area, even at club level. The executive have to make sure they are on the same hymn sheet as the players, team, and management. It creates a happy environment and it creates an environment where you can succeed.

It was very hard to do back-to-back at that time.

We were the first team to do it in that era.

I know the Dubs have blown that out of the water, but at that time there were so many competitive teams. You had Galway, you had Armagh, you'd Tyrone... and Meath were winning All-Irelands at that time, so it was very difficult to win back-to-back.

Nobody had managed it since 1989 and '90 when Cork did it, so to do it in 2006 and '07, which was 17 or 18 years later was brilliant.

Tyrone weren't able to do that... or Armagh, or Meath... or Galway, and that tells you how difficult it was to hold onto your All-Ireland title.

SEAMUS MOYNIHAN

KERRY 2-11 ARMAGH 2-11
All-Ireland SFC Semi-Final
Croke Park
AUGUST 20, 2000

Seamus Moynihan races out of defence with the ball and away from the clutches of Armagh's Diarmuid Marsden during the drawn All-Ireland semi-final in 2000.

★ **KERRY:** D O'Keeffe; K Burns, **S Moynihan**, M McCarthy; T O'Sullivan, E Fitzmaurice, T Ó Sé; D Ó Sé (0-1), D Daly (0-1); A MacGearailt (0-1), L Hassett, N Kennelly (0-1); MF Russell (0-3), D Ó Cinneide (1-2), J Crowley (0-1). Subs: M Fitzgerald (1-1) for Hassett, M Hassett for Burns, D O'Dwyer for MacGearailt, E Galvin for Kennelly.

★ **ARMAGH:** B Tierney; E McNulty, G Reid, J McNulty; K Hughes, K McGeeney (0-1), A McCann (1-0); J McEntee, T McEntee (0-1); C O'Rourke (0-3), P McGrane (0-1), P McKeever (0-1); S McDonnell, B O'Hagan (1-1), O McConville (0-3).

THE ACTION

A NEW MILLENNIUM, a new era, but it was a familiar face who stole the show when it mattered most, as Maurice Fitzgerald's genius from the bench forced a draw for Kerry.

A topsy-turvy game packed with incidents and scores went the distance but when the towering Cahersiveen corner-forward pointed a dramatic late free, Kerry's All-Ireland dreams were kept alive.

Kerry got off to a flying start. Mike Frank Russell brushed aside Enda McNulty with ease to put the Kingdom one point to the good after just 15 seconds. With the supporters still settling in their seats, Johnny Crowley was taken down as he bore down on goal. Dara Ó Cinnéide coolly found the net with the resulting penalty.

Kerry's best possible start continued. and the men in green and gold concluded their early blitz when Crowley and Ó Cinnéide added further points, but their northern counterparts, to their credit, responded wonderfully and when Barry O'Hagan found the net in the ninth minute – his first ever championship goal – Armagh reduced the deficit to two.

Fifteen minutes in, the sides were level at 1-3 apiece. The game settled down from there, and it took another 10 minutes for the 50,449 in attendance to be treated to another point when Liam Hassett set up Russell for a much-needed score, Kerry's first in 20 minutes.

It was a two-point game at half-time – 1-7 to 1-5 in favour of Kerry.

The all-important goal in the second-half came from substitute Fitzgerald, who linked up well with Crowley before sending Tierney the wrong way But Andrew McCann was the hero when he drew Armagh level in the final minute of regular time, easing past Mike Hassett to break Kerry hearts.

Kieran McGeeney popped up from centre-back a minute later to put Armagh ahead for the first time, and it looked like the Orchard County captain had done enough! However, the drama wasn't over just yet and Fitzgerald saved Kerry blushes with a well-taken free to draw the sides level for the sixth time with the second last kick of the game after Ó Cinnéide had been adjudged to be fouled just inside the 'D'. In the replay, Kerry prevailed by 2-15 to 1-15 after extra time to reach their second All-Ireland final in four years.

★ ★ ★ ★ ★

66

IT WAS THE first time I had to go full-back in a major game, because Barry O'Shea had done his cruciate that year. Barry was always our mainstay full-back. He had been playing there since 1997.

I was put back in there as a makeshift full-back to try and do a job. That's why the drawn game against Armagh in the All-Ireland semi-final in 2000 was a defining moment in my career.

Certain mistakes were made, and in the second-half Armagh completely took over the game, but we were still able to hold out… but only after a lot of red buttons were pushed, just to get ourselves over the line. It was a day that some things fell to me and I took chances on other things… and it worked out, but we were lucky to get our draw and get a second chance.

There were a lot of questions over decisions made by the referee John Bannon in the second-half, but at least he gave us an opportunity to level the game with Maurice Fitzgerald kicking the ball over the bar from a free. That was probably the only break he gave us in the second-half.

From my point of view, we had to do a lot of fire-fighting and absorb a lot from Armagh in that second-half, which we did to a point.

I was thrown in that summer… I was parachuted in full-back.

I played there in the Munster final against Clare, who put up a no-show. Cork were poor that year too. The Armagh game was the first real test against quality opposition, against quality forwards… in Croke Park.

The replay went to extra time, and we ultimately won by three points.

But the first day was the defining moment for me because, for the next three years, I played full-back. Páidí Ó Sé was slow to change and he was happy with me playing full-back, but it was a dramatic moment for me in the sense that I was anchored at No 3 for the remainder of Páidí's managerial role.

We went on to play Galway in the All-Ireland final, which also was a draw and went to a replay. We certainly did it the hard way that year and it was fantastic when we did win it. Obviously, winning any All-Ireland is great, but I think that one certainly wasn't handed to us in any shape or form; we earned it because we were put to the pin of our collar so many times.

From my own point of view, to win it while being captain and being parachuted into a position that wouldn't be the norm for me, made it even more satisfying.

In the media at the time, they were saying I wasn't a full-back and whatnot. When you are told you can't do something, or you aren't able to do something, and you go and do it... there is a real sense of achievement.

The doubters would drive you on beforehand. Anytime you are told you can't do something, or you're not good enough... or you're too small, or you're too this or too that... I think as a sportsperson that is an invitation to go out and rise to the occasion.

To be fair to Armagh back at that time, they were kicking the ball in long and even in 2000 the time of the blanket defence or anything like that wasn't really there.

Armagh played a very, *very* physical game, but they were able to take it too.

They played a hard brand of football, and they were getting the ball in as fast and furious to the forward line as they physically could. No different to what we were doing.

The game has changed dramatically since. Within two years the game had changed, but at that stage it was still very much man-on-man, and everyone minded their own corner. If you had a little bit more to offer, well and good. Forwards were only beginning to tackle up front and put pressure on backs.

There were certainly no corner-forwards in defence or double-sweepers, or sweepers in any shape or form. If you were a full-back, you had a full-forward to mark and you had 70 yards of space in front of you to mind.

I played full-back with Páidí up until 2003; after that, Jack O'Connor had me back out wing-back again.

For three more years then, I was utilised in the half-back line until I retired.

Playing well that day against Armagh justified Páidí's selection of me at full-back, and on top of that we went on to win the All-Ireland... and I got Player of the Year that year in 2000 as well. So Páidí was well justified in what he did.

Páidí had said, 'Do you want to play wing-back and play well and lose the All-Ireland... or do you want to play full-back and do a job and win?'

Ultimately it is a team game and you do what it takes to win for the team. It is not about personal prizes or winning All Stars; it was about putting in a shift for the team in a position that was required, and that's what happened that year.

I certainly enjoyed playing there. It was a challenge.

Was it my best position? Probably not, but look, at the end of the day it is a team and it is an honour to wear the Kerry jersey wherever you're given it.

Centre-back was probably my favourite position.

The end result is winning and thankfully in 2000, that's what happened. Unfortunately, after that we didn't win All-Irelands, but we went very close.

We should have won one in 2002… we left that after us, whereas 2001 was just one of those days when it was a bad day at the office against Meath and poor preparation in terms of the county championships being played 10 days prior to the All-Ireland semi-final, which didn't make sense.

I've such great memories, but the first few years weren't very fruitful. It was a team in transition from 1992 up… so it was '96 before we got any silverware when we won the Munster title.

It took four or five years before we won anything. But that's the way sport goes and there are players that go through their careers without winning anything. I played 14 years and won eight Munsters and four All-Irelands so, at the end of the day, I was lucky.

The one thing every player wants is to win an All-Ireland and be remembered as an All-Ireland winner. That's the driving force from word go.

The benefits that come with it… whether you get an opportunity to win an All Star… whether you get a trip away at the end of the year, while they are nice… they're not the be-all and end-all. The driving force is that you are playing at your best, you are playing with the best players, and you give yourself an opportunity to win All-Ireland and Munster titles.

Everyone I played with… there are very few that didn't do that. When you get that chance you just go for the jugular.

I started playing football when I was eight.

Back then, under-12s was the earliest you could actually play football.

We were tight on numbers and whatnot, but we had good men looking after us… Liam Bartlett, Pa Deady and Mike O'Donoghue. They started what became a very strong senior team. It was a good mix, and we went on to win five O'Donoghue Cups and a Millennium Cup with Glenflesk. From 1992 on, Glenflesk had a fantastic run for 10 or 15 years.

I went into St Brendan's in 1986. The Sem is a really great school, and that is where I got the opportunity to play with great players and to learn from good people… the likes of Fr Jim Kennelly and Fr Larry Kelly, who were very dedicated and had great knowledge of the game. We trained Monday, Wednesday and Friday… that was set in stone from first year and that never changed until the time I left.

That's why I felt the Sem stands out… they put football first and they put a great structure in place there.

I played midfield with Glenflesk for 20 years, but as a midfielder you kind of have to be a utility player. You have to defend, and you have to have the ability to go box-to-box.

Playing that *game* gave me the opportunity at club level to work on certain things in terms of defending… and if I wanted to attack I could attack. Glenflesk were always giving me that flexibility to just go out and express myself.

At underage now, I'm trying to do that same thing where I'm trying to get players to play in different positions… whether it is full-back or up the field. I feel the way football has gone, and maybe it was even that way in my time, you have to be as comfortable playing full-back as you are full-forward.

If you are going to pin yourself as just a corner-back, or a corner-forward… trying to make Kerry teams just in those positions is going to be very hard. Managers are looking for players who can play in multiple positions.

Can he play wing-back? Can he play midfield?

Can he play centre-back?

Can he play corner-forward or wing-forward?

It was a strange year in 2000, in the sense that the All-Ireland final replay was on a Saturday because the International Rules was due the following day.

That was strange, and Croke Park was also strange because the Hogan Stand was non-existent since they were redeveloping Croke Park at the time… and it was *strange* being presented with the cup in the middle of the field, and not going up the steps of the Hogan Stand.

Then we got a flight home from Dublin on the Sunday, as opposed to getting the train like we'd normally do... always stopping at Rathmore, Killarney and Tralee, before heading back to Killarney.

Our initial welcome home from supporters was in Farranfore airport... we were the first Kerry team to fly home.

It was all strange and different, but memorable and fantastic.

John Crowley had been captain of Kerry before me, but I had the honour of being the first Glenfesk man to bring the Sam Maguire Cup home to our parish.

I felt one lucky man.

99

MIKE FRANK RUSSELL

KERRY 0-14 GALWAY 0-14
All-Ireland SFC Final
Croke Park
SEPTEMBER 24, 2000

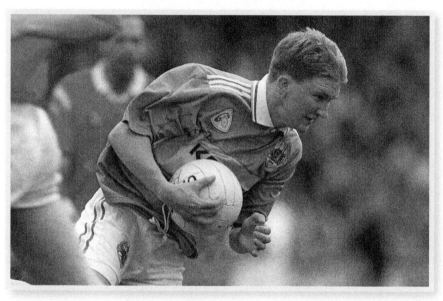

Mike Frank Russell (above in championship action against Cork in 2000) was told by manager Páidí Ó Sé there were only two dates in the diary of every Kerry footballer... the Munster final against Cork and the All-Ireland final.

★ **KERRY:** D O'Keeffe; M Hassett, S Moynihan, M McCarthy; T Ó Sé; É Fitzmaurice, T O'Sullivan; D Ó Sé (0-1), D Daly; A MacGearailt, L Hassett (0-2), N Kennelly (0-2); MF Russell (0-3), D Ó Cinnéide (0-4), J Crowley (0-2). Subs: M Fitzgerald for Crowley, D O'Dwyer for Kennelly.

★ **GALWAY:** M McNamara; T Meehan, G Fahey, R Silke; D Meehan, J Divilly, S Óg De Paor; S Ó Dómhnaill, J Bergin; P Clancy, T Joyce (0-1), M Donnellan; D Savage (0-2), P Joyce (0-6), N Finnegan (0-3). Subs: K Walsh (0-1) for Bergin, R Fahey for Silke, J Donnelllan (0-1) for T Joyce.

THE ACTION

IT WAS KERRY and Galway meeting in the All-Ireland final for the first time since 1965. Very old foes, but for Kerry it was a Jekyll and Hyde performance – a rampant show in the first-half but sheer relief at the end.

The game saw Páidí Ó Sé's side take a seven-point lead; however, it was the Kingdom who *survived* a second-half comeback by the Tribesmen.

Kerry controlled the game in the opening quarter with the full-forward line of Dara Ó Cinnéide, Johnny Crowley and Mike Frank Russell in impressive form; the latter causing Ray Silke all sorts of trouble with his pace and trademark craft. At the other end, Seamus Moynihan was in top-class form, succeeding in the not so easy task of trying to keep Pádraic Joyce quiet in front of goals.

It was 0-10 to 0-7 in favour of the Kingdom at the break. But Galway surged into the game on the restart and had narrowed the deficit to a single point by the 48th minute. However, they had to wait another 18 minutes to draw level. Kerry now had to hang on for dear life in their bid for their 32nd All-Ireland title.

Just like in the semi-final against Armagh, Kerry stalwart Maurice Fitzgerald was introduced not long after the half-time break, albeit to a lesser effect than four weeks previously. In contrast, towering midfielder Kevin Walsh was the main inspiration behind Galway's rally when he was introduced in the 20th minute, as was the decision to move Joyce to centre-forward.

Seán Óg de Paor, Michael Donnellan and Derek Savage wasted late chances for Galway.

Despite being a really end-to-end attacking game of football, it was the first time since 1992 that either side failed to score a goal in the All-Ireland final. Questions were asked when a mere 39 seconds were added on, but in the end both sides were delighted with the second opportunity for glory.

Kerry went on to claim the title with a 0-17 to 1-10 win in the replay.

★★★★★

"

I GOT MAN of the Match on the day and, I suppose, it is hard to overlook receiving that honour in an All-Ireland final for Kerry, but we had a great team at the end of the 90s and early 2000s... we were lucky in that there were lots of memorable days for so many of us.

We grew up watching Jacko, Mikey Sheehy and Pat Spillane... all these lads, and you always dream that one day you'll get to play in an All-Ireland final for Kerry. But to play in one, and play to the best of my ability was very special.

That was my first All-Ireland senior final on the starting team. I came on in the 1997 final, but I was very young. I was only 18.

That year in 2000 was a long year... we got through the semi-final against Armagh after two very tough games, and we went to a replay against Galway in the final as well.

Things were going well for me that summer.

I had played well in the semi-final, so coming into the final I was confident enough, but obviously on the day you still don't know how things are going to go until that ball is thrown in. It was a great game the first day... both teams were thinking *attack*. This was before blanket defences or anything like that. I got three points the same day... it worked out great.

We went into a big lead. We were up seven points at one stage.

With Pádraic Joyce and Michael Donnellan, they clawed it back. We were probably lucky to hang on in the end, and win the replay.

That was a great game of football. It was man-on-man. As a forward it was... *Beat your man, and get a score...* whereas now there are systems and sweepers. It seems simple to say it now, but it was all about beating your man and getting a score. In fairness to Galway, they played football too. They were never resorting to very physical stuff or anything like that. They were what I'd call a pure football team.

High scoring... two great games.

You hit a peak in your career sometimes where everything you touch turns to gold, and I definitely had that that summer... I was blessed. A county career has its steps.

You come in first, and you have to establish yourself in training.

You have to prove yourself to your teammates.

You have to get on the team.

And then you have to stay on the team… and finally, cement your place on the team.

It comes full cycle as well, because towards the end of your career there are young lads taking their important steps forward, and trying to take your jersey.

At that stage of my career, in 2000, I was comfortable and a permanent fixture in the team. It was a time to perform.

My first Munster final in Killarney against Cork was a great day out as well… I always wanted to play for Kerry against Cork in a Munster final. They say sometimes you are judged as a Kerry player on how you played against Cork in the Munster final.

Páidí had that drilled into us.

I really loved playing in Killarney, especially when it was a full house… especially against Cork.

We had a fine team back then… the Ó Sés, Dara Ó Cinnéide… Seamus Moynihan… outstanding players. The Ó Sés went on to be once in a lifetime footballers, so we were blessed really. Maurice Fitzgerald was coming to the end of his career, but he got his second All-Ireland that year which was great for him.

The rest of the team was fairly young… 21, 22, 23 and a lot of us had just come through from the under-21s. That team stayed together for a few years, but it was great for the older lads.

That was Mike Hassett's last year.

He was dropped, unfortunately, for the 1997 final. And that led to some controversy, because at that time there were only 21 medals given out. It was unfortunate… Mike got an injury before the semi-final against Cavan and was dropped for the final. It was great for him to come back and start that final in 2000 and win his All-Ireland on the field.

I got Man of the Match, but I was allowed to feel good about myself for about 10 minutes… because we had Páidí Ó Sé roaring at us that we were back training on the Tuesday night. My *moment* was fairly short-lived.

We were back into it then. There was a two-week gap for the replay which was on the following Saturday week… another great game.

I played well enough the second game… I got three points the first day and two the second day, but I still played well enough.

It was difficult though. You are going from a serious high… and going back at it again, but we did that and it was great for Seamus Moynihan, such a fantastic footballer, to lift the Sam Maguire Cup. He was a great captain.

Seamus Moynihan was one of the lads who looked after me, when I came into the Kerry team in 1997… you'd Seamus, Liam O'Flaherty, Eamonn Breen, Darragh Ó Sé… and clubmates Billy O'Shea and Liam Hassett. In fairness, they looked out for us, they backed us up. I couldn't speak highly enough of them.

Our own club team was going quite well at the time too. We had won the All-Ireland in 1996, so I'd a lot of older senior players minding me when I started out in my career.

I got kind of lucky. I come in for my first year playing with Kerry… and we win the All-Ireland. With that and with Laune Rangers winning an All-Ireland club, I was around at the right time with two great teams.

I started in 1997 with Kerry, and finished in 2010, so it was a golden era. Some lads, even throughout the country, not just in Kerry, have gone through 16 years of senior football and haven't won a whole pile. I was lucky to be born and reared in Kerry.

We had the two Hassetts and myself from Laune Rangers on that Kerry team in 1997, and Liam was captain. Maybe I was too young in '97 to appreciate it as much… I was thinking game-to-game, but in 2000 it was just fantastic.

I loved bringing the cup back to our town… to the people who coached us, the people you meet every day. There was a fierce crowd in Killorglin that night.

You get to bring Sam back to your people, your family… and I loved bringing it back to my old primary school, where I grew up and learned to play football.

I'm a teacher myself now, and I get to see lads when they bring in the cup, and I see how brilliant it is for the students. I suppose when you're playing, you don't realise how much enjoyment you actually bring to people locally.

It's only afterwards, when you are reminiscing, that you fully realise the pride people have in lads who have given it their all.

Páidí Ó Sé, God rest him… I'll always be indebted to Páidí.

He gave me my first Kerry jersey. Sure an icon in Kerry, and for him to trust me enough to give me a championship debut… *I'll never forget that.*

I'll always remember him for that, but Páidí was also a great character. He loved football. He liked to enjoy himself in the off season, but Kerry football meant everything to him and he expected the same from us.

He instilled responsibility in us… he expected us to look after ourselves off the field as well. He made us understand we were role models for young lads. On and off the field… he expected us to honour the jersey.

I just loved going out every Tuesday and Thursday night with my gear bag, and playing football. There was no better place for me to be going on a Tuesday night than down to Killarney during the summer. That made the training easy… the fact that I was in love with football.

I am lucky to have played the game with some of the best players that ever played the game. It is only as you get older and look back, that you appreciate it all the more. When you are playing, there is pressure to perform… and you are just thinking about the next game… the next training session… and the next game after that.

It's not until you get older that you realise… *It was such a good time…* a time you'll always be able to tell the children and the grandchildren about, hopefully, in the future.

Páidí once said to me… 'There are two dates in the diary for a Kerry footballer. The Munster final against Cork… and the All-Ireland final!'

Nothing else mattered to Páidí. He instilled into us that every year we wanted to be competing to win Munster Championships and win All-Irelands.

There is a fierce commitment there and you are *committing* to the cause. A lot of things outside of football take a back seat, but you know what you are signing up to, and we all wanted to be there.

All-Ireland final day… it can be very hard.

We'd gone through our first final in 1997 so we knew all about the pressure… starting with people looking for tickets! By the time you play in the second one, you are a bit more relaxed, and you know how to deal with the 'sideshows', as we used to call them.

You don't want to be getting involved in those *shows*... you want to be concentrating only on performing.

You get more experience as well playing in front of big crowds... playing in Croke Park and the routine around the big game... the trip from the hotel to the stadium, and all the little things like that.

As a player, your job is to play and perform.

Looking back, we also have to remember that a lot of lads were unlucky and went through the early-90s with Kerry... and they weren't getting past Cork. They had no backdoor either.

Kerry went through a barren period, so we are lucky.

We were part of a good team, at a good time. There are some great Kerry footballers who didn't get that All-Ireland medal.

I loved playing in Croke Park.

There is a lot of space there, and in 2000 I got a *lot* of space. It was a time before blanket defences and when you've got balls supplied by Darragh Ó Sé and these lads... it sure helps!

Things went well for me those days against Galway.

I got a good start the first day and got a point very early, and that's a big thing in an All-Ireland final... *Get your hands on the ball early*. It just took off from there. The confidence was up. When you are on the team starting for years, you are not looking over your shoulder... and when you have that confidence you feel nothing can stop you!

That first game in 2000 and winning the replay cemented my place in the Kerry team for years to come. I went on to play for Kerry for another eight years.

The big thing in Kerry football is when lads talk about their first All-Ireland... they're talking about their first one in the starting team. That's the big one!

Not everyone can start. Some lads are unlucky and come on, but to start on the team and walk behind the band and meet the President... *That's what you want*. You can always say you got to play in an All-Ireland final, but you want to *start* and if you don't start, you just work even harder to get on the team the next year.

It defines your career, and your life.

Two years later, we lost the final to Armagh. I actually played okay the same day as well, but you never forget the games you lose too.

I think any fella who says he doesn't have any regrets, he'd be lying… we all definitely have some regrets. But overall, I'm lucky to have been part of that team in a great era where we were competing and winning things.

We lost finals, but thank God, we won more than we lost.

My dad was my main influence growing up. I had a younger brother Francis. When he came along, he was kicking ball out the back as well.

In the club there were some great underage mentors… former principal Jerome Conway in Killorglin; he was over the underage structure in the club and he was making sure we were all playing.

We had Patsy Joy and Seamus Murphy, God rest them. Great men and we had a great tradition in Laune Rangers, but it starts with your parents… my mum and dad, Frank and Mary.

I'm indebted to them. My sister Mary and my brother Francis were a great support as well.

My dad played with Kerry. He played minor and then National League.

We always had a ball out in the yard, and we grew up idolising and hearing about… and rewinding the *Kerry's Golden Years* tape… we wanted to be Jacko, we wanted to be Pat Spillane, we wanted to be Mikey Sheehy, we wanted to be 'Bomber' and we wanted to be 'Ogie'.

After my dad finished playing with Laune Rangers he was a selector so I was going along to the games. Back then the underage at Laune Rangers was strong. We went to a Féile, our under-14 team, and we were playing Division 1 up to minor level.

We'd lads from the club who represented Kerry… Joe Shannon, Timmy Fleming, Gerard Murphy, Billy O'Shea and the Hassetts, so there were always role models for us to look up to… not just from the county but from within my club as well. I'd want to be these boys as well.

There's that pedigree and ambition in Kerry… there are always fellas to look up to. There are young lads going around now and they are looking at David Clifford. At the time we were watching Mikey, 'Bomber' and Spillane. It's a great culture.

And also, you won't get too big for your boots, because there is always another fella coming up behind you.

I'm still playing a bit of football.

Whether it is the 'A' team or the 'B' team, it is just great to be involved, just kicking that ball… staying out there, enjoying it.

As a primary school teacher, I'm involved in coaching in the school, and I'm also training the Laune Rangers minor team.

I like the coaching side of things more so than management. I especially like coaching the underage kids. I like that side of it a lot. And I haven't taken up the golf yet.

Playing with the club means a lot to me. I'd say if I gave it up now, I'd definitely have to take up the golf.

I feel sometimes it is expected of you to give something back. A lot of lads – some of them have passed on now, God rest them – gave up their time to coach us and I think it is only the right thing to do to go back and give *something back* to the young kids.

SEÁN O'SULLIVAN

KERRY 2-17 GALWAY 1-12
All-Ireland SFC Quarter-Final
Croke Park
AUGUST 4, 2002

Seán O'Sullivan celebrates after scoring against Galway in Croke Park in the All-Ireland quarter-final, in the defining game of his career in green and gold.

★ **KERRY:** D O'Keeffe; M Ó Sé, S Moynihan, M McCarthy; T Ó Sé (0-1), E Fitzmaurice, J Sheehan (0-1); D Ó Sé (0-1), D Daly; **S O'Sullivan (1-1)**, E Brosnan (0-1), L Hassett; MF Russell (0-4), D Ó Cinneide (0-3), C Cooper (0-4). Subs: A MacGearailt (1-1) for Daly, T O'Sullivan for Fitzmaurice, J Crowley for Russell.

★ **GALWAY:** A Keane; K Fitzgerald, G Fahey, R Fahey; D Meehan, T Mannion, S Óg de Paor; K Walsh (0-1), M Donnellan (1-0); P Clancy, J Fallon, J Bergin (0-1); D Savage (0-2), P Joyce (0-6), M Clancy (0-1). Subs: T Joyce for Fallon, T Meehan for de Paor, M Colleran (0-1) for Fitzgerald, L Colleran for Donnellan, J Donnellan for P Clancy.

THE ACTION

GALWAY'S HOPES OF landing two All-Ireland titles in-a-row for the first time since 1965 were dashed by Kerry after the jaded looking Tribesmen faded out of contention of this quarter-final clash in the second-half. Galway were quickly left staring at a five-point deficit when substitute Aodhán MacGearailt found the net in the 62nd minute.

While MacGearailt's score killed the game, it was Seán O'Sullivan's first-half goal that *killed* the Tribesmen. The moment Eoin Brosnan put O'Sullivan on a collision course with the Galway goal, it was game over for the All-Ireland champions.

Both sides had started hell for leather and treated the crowd of 59,252 to a game of open, attacking football. But as the game went on, a much-improved Kerry side, who overcame Wicklow, Fermanagh and Kildare in the qualifiers, after defeat to Cork in the Munster SFC semi-finals, looked far more alert and exposed a rusty Galway side. Galway had not played a championship match since their Connacht final victory over Sligo five weeks previous.

Kerry opened the scoring and were two points up with five minutes gone, but Galway stunned Páidí Ó Sé's side a minute later when Michael Donnellan burst through the Kingdom defence before flicking the ball past Declan O'Keeffe to raise the green flag.

Kerry's lethal corner-forward duo of Mike Frank Russell and Colm 'Gooch' Cooper kept the Kingdom ticking along with a platter of scores in what proved a fruitful opening period for the Kerry attack. And as half-time fast approached, Eoin Brosnan did well to find Seán O'Sullivan and the Cromane man brushed aside several tackles before blasting the ball past Alan Keane to give Kerry a five point lead. It was 1-9 to 1-6 in favour of Kerry at half-time.

The game slackened in the second-half as Galway's lack of competitive action in recent weeks started to show.

The excellent Darragh Ó Sé, Dara O'Cinnéide and Cooper put the game to bed as they carved open a tiring Galway defence to confirm Kerry's place in the All-Ireland semi-finals and set up a rematch against Munster champions Cork.

★★★★★

66

I HAD JUST broken into the Kerry set-up in 2002.

I had been on the senior panel about three years before that, but I had drifted off it… and played with the under-21s for a couple of years.

It was Páidí Ó Sé who called me in. That summer we lost the Munster semi-final to Cork after a replay and I wasn't making the team. I was a sub… getting a little bit of a look in, here and there.

We went in through the backdoor, in through the qualifiers after losing in Munster, and Páidí wanted to shake things up a little bit so he changed the team around.

I got my chance… and the qualifiers went well for me.

In the last round of the qualifiers we were playing Kildare in Thurles, in Semple Stadium… and I didn't have a great out, I have to say. I was being marked by Anthony Rainbow, who at the time was one of the best wing-backs in the country… a great player, Anthony. He kept me fairly quiet. I was taken off.

Páidí gave me the curly finger with about 15 minutes to go and I was very, *very* disappointed.

That evening, coming back down home, we got back as far as Killorglin.

We knew we were playing Galway the following weekend in the quarter-final in Croke Park, but I really feared for my place. I was very, *very* down on myself.

I was going to go away home… *I was going to just go away home and close the door of my bedroom behind me…* and not talk to anybody about it.

I'll never forget… Liam Hassett messaged me to tell me to stop in Killorglin… that we were going to go for a few pints. Now, I thought that was probably a bad call because we were playing again the following weekend. I don't think it would be done nowadays, to be honest with you, but Liam, in fairness to him, he was a great experienced head around the panel. The two of us went for a few quiet pints in Killorglin that evening, the night of the Kildare game. Liam had a good chat with me about how I was going to react to having a poor game against Kildare… *There was no point feeling sorry for myself.*

That was his direct message.

I was only 22 at the time, and I thought it was the end of the world. I thought…

No way was I going to get picked the following weekend! I really thought I was gone down the pecking order in the management's eyes.

So, Liam said to me, 'There is only one thing you can do now and that's go in training Tuesday and Thursday night and just throw your lot in, give it everything you have… just try and hang onto your jersey for the game against Galway'.

I remember waking up the following day, thinking… *I'm in a better place now!*

I went in and had a good week of training and convinced the management… Páidí and the selectors, to take another chance with me.

It wasn't all about the few pints; it was more all about the man I was having the few pints with… that's why leaders in a dressing-room, leaders around a squad, are so vital. Liam Hassett… and I've often said it to Liam since! He didn't have to worry, he was playing well. But he took the time and he realised that here was a young fella from a neighbouring club – Liam is Laune Rangers, and I'm Cromane – who had suffered a bit of a confidence drop after a poor performance.

Liam didn't have to take the time to pick up the phone to me and tell me to meet him in Killorglin. And it was more the advice I got from Liam really, more than anything else. It's not like we went mad altogether. We only had a couple of pints.

It was more the chat and the little bit of guidance from a senior player, a man who had All-Irelands and All Stars in his pocket already. He was just directing a young fella, and it really brought it home to me.

I've been involved with a lot of teams since… I'm the other side of 40 and I'm still playing with my club team, and people often ask, 'Would you walk away from it now?' But I see young fellas coming into the club and they need a little bit of leadership. Young guys need guidance.

If Liam hadn't phoned me, I could have gone home, felt sorry for myself… and I could have brought that baggage into training with me the following Tuesday night.

And who knows? I might have given off the wrong impression at training and I might not have been picked for the Galway game.

I was also proud of myself as well, in the way I reacted.

I went into training and I worked hard that week, and got my place. *And then the game itself?* I knew I had a bad day the week before, but I hadn't turned into a bad player overnight… *Just to go out onto Croke Park and prove to myself and everyone else that I could do a job for Kerry.*

I ended up playing my best game for Kerry. I got a goal and a point off Seán Óg de Paor from play. Everything just went right for me because I just went in with an air of confidence that the management – even though I had a bad game the week before – really had faith in me and saw that I could bring something to the table.

I'll never forget. It was a beautiful, hot summer's day in Croke Park, and I just ran myself into the ground. I came off with about five minutes to go… absolutely shattered because I had given it everything.

For me, that day stands out as my most memorable game for Kerry.

We won, we got through to the All-Ireland semi-final where we were going to meet Cork. It was the stand-out game in my career.

Páidí was a real players' man.

He was a great motivator, and he had no problem in telling me when I got into training after the Kildare game, 'Look you didn't have a great day now out Sunday but, you know, you need to drive on again'.

He pulled no punches. He was direct… 'Look, we need more from you!' That was a little kick up the behind I needed as well.

After we beat Galway, we ended up – usually we used to get the train to games – getting the bus home. I'm not sure why we decided to get the bus.

We had a few weeks off before the Cork match, so Páidí decided to organise a bus from Dublin back down to Killarney, and as you can imagine it was a fairly happy bus. We stopped for a meal in An Poitín Stil – it is just on the way out of Dublin, in Rathcoole on the left as you're coming onto the motorway. We had our food and there were a few slabs thrown onto the bus for us as we drove down.

I was sitting with Páidí up the front of the bus for a couple of minutes. He told me how delighted he was for me and how happy he was with my performance, but he also told me that one swallow doesn't make a summer… that we had Cork in a couple of weeks, and I had to drive on again to get my place.

That was the ship Páidí Ó Sé ran. It was a competitive ship.

You could never rest on your laurels. You always had to go and prove yourself. That's why he was so successful. We didn't end up winning the All-Ireland that year, but we came very close. We were beaten by Armagh in a game that, when you look back, we probably shouldn't have lost, but definitely for me that Galway game stands out as one of the greatest games that I've ever played in the green and gold.

I'll remember it especially for my goal in the first-half.

It was just one of those shots where the minute it left my boot, I knew it was flying into the top corner. It was my first ever goal in Croke Park. It was exhilarating really to see it nestle in the top corner.

I knew I was going to be marked by either Declan Meehan or Seán Óg de Paor. That Galway team from the early 2000s were a superb outfit. They had won the All-Ireland in 1998, and they had won the final against Meath in 2001. They were a fantastic team.

I knew I was going to be up against one of the top wing-backs in the country and, as it turned out, it was Seán Óg. But I knew Seán Óg was coming to the end of his career at that stage and I knew I had legs, I had speed… and that I was going to use that to my advantage.

I just swore to myself going out that day, whether I came off the field after 15 minutes, 25 minutes or 55 minutes… I was going to run myself into the ground. I remember getting in at half-time and I was getting my water on board. I was sitting next to Rónán O'Connor from St Michael's/Foilmore… he was on the panel.

Páidí was giving his instructions, and I turned to Rónán and told him that I felt I was going to be sick because it was just a really hot day.

It was a game played with real pace and intensity. I was just on the move all of the time, and I just felt physically sick, but once I got my bearings and got out for the second-half, I was fine again.

It was a double-header in Croke Park. There was a decent crowd in for our game. There was a nice Kerry crowd in at the time, because I remember after I scored the goal down into the Cusack Stand side, as I ran away and gave a little fist pump there was a nice batch of green and gold jerseys over in the corner. That moment stands out for me as well.

Kerry supporters at that time were so used to getting to finals and getting to semi-finals, so they probably got a bit of criticism for not making the journey to the quarter-finals, but I must say there was a good Kerry crowd there that day.

My father Danny and my uncle Patrick always had an interest in football so, from a young age, I was brought to Munster finals in Killarney and Cork.

Unfortunately, as I grew up in the late-80s and early-90s when Kerry were going through a bit of a famine and Cork were the dominant force in Munster. There was no backdoor. When we were beaten in Munster finals, we were gone!

So, there were no regular trips to Croke Park, but I was often brought to Páirc Uí Chaoimh. We'd go up the old Cork road and we'd stop to have our sandwiches before the match.

And we'd go into Killarney for Munster finals, of course. There are photos of me, when I was five or six, with the full Kerry kit on.

I actually started off as a corner-back. My under-12 manager thought there was a back in me, but I think he wasn't long changing his mind. You were literally thrown into it, and you had no choice. You either went with it or you didn't.

Maurice Fitzgerald for me was my hero.

I used to go up to Páirc Uí Chaoimh and watch Maurice kick 10 or 12 points for Kerry and end up on a losing team, but he was always the footballer I aspired to be.

Young fellas always want to be somebody they see!

My young fellas – I've three kids – and other young fellas around Cromane now want to be the next David Clifford. That's the way it works and for as long as time, it will always be like that!

You are never too far away in Kerry from greatness.

I have four All-Ireland medals and I'm very honoured and privileged to have them, but I could walk around the corner in Tralee and bump into Mikey Sheehy, who has eight. *Do you know what I love about it?* There are no agendas, there is no big-headedness… no egos. Tomorrow, or the next day, you could bump into one of the all-time greats, someone like 'Ogie' Moran or 'Bomber' Liston.

The Ó'Sés, 'Gooch'… I'm currently working with Declan O'Sullivan with the Kerry under-20s… no egos!

You only get a short stint at it. I played from 2002 to '09. That seven years went by in a blink of an eye, because it was just a phenomenal seven years. We got to six finals in-a-row. You were really only a caretaker. You were only in the jersey keeping it for the next fella. I was lucky to either wear the No 10 or No 12. Paul

Galvin was usually on the other wing, or Darran, or Eoin Brosnan.

You were always only looking after it for somebody because when I left, the next bunch came through. My own clubmate Donnacha Walsh started wearing 10 or 12, and now he's gone. Now you've got the likes of Dara Moynihan wearing 10 or 12. It is passed on from man to man, and regardless of who is wearing it, we all hope that they do it justice and do their best for the Kingdom.

It flies, and that's the one thing I would say to any Kerry player or any fella who is lucky enough to get on a team or get a jersey... *Treasure it.* Cherish those days because they do fly by. You try your best to extend them as much as you can but the body eventually tells you it's time to walk away, or you might be forced to walk away with injury. But every time you get to run out with Kerry is a special day.

That day in 2002 was one of many for me, but it definitely stands out as my most memorable game in the green and gold.

I played for Mid-Kerry in Beaufort against Laune Rangers in the county championship in 2009 and I kicked 10 points. It was just one of those days where everything just clicked. Everything I kicked went over the bar.

I could have kicked it from the dressing-room door and it would have gone over the bar.

But for me, when I look back at my career, the feeling of performing for Kerry to my best in Croke Park, up against the best footballers in the country in Galway at the time, for me that definitely stands out.

It was a day for me that proved that I belonged at that level, and that I could do it at that level because after the Kildare game I did start questioning myself. I was only 22. You kind of start saying to yourself... *Am I being found out here?*

The All-Ireland final day itself... don't get me wrong, some lads have great days on All-Ireland final days... but you just want to get the win and get out of town.

The closer we got to All-Ireland finals, the more pressure you put on yourself. To the point where you didn't really enjoy it. You just wanted to get your win and have Sam Maguire going down on the train, which we were lucky enough to do on many occasions. None of the finals would stand out for me, but certainly that Galway game was just a great day out for myself and Kerry.

I left in 2009 after we beat Cork and Jack O'Connor asked me back in… in 2011.

I had been playing good football with Mid Kerry, and I went back in. I was actually a selector with Kerry minors at the time and I left that role to go back in and play with the seniors. I didn't last long with the seniors. I quickly knew that it was a bad move, so if I have one regret it is probably making the decision to go back in.

But to be honest with you, it's not even a regret either because when Kerry football comes knocking, you don't say no. I had been playing well, and obviously Jack realised that, but it was probably the wrong move at the time. Hindsight is a great thing.

I felt it might have hindered my chances of coaching for Kerry at some stage. It did for a while, but now I'm back. I went back with development squads and worked myself back in. Now I'm in with Declan O'Sullivan as a coach with the under-20s.

The most natural step when you stop playing is to go coaching, and that would be my long-term aim. This is a start. Obviously, I have to prove myself with the 20s and show what I can do and hopefully take it from there.

It is a huge dedication and it is certainly something you have to enjoy. It is the same as playing, you *have* to enjoy it. You give up all of these social events… weddings, birthday parties and stags with the lads. Don't get me wrong, you did… you missed them, but you were doing it out of choice. Nobody put a gun to our heads and said… 'You're going playing with Kerry!'

You did it because you wanted to do it, you wanted to represent Kerry… you wanted to play at the top level of gaelic football, and you knew going into it what the pit-falls were in terms of having to sacrifice so much.

I'm 41 now and the club have asked me what my plans are? I've told them I'm going to play until my body tells me I can't play anymore. When that day comes, which I hope won't be for a while yet, I'll walk away from it, but I know for a fact that I won't just walk away.

I'll say… *Okay I can't play anymore, what can I do for the club now?* That comes from within. That comes from a passion for the game.

Everyone doesn't have that.

I know fellas that I played with… with Kerry, who I meet now and they haven't even gone to a game since. They were in it while they were in it, but once they finished they had their other interests. You either throw yourself into the passion of it and throw yourself into it lock stock and two smoking barrels, or you are the type of person who says… 'Yes I was there for a period of my life, I enjoyed it, I got great reward from it… but now I've moved on to something else'.

For Cromane, for such a small community to have two men… myself and Donnacha Walsh… bring home seven All-Ireland medals between the two of us to such a small area is amazing. Myself and Donnacha pinch ourselves sometimes when we are talking about it. We look back with very fond memories. It makes us proud.

With Cromane we are always trying to fight for numbers with such a small pick, so we'd like to think that what myself and Donnacha have done with Kerry in the past would inspire young guys to go on and maybe follow in our footsteps. We had a Kerry minor a couple of years ago, Kieran O'Sullivan… no relation. He is on the under-20 provisional panel at the moment. He is a guy who is carrying the torch. We have other young lads on development squads, who are also trying to pave a way in the game themselves, so if myself and Donnacha play any small part in those guys making it through to play with Kerry, then we'd be delighted.

EOIN BROSNAN

KERRY 1-20 MAYO 2-9
All-Ireland SFC Final
Croke Park
SEPTEMBER 26, 2004

Eoin Brosnan in full flight against Mayo in the 2004 All-Ireland final.

★ **KERRY:** D Murphy; A O'Mahony, M McCarthy, T O'Sullivan; T Ó Sé, É Fitzmaurice, M Ó Sé (0-1); **E Brosnan**, W Kirby (0-3); L Hassett, D O'Sullivan (0-1), P Galvin (0-1); C Cooper (1-5), D Ó Cinnéide (0-8), J Crowley. Subs: S Moynihan for L. Hassett, MF Russell (0-1) for Crowley, R O'Connor for Ó Cinnéide, P Kelly for Galvin, B Guiney for T Ó Sé.

★ **MAYO:** P Burke; D Geraghty, D Heaney, G Ruane; P Gardiner, J Nallen, P Kelly; R McGarrity, F Kelly; J Gill, C McDonald (0-3), A Dillon (1-2); C Mortimer, T Mortimer, B Maloney (0-1). Subs: D Brady for Kelly, C Moran for Geraghty, M Conroy (1-1) for Gill, A Moran (0-1) for C Mortimer (0-1), P Navin for D Heaney.

THE ACTION

AFTER THREE YEARS of heartbreak in Croke Park, Kerry finally got back to the summit in 2004, winning the National League, Munster and All-Ireland treble for the first time since 1997.

John Maughan's men couldn't capitalise on an early Alan Dillon goal. And nobody expected such an easy win, as Kerry were missing the hugely influential duo of Darragh Ó Sé and Seamus Moynihan through injury. Moynihan, who was on the bench, did come on towards the end of the game, when the result was beyond any doubt.

An ever impressive Colm Cooper scored 1-4 from play in a Man of the Match contribution, while Dara Ó Cinnéide kicked eight points, two from play.

Kerry had the game wrapped up by half-time when they led by eight points, 1-12 to 1-4.

Kerry's domination drove Mayo spectators to leave the stadium in their thousands long before the finish.

Kerry extended their advantage in the second-half and Mayo, playing for respectability at this stage, trailed by 11 points with 20 minutes to go in the second-half as Jack O'Connor's men continued to put on an exhibition for their travelling support.

There was a late consolation goal by substitute Michael Conroy, who tapped home a Trevor Mortimer rebound in the last minute of regular time, but Mayo only managed four points from play in the second-half.

Mike Frank Russell, who replaced Johnny Crowley 10 minutes earlier, took a great point in stoppage time to close out a game that had since early in the second-half been a foregone conclusion.

O'Connor watched his team lift the title in his first season in charge, and watched Kerry rack up a total of 1-20 – the highest score in an All-Ireland football final since 'Bomber' Liston got 3-2 in his team's 5-11 destruction of Dublin in 1978.

★★★★★

66

WE SHOULD HAVE won the All-Ireland in 2002. We played fantastic football the whole way through the first-half against Armagh, and went in comfortable enough at half-time, but we just didn't show up in the second half.

Armagh took it to us. They were dominant in the second-half really, and left us scraps.

We met Tyrone in the semi-final the next year, and we'd never come across anything like that before.

Páidí Ó Sé finished up then. He had brought me into the panel in 2000.

Jack O'Connor came in. I'd had no dealings with Jack previously, but a lot of the team had played under Jack between vocational schools and Kerry under-21s, and he was a selector going back before that.

There was a new regime. Pat Flanagan came in too, as a fitness trainer. We trained hard enough before Christmas, and then we went to Lanzarote, to Club La Santa just after New Year's for the first week in January. We trained full-time over there. That was the first dedicated training camp that Kerry ever went on.

It was a different environment really. We were training three or four times a day. We were there for a week, and we had just one day off.

The Leeds Rhinos rugby league team were in the same resort as us. These lads were eating weights in the gym. We were only really starting off, but these fellas were animals. They were way more advanced than we were.

Pat Flanagan said that it was a three-year project to get up to the level that he wanted us at. We bought into it that year. We played well and we won the National League. We then won the Munster Championship… and we won the All-Ireland.

It happened fast.

We had played Derry in the semi-final. We were playing great football… there was a lot of confidence running through the team.

Seamus Moynihan and Darragh Ó Sé were our two talismen, but both of them were missing for the final. That was a big blow for us really, going into the final without the two boys. Seamus was on the bench that day, but Darragh had broken his foot. He was out!

Going up to the game, I remember Jack O'Connor telling us to relax. 'Enjoy the parade... just take it in,' he told us. For a lot of the lads, it was a first All-Ireland final.

It is different in a final, because you are out on the field nearly 35 minutes before the game. You've your warm-up done beforehand, and then there is a lot of pageantry. There is the parade, meeting the President... there is the National Anthem, there is a lot going on before the game. It can take a bit out of you... that 35 minutes.

What Jack said stuck with me.

I said I'd just switch on afterwards.

Don't be switched on... Getting nervous and uptight and what not!

We performed fairly well. It was a comprehensive win in the end.

Marc Ó Sé and myself were roommates... we were close. We'd lost in 2001, in '02... and we lost in 2003. We won very little at minor, and we won nothing at under-21. We were both thinking... *Are we ever going to win anything?*

Doubts do start to come in... and All-Irelands are so hard to win.

Winning was a fantastic feeling... something better than we had ever imagined. Winning an All-Ireland does define your career. The first one is always the special one.

The second and the third, and whatever comes after that are great... they are brilliant, they are a bonus, but it is nice to get one over the line the first time.

If we had lost to Mayo that would have been four years with four bad losses.

Suddenly, a manager might be thinking... *This fella is involved for four losses... There might be something up here.* He might think of slipping in a new player or a younger player.

Or the manager might be changed, and a new manager mightn't favour you. Sport is fickle enough. You could pick up an injury the following day... every day you go out could be your last.

It was great having William Kirby beside me in midfield. We wouldn't have played a whole pile together in matches beforehand, but obviously when Darragh got injured, Jack had a plan. He told me pretty much straightaway that I was going in midfield with William.

I would have been in the half-forward line all along, but for the three or four weeks in training that's where the two of us were… and we were geared up for it.

William had a fantastic game that day. He kicked three points from play which for a midfielder is amazing. Only for 'Gooch' going on fire altogether, William would have been Man of the Match.

Mayo came in with good expectations. They were a decent side. They had good players. The likes of James Nallen, David Heaney, Ciarán McDonald and Trevor Mortimer… but we blew them away really.

The first year I was involved, in 2000, we played a tough Armagh side.

And in '02 Armagh got the better of us in the final. They were tough nuts… the likes of McGeeney, McGrane and Diarmuid Marsden, all big strong fellas… Francie Bellew, and you had the McEntees. I think up north they probably had a couple of years head start physically, before we caught up with them.

There was a fantastic Tyrone side at that time. They blew us away in 2003, and in '05 and '08 they beat us in two finals, so there were high quality sides back then.

In the last number of years you've had Dublin far ahead of everyone and Kerry getting close but not close enough, but at the time I was playing you'd a brilliant Tyrone team, a good Mayo team, a brilliant Kerry team, a good Cork team… there was a whole pile of teams competing. Dublin were never too far away.

There were a lot of teams that were good, *good* sides, but we had an exceptional side really when you look at six All-Ireland finals in-a-row from 2004 to '09. They were long years but to keep going back and keep doing it again and again? When you look back, you realise we had a fantastic side.

I was playing in the forwards and I wasn't really enjoying my football as much in the 2007 and '08 seasons. I'd been on the road a long time, had got married and started a family, and I was self-employed in effect, so it was hard going… long years.

I'd lost a yard of pace. I wasn't really getting away from fellas in the forwards. So I stepped aside.

When I came back with the club, I really enjoyed it and we'd good success. In 2010 we won the county championship with Dr Crokes. I remember Jack gave me a call after we played Nemo Rangers in a Munster club final. The game was meant to be played before Christmas, in December 2010, but it was frozen off.

It was finally played in late-January 2011. We were 12 or 13 points down at half-time, but things had been going well enough for myself at centre-back. I had settled into that position with the Crokes and I was enjoying it. We pinned them back to about two or three points in the end. They dominated the first-half... we dominated the second-half. It was a funny game because it wasn't a game where there was a huge gale or anything like that.

Coming down on the bus after the game disappointed, I got a text from Jack saying he'd been watching the game and he'd give me a buzz during the week.

We had a chat, and the following week we were playing Mayo in Castlebar and I was No 6 for Kerry, which two weeks previously I wouldn't even have been dreaming of... and I was marking Andy Moran.

We won that game. It nearly ended up being a dream comeback but unfortunately it didn't work out like that... it all changed in the last 10 minutes in the 2011 All-Ireland final against Dublin.

I was fairly versatile. I would have played every line, and I started a county championship final in every line.

I started in the full-forward line in an All-Ireland final against Tyrone... I played in half-forward lines, midfield... and the half-back line with Kerry. Now, I never played in the full-back line with Kerry, but I remember a few years ago we played Kenmare in the championship and Pat O'Shea told me I was going in on Adrian Spillane, and wherever Adrian was going... I was going.

And the next thing, Adrian trotted into No 13 or 15, so I started the game at corner-back... *Jesus*, I thought... *I'm out of my depth here.*

I kept moving further back, but I never made it as far as the goalkeeper.

My father would have always been Crokes. That's where playing with Crokes came from really. I remember as a young fella... four, five, six years of age, getting on the bus. There used to be a bus going around that would bring you up to the small field in Fitzgerald Stadium, and I'd be kicking the ball around.

It wasn't as structured as it is now, and the club wouldn't have had the facilities they have now. So, I would have been inside in the small field and when I was around 10, I remember... I don't know did I lose interest or what, but I didn't go up for a while.

Patrick 'Tatler' O'Sullivan called to the house and said, 'Listen, you're back up!' He nearly pulled me out of the house.

He threw me into a game above in the small field. It was a final against Kilcummin. It was possibly an under-12 'B' game. We hadn't much success at under-12 but at under-14 then Patrick 'Tatler' took charge of the team and took us all the way up to minor. We had great times and great success.

We won a county championship at under-15. It was a straight knockout... we played Listowel in the final in Ballymac. It was a good Listowel team with Tadhg Kennelly and Noel Kennelly, so to win that championship was a huge result.

That was in the 90s and the Crokes senior team at the time won a county championship in '91, won the All-Ireland club championship in '92, and were in another county final in '94.

I started then in 1998 against Mid Kerry in midfield, when I was 18. The late Martin Beckett was playing with us. You are seeing the likes of John Galvin, Liam Hartnett, Pat O'Shea, Connie Murphy, Noel O'Leary... all these fellas that would have played in the 1992 team with the Crokes.

I finished college quite young... I was only 19 doing my finals, and around May or early-June in 2000 we played An Ghaeltacht back in Gallaras in a county league game. After the game Eddie 'Tatler' told me that Páidí Ó Sé was at the game and Kerry were playing a challenge game, or a pitch opener against Laois, the following day in Stradbally and they wanted me to travel.

I went up and I kicked four points that day. I played well. I'd a great bit of pace when I was younger. I slowed down in my older days alright, but speed was always a huge asset of mine.

Next thing, I was called into the panel. The team ended up winning the All-Ireland that year which was super, but it was hard to break into a winning side. The final went to a replay, so we won the All-Ireland in October and a week or two later we were out in the National League against Louth... there were three games before Christmas. That was my first start.

It was the defending All-Ireland champions against Louth in Fitzgerald Stadium. Most of the boys were still in celebration mode so it was hard enough to put a team together. We were actually beaten by Louth by a point.

I always loved playing with the club. I suppose it was fairly easy when we had the success that we had.

Sometimes, with Kerry, the pressure might have been a bit too much, and the commitment might have been a little bit too much, but to be fair I think it will make it a little bit easier in time to come when you have the split season… we didn't really have a split season.

For years we'd be constantly on the go.

On St Patrick's Day in 2019, we were beaten by Corofin and I retired. I was turning 39 later that year… I'd enough done. I was still playing okay, but injuries were becoming more and more common, and being with the Crokes the level isn't a million miles off inter-county. It is certainly not social football, because you are training fairly hard.

Patrick 'Tatler' rang me the next day and said, 'Remember we'd a chat over Christmas and you said you'd get involved in an underage side? Well you are now involved with the under-14s'.

This was a day after retiring.

I got involved with the under-14s in 2019, and I haven't taken any break from the game since.

MARC Ó SÉ

KERRY 3-15 ARMAGH 1-13
All-Ireland SFC Quarter-Final
Croke Park
AUGUST 5, 2006

Marc Ó Sé wins the ball from Andy Mallon in the epic All-Ireland quarter-final meeting with Armagh in 2006 which proclaimed Kerry as the team to beat that summer.

★ **KERRY:** D Murphy; **M Ó Sé (0-2)**, M McCarthy, T O'Sullivan; T Ó Sé (0-1), S Moynihan, A O'Mahony; D Ó Sé, T Griffin; S O'Sullivan (0-2), E Brosnan (1-0), P Galvin (0-1); C Cooper (0-3), K Donaghy (1-0), MF Russell (0-2) Subs: Darran O'Sullivan (1-0) for S O'Sullivan, Declan O'Sullivan (0-1) for Griffin, B Sheehan (0-2) for Russell, E Fitzmaurice (0-1) for Brosnan.

★ **ARMAGH:** P Hearty; A Mallon, F Bellew, E McNulty; P Duffy, A Kernan (0-1), C McKeever; K McGeeney, P McGrane; M O'Rourke, J McEntee (0-1), M Mackin, S McDonnell (1-5), R Clarke (0-3), O McConville (0-3). Subs: P Loughran for Mackin, B Mallon for McEntee, P McKeever for O'Rourke.

THE ACTION

BORN-AGAIN KERRY lit up Croke Park as Darragh Ó Sé and Kieran Donaghy helped pull the Northern Lights down to earth in an epic battle to last the ages. Putting in their classiest championship display for some time, the Kingdom crushed Armagh's All-Ireland hopes.

Led by the outstanding Darragh Ó Sé, the Kingdom scored 2-10 in the second-half to totally swamp the Ulster champions in game six of eight along the way to securing their 34th All-Ireland.

Jack O'Connor and Joe Kernan sent their men out to attack from the get-go and the clash between Francie Bellew and Kieran Donaghy quickly caught the attention, with both players battling for the ball around the square, but with the impressive Steven McDonnell hitting 1-3 Armagh led 1-7 to 1-5 at the interval.

Eoin Brosnan had toe-poked into the net to put Kerry in front after just three minutes, but McDonnell's 23rd-minute strike saw his side lead by four at one stage.

Three minutes into the second-half, Donaghy found the back of the net to put Kerry three points ahead, 2-7 to 1-7. After a superb diagonal centre from the classy Seán O'Sullivan, Donaghy soared to the clouds, fielded superbly, and left Bellew sprawling on the grass before giving Paul Hearty no chance.

Despite having Paul Galvin sent-off on the hour mark for a second bookable offence, Kerry held their nerve and good substitutions gave them a second wind.

With 10 minutes to go, Armagh were still only a goal behind with McDonnell and Ronan Clarke keeping them in touch, yet despite their numerical disadvantage, Kerry's play continued to be wonderfully expansive, with the Ó Sé brothers, Marc (two) and Tomás, racing forward from the back to land three successive scores.

The score that sank Armagh hearts was a Darran O'Sullivan goal five minutes from time. From there, Kerry never looked back. The resulting prize was a semi-final spot against their arch-rivals Cork.

★ ★ ★ ★ ★

66

KERRY'S GOLDEN YEARS came out in 1988 or '89, and it was an incredible production. Every person in the county interested in gaelic football would have a copy of *Kerry's Golden Years* at home. It was great… I could memorise every bit of that video… Michael O'Hehir's voice… and Kerry winning All-Irelands upon All-Irelands.

Great times we'll never forget.

Páidí and my dad, of course, were huge influences on us growing up.

But when Páidí took charge of Kerry then, that drove it on even further and we desperately wanted to play with Kerry. Darragh was on the team before Páidí took charge. That was the inspiration.

At the start of the Armagh game, we were taking on huge water. Armagh were coming at us in droves, and it was end-to-end stuff.

They talk about the 2008 game between Kerry and Galway and how end-to-end that was… this game was something similar.

Coming into that game, you'd be lying if you said we didn't want to avenge the 2002 defeat. We were four points up at half-time against Armagh in 2002 in the All-Ireland final, going well but, in fairness to Armagh they really rallied in the second-half… and they came back.

It was hugely disappointing for us that year, because it was the year we buried our father, and as well as that Darragh was captain. It would have been a great year to win Sam and bring the cup back to Ventry… and add in the fact that that year we played the best football we ever played.

We had nine games in the Championship in 2002, and to lose at the final hurdle was bitterly disappointing.

The Armagh game in 2006 had a similar backdrop. We had lost to Cork in the Munster final replay and we went through the backdoor again… and again we came up against Armagh in the quarter-final. It was a huge game for us. The minute the draw was made we were thrilled in a way because we knew there was no need for motivation.

In the first-half, they were totally in control. There were great battles all over the field… beginning with Francie Bellew and Kieran Donaghy. The week previous to this game, Donaghy had an outstanding game in Killarney against Longford. Eoin Brosnan got three goals the same day, but Donaghy was the fella who was putting them all on a plate.

The training session before the Longford game, Jack O'Connor had asked myself and Kieran to stick around after… and Jack put a few balls into Kieran inside in the full-forward line. It definitely changed our season, the fact we had a focal point inside there for that Longford game… and then for the Armagh game.

We had 'Gooch' around him, we had Mike Frank Russell around him… so he was the perfect foil for those fellas. He was winning ball against Armagh, but the funny thing about it was, it wasn't all that plain sailing in the first-half. Francie Bellew was coming out on top a bit.

But 'Gooch' kept Donaghy going!

He'd say to him… 'Keep going, you're doing grand'.

At the other end of the field, we were under serious pressure. It was end-to-end stuff. All you have to do is walk around Croke Park and see the dynamics and how big the pitch is, and if good ball is coming in, it is very hard to get out in front and win that ball against your man.

Armagh definitely posed questions that day.

What a serious side they had! They had Paul McGrane, Kieran McGeeney, Stevie McDonnell… they'd Aaron Kernan and Bellew. They had quality players all over the pitch. We were definitely up against it.

Then McDonnell got the goal to put them 1-6 to 1-3 up. After that, we needed to do *something*. We needed to tweak something. What we did was… we brought Tommy Griffin, who was midfield, back a small bit. We brought Seamus Moynihan covering back a small bit as well.

That gave us a better structure… we were able to build from the back then, because you'd someone like Moynihan who could carry ball. We were able to get the ball in that bit quicker as well. What we also had that day was, we had the likes of Paul Galvin working furiously off the ball. His work ethic was frightening. The unbelievable thing about him was he was kicking in a few scores as well, so he was giving us a bit of both which really, *really* helped.

Any chance he got to get back, he was making tackles… pulling balls off the likes of McGeeney and these fellas.

In those situations when you go 1-6 to 1-3 down, your mental strength is definitely brought into play to try and stay in touch. The big thing about it, that's exactly what we did; we stayed in touch. We went in at half-time two points down.

Once we could weather that Armagh storm, and get bodies back, we felt that we were in a good position at half-time. We had opportunities and we knew that.

Right on half-time, Donaghy had laid it on a plate for 'Gooch' and he forced a great save by Hearty. Mike Frank went at it again… and it was another great save by Hearty.

Over the bar it went.

So, we knew we were creating scoring opportunities.

The second-half came, and we were a different animal.

Tomás, myself and Darragh really stood up in the second-half. I was delighted with that from a family point of view, but Darragh was just phenomenal. He totally took over around that midfield area. He was *everywhere.*

Armagh had no answer to him. Any ball that was kicked out, Darragh was fielding it. He was all over the place.

We were also getting breaks. Donaghy was staying mentally tough, picking away at the scores, and drawing the odd free or two from Bellew.

Do you know what was a real significant moment in that game? In the first-half, there was a ball played into Donaghy. He had Bellew and McGeeney marking him… and Donaghy won a free against the two of them. I thought it was a huge moment just for Donaghy himself because it kept him in the game mentally.

It really showed his mental resolve.

Donaghy got his goal then. Seán O'Sullivan came in…. he was probably going for a point. He put that ball in and Donaghy just at the edge of the post slipped, got back up on his feet and had the composure. He gave Paul Hearty a bit of an earful straight after, but that goal got us going. That goal is what kick-started the whole thing for us.

I was pushed out the field after that. I was moved out to the half-back line on O'Rourke. He was getting on a few breaks so I was moved out. I said the moment I go out… *I'm going to bring him down the field.* I was mindful of the fact as well that I didn't want to be occupying space.

I got in then for a point.

'Gooch' got the ball and he slipped it to me, and I popped it over the bar. That kept the scoreboard ticking over. We were still the goal up. I felt at that stage there were scores to be got, that we could pop up and get the odd score because there were holes being punched.

Darragh had a great catch then. Tomás popped up; he saw me getting a score and he probably wanted to pop up and get a score. *Great score by him, over the bar.*

All of a sudden, we had gone four points up and Armagh had to come out and play.

My favourite score that I ever scored was on that day. We worked it from one end of the field and we were totally patient with the ball… and then, all of a sudden, we had numbers and Armagh couldn't get bodies back.

I saw Bellew coming at me like a train, so I showed him the dummy… and over the bar it went.

That was my favourite point that I ever scored in the championship. There were opportunities to get up the field, and I think from that moment we didn't really look back. We were now five points up, in a great position… and we were able to empty the bench then as well. Ronan Clarke got a great score, so they did keep in touch.

They did keep that goal between the two teams.

It kind of got a bit messy because Galvin got sent off. John Toal came onto the field and he was getting at Galvin.

There was real danger when Galvin got sent off. It was in the 60th minute, and the game was still in the balance. It was end-to-end stuff. McDonnell was a real thorn in the side for us, and was single-handedly getting them back into the game.

The fight started around that time.

Toal was no help to the cause. He was the waterboy and he was coming in. The referee wasn't looking and Toal was going at Galvin. I think the ref needed to take control. Paul took matters into his own hands.

Waterboys shouldn't be getting involved like that.

For us, Galvin being sent off was a disaster. The game was in the balance, we'd 10 minutes plus left… it's only a three-point game.

This was a key point in that game when temperatures were definitely high. But we had Declan O'Sullivan in… and we still had real leaders on that field. The likes of Declan, the likes of 'Gooch', the likes of Darragh... and Tomás.

The last 10 minutes is when we really took over! In the last 10 minutes we were able to bring fellas on that were able to cause serious damage. The likes of Darran O'Sullivan.

But the questions were still being asked... all of a sudden, it's a two-point game, we are playing with 14 men... 62 minutes gone on the clock, and now it's really backs-to-the-walls stuff.

It was McDonnell and Clarke who were really causing problems, but we never panicked. We brought it back to three points. Tomás tore up the field then and we got an important score... through the lines, simple... we never panicked.

A lovely little ball again through the lines, and Darran O'Sullivan got his goal. Fortuitous alright in a way, but that was the one.

We really took off then. A six-point cushion... 65 minutes on the clock, and it wasn't until that goal that you could actually say... *Do you know what, this game is won!*

We never looked back after that goal. Darran was young at the time as well, he would have only been 19 or 20 so to get that goal... it was special.

It was an excellent Kerry team. That 2006 team I reckon was our best team of that period.

In the full-back line there was myself, there was Mike McCarthy, Tom O' Sullivan... you'd Tomás, Seamus Moynihan, Aidan O'Mahony... you'd Darragh out in midfield. Diarmuid Murphy in goals. That's as strong a 1-8 as you are going to get. All characters too.

I definitely believe that game was a turning point because there were serious questions asked of us. We were really put up against it.

Maybe we might have folded in previous years, like in 2002 when Armagh got the goal... but when they got the goal in '06 we continued to rally and we continued to stay strong. There was a great team ethos at that time.

We'd Bryan Sheehan, we'd Darran O'Sullivan, and we'd Declan to come off the bench. Declan had been dropped for two games – he was going through a tough period at the time, football-wise – but to have a player of his calibre coming off the bench was absolutely incredible.

We never really looked back after that. It was a great game.

Darragh was the real catalyst; he kept the whole thing going. He got Man of the Match that day… he had a whale of a game. I'd never seen anyone to lord the game out around the middle. Paul McGrane was a huge player for Armagh, but Darragh absolutely lorded it that day.

It was great to win All-Irelands together with Darragh and Tomás on the field.

I used to go to the games with my dad watching the two lads in 1997… their first All-Ireland. Darragh was playing, Tomás was a sub… and then in 2000, watching them in the drawn game and the replayed All-Ireland. It was fairly nerve-racking now for my dad having two lads playing… *What must it have been like for him watching the three of us playing?*

It was great to go on and win All-Irelands with the lads. We won in 2004, '06, '07 and '09… four All-Irelands together on the field. Obviously Darragh won it in 1997, and Tomás and Darragh won it together in 2000… and I won it in 2014.

As I said, it wasn't about just us three… we had a team of characters. In defence… the likes of Tom O'Sullivan, Mike McCarthy, Diarmuid Murphy, Seamus Moynihan and Aidan O'Mahony… all real leaders. You'd Darragh. You look in the forwards… you look at Declan, you look at Paul Galvin… and you're looking at 'Gooch', Eoin Brosnan, Mike Frank and Kieran Donaghy… absolute leaders everywhere you look.

The Northern teams at the time were playing a more direct style of football.

If you can't beat them, you've got to join them… and you've got to think outside the box and try to come up with new ideas of playing. With Donaghy inside, it just gave us a different focal point. The thing about that is, we were able to change the system midway through the season. In fairness to Jack O'Connor, it was great to be able to change the dynamics of the whole thing. It just gave us something different.

All of a sudden, it was a different Kerry team.

It just gave us more options. You could put the short ball in… or you could put the high ball in. We could ask more questions than we could have asked at the start of the year, because we weren't going well at the start of the year.

We hadn't really beaten the Northern teams up until that point. Kerry did beat Armagh in 2000, but in '02 Armagh beat us, in '03 Tyrone beat us, and again in

'05 Tyrone beat us, so this was a huge match for us.

The story had been… *Kerry struggle against the Northern teams.*

So in 2006 that was another carrot that we were really going after, to try and right the wrongs.

We got to six finals in-a-row at that time… 2004 to '09.

Winning four out of six; that in itself was a huge achievement. You had to go back as far as the 70s to find a team that had done that. Dublin had got to the final in 1974, '75, '76, '77, '78 and '79. But we got to six, and won to four! Dublin won three in the 70s. I never saw it as a chore because it was just something that we always loved doing.

The honour of playing with Kerry… after watching Páidí before us in the Kerry team coming back to Ventry with the Sam Maguire… all we ever wanted to do was play with Kerry. To get the opportunity then and to be able to play championship… I was lucky enough to get to play championship on 88 occasions which was just incredible.

I look back on those days now and they are days I'll never forget; just running out onto Fitzgerald Stadium, running out onto Croke Park… *What days!*

I'd go to war with those fellas all day long. They were just incredible footballers, and great teammates.

Yeah, there is huge sacrifice, but we were so lucky that the players that came around at the same time did so. Obviously, we had bad days as well. I won five All-Irelands, but I lost five All-Ireland finals… 2002, '05, '08, '11 and '15.

But I do think of those days where we won those great games… and it is not always a final. It might be a Munster final that gets you over the line, and in this case the 2006 quarter-final was one that really got us *over the line.*

To go and win it… and win it 3-15 to 1-13, the scoreboard didn't reflect where the game was at. We'd been on the other end of those types of scores as well where the game was really tight. The Armagh game was certainly a game like that where it was nip and tuck and we finished up then winning by eight.

We were very lucky, but mentally we were strong.

We were well up for the battle. And we didn't lie down.

99

KILLIAN YOUNG

MAYO 1-11 KERRY 0-11
National Football League Round One
McHale Park, Castlebar
FEBRUARY 4, 2007

Killian Young wins the ball against Mayo's Peadar Gardiner, in his first start for Kerry in the first round of the National League in Castlebar.

★ **KERRY:** D Murphy; M Ó Sé, T O'Sullivan, **K Young**; T Ó Sé, A O'Mahony, B Guiney; D Ó Sé, K Donaghy (0-1); S O'Sullivan, E Brosnan, P Kelly; C Cooper (0-3), M Quirke, B Sheehan (0-5). Subs: D Walsh for Kelly, T Griffin for T. Ó Sé, S Scanlon for S O'Sullivan, Darran O'Sullivan for Quirke, D Quill (0-2) for Darran O'Sullivan.

★ **MAYO:** D Clarke; D Heaney, L O'Malley, K Higgins; A Moran, BJ Padden, P Gardiner (0-3); D Brady, J Kilcullen; P Harte (1-0), T Mortimer (0-1), A Dillon (0-4); C Mortimer (0-1), A O'Malley (0-1), K O'Neill (0-1). Subs: M Conroy for O'Malley, G Brady for Conroy, A Kilcoyne for Dillon, J Nallen for Heaney.

THE ACTION

A PAT HARTE goal proved to be the difference as Mayo got revenge after the previous year's crushing 13-point All-Ireland final defeat to Kerry. Despite the early stage of the season, Mayo looked well-drilled and business-like, and ready to impress following the return of their prodigal son John O'Mahony.

Under the new management of Pat O'Shea, Kieran Donaghy's double yellow card sending off in the 43rd minute was the obvious turning point in the game, although Kerry trailed by 0-6 to 0-5 at the time. Mayo, who also had Trevor Mortimer sent off in the second-half, controlled the game from start to finish with Peadar Gardiner kicking the opening score after just 70 seconds to set the tone. The hard working Austin O'Malley and Trevor Mortimer added early points to make it 0-3 to 0-1 on 13 minutes, the Kerry point coming via a free from Bryan Sheehan.

Kerry responded well and just shy of the 20th minute mark were level thanks to Colm Cooper and another Sheehan free, the former adding an excellent point from play from a Mike Quirke knock down. Kevin O'Neill and Alan Dillon exchanged points with Kieran Donaghy and Cooper (free) to draw level for the third time at 0-5 apiece. However, a late injury time Conor Mortimer free ensured a one-point interval advantage for the hosts.

The first eight minutes of the second-half proved to be decisive as Mayo added four vital points without response to open up a comfortable five-point lead; a purple patch Kerry never really recovered from. Things went from bad to worse for the visitors when Donaghy was sent for an early shower for a second bookable offence. Being reduced to 14 did seem to awaken Kerry from their second-half nap, however. Sheehan slotted over another free – his third – and substitute Declan Quill, who came on for the injured Darran O'Sullivan, nailed a fine score to narrow the deficit to three points with 20 minutes to play.

Just as it looked like the momentum was swinging in favour of the men in green and gold, that all-decisive goal broke Kerry's impetus 10 minutes from time when an unmarked Harte lashed the ball into the net. The crafty Kevin O'Neill and Gardiner linked up well before finding Harte in space at the edge of the parallelogram.

★★★★★

66

ONE OF THE biggest moments really for me, understanding what it was all about, was in 1997. That is when I understood this is something that I want to be a part of.

I'll never forget it. We were at home.

I was wearing my Kerry jersey, but of course my mother had it all set up... making sure I was wearing my Kerry jersey when the doorbell rang. I opened the front door... and the Sam Maguire Cup was just sitting there on the doorstep.

I was in shock... Maurice Fitzgerald and Denis O'Dwyer were both hiding around the side of the house. I was just staring at the cup, and I picked it up... and just had that moment looking at it.

We then all took photos with the cup, along with my sister Caoimhe.

When Kerry won that All-Ireland in 1997 it had an influence on so many young people... allowing us to dream. Then coming into Coláiste na Sceilge where the underage structure was so strong under Jack O'Connor, and John Dorgan, we started to put those dreams to work.

I won a Corn Uí Mhuirí medal, so all that development was happening with Coláiste na Sceilge and at the same time more was happening with South Kerry, and with the club. It was all games and *games*, which was crucial.

Going to Coláiste na Sceilge as well was something that happened at the right time... the school was just built at the time I went into first year, so effectively we came into a stronger, and a more senior set-up in relation to having all of the South Kerry secondary schools joined together and forming Coláiste na Sceilge.

It is amazing how things happen for a reason.

In 2006, I went in with Kerry and at the time you just had this unbelievable team and all of a sudden you are part of this as a young man, thinking... *Am I really up to this at all?* Questioning yourself... *Is it time for me?*

It's mad how things just happened and developed from there. The timing of Seamus Moynihan retiring in 2006, too. I was considered a corner-back, but suddenly there was a vacancy in the half-back line.

A big moment for me was making my debut. I actually made my debut in the championship before I made my debut in the league... it was very strange.

I played for five minutes against Tipperary in the Munster semi-final in 2006. It was such an unbelievable feeling to wear the jersey... and then we won the All-Ireland in '06.

But in 2007, in the first game in the league, suddenly there was an opportunity to really fight for my place.

There was no time to make mistakes, because there was such a strong squad.

We went to Castlebar. Mayo were really, *really* strong at the time as well. They were competing for All-Irelands... we had beaten them in the final in 2006.

Conor Mortimer was in the corner. We never had a great record in Castlebar, and he was the hottest property at the time. He was the best player in Ireland, and suddenly I was marking him. I kept him scoreless from play.

That was a huge moment for me. I don't even know what the outcome of the game was, but for me personally making a stamp on it at such a young age in a robust game, that was when I felt... *Yeah, do you know what, I can actually mix it here!* More so after playing well against Conor Mortimer... *I'm actually here and I'm ready!*

I was starting every game from that point on into the championship... and winning the All-Ireland, that was the real defining moment for me in my Kerry career.

I was very nervous going into the game, knowing the responsibility.

It is kind of a numbness when you start out. You've been in the stands waving your Kerry flag, watching your heroes and, suddenly, you are out there... beside them, and you are aware of the responsibility. Very aware of the daunting task ahead in marking Conor Mortimer.

I remember vividly going into that game thinking... *I know Conor Mortimer, I've seen him on TV.* That was the other side of it as well. This was my first time standing beside these players that I'd been watching on TV.

I knew... *If he gets his hand on the ball, he's going to shoot.* At the time, Mortimer was scoring... he couldn't stop scoring, when he got an opportunity or a yard, it was an automatic score. If he could get a shot away, it was a score.

So, I competed for everything.

When he got the ball, I was closing him off from shooting on the spot. That happened on three different occasions. I got a block at one stage and I turned him back onto his right. He wasn't comfortable shooting so he off-loaded it, which was unusual for Mortimer.

From such a young age I was very, *very* mature in how I was positioning myself, and setting myself up, which came from playing so many games so fast... developing at Coláiste Na Sceilge, South Kerry, Reenard and the Kerry minors. There were so many teams to play with.

People have asked me did I burn out, or did I play too much... but it just helped me. It matured me at a younger age, and that's why at that age, breaking into the team, I was able to bed myself in so quickly.

Afterwards, I felt the joy of others. I don't know if it was other people thinking... *Oh, let's see how Killian gets on for 10 minutes!* And they thought Marc Ó Sé or someone might be needed to finish the job. Afterwards, there was a sense of acceptance.

Major players were coming up to me, giving me high-fives, complimenting me... I just felt on top of the world. I felt accepted within the group, there and then. For me, that was the real stepping-stone... *I'm a part of this group.*

It set me up for life.

I progressed out towards the half-back line that year. Then, suddenly, I had such enthusiasm and such confidence inside me.

I was so excited every time I went into training, to actually have the opportunity to be there. I was wound up. All I wanted to do was run. I was so light and agile. All I wanted to do was run, run... *RUN*, and at that time football was different. It was very structured and rigid. It was very much breaking ball and long kick-outs.

It was... *Put down the tee and let's all come underneath the ball.*

That was what it was like. But when I was out there, I thought... *You know what, why can't I just keep running?*

I started to do this and it started to work... I was up past the half-forward line.

I was thinking... *How am I getting so much space?*

It was because my man didn't know what to do. He just couldn't comprehend what I was actually doing. It was high-risk, but it was high reward, and that's why 2007 worked so well for me until such time that people started to cop on to it... and started to defend against that type of attacking half-back. But for that year,

KERRY'S GREATEST FOOTBALLERS

nobody knew how to defend it. I just took the risk every time.

I can remember forwards trying to be very offensive and staying inside the '45', which is worse again for them, because I had two or three yards… and I was gone. I'd just run my 100 yards, get to the ball… I was just in acres of space.

Tomás Ó Sé really brought it to everyone's awareness. He definitely excelled from there as well. He was a huge mentor at the time on how to do things and implement runs. We both had this belief in taking risks.

And it worked!

There were unbelievable leaders in that group. It was such a mature team and when you look back on it, for the strength and the quality we had on that team, we should have been doing what Dublin are doing today.

What we left behind was criminal in that sense, yet we were very, *very* successful. When you see how Dublin have raised the bar now? We should have achieved more. It was just an absolutely unbelievable team.

It was a huge honour coming into that team.

These are all my heroes… and you are getting to know them and building strong relationships with them.

It is easy when you are winning… it is so enjoyable. That's the easy part, but one of the biggest moments for that team was in 2009 when we took a serious wobble for such a powerful team that everyone wanted to beat.

From my perspective, that was the first time my form dipped, where things weren't happening as naturally as they were previous. It was a difficult year.

At that time, I was soul-searching, trying to figure things out and get through that period, and it was the first time that I really had to think about my game… and what I was doing.

We struggled with games. We were very lucky. It was through the qualifiers we went. I recall vividly that I didn't play one minute for the first time. I was dropped against Sligo in Tralee. Diarmuid Murphy saved a penalty in the last minute from David Kelly to keep us in the championship. It was a time of turmoil in the sense that we couldn't find form… pressure was on and people were saying we were finished.

We were up in Offaly playing Antrim, and once again stumbled over the line and got through it. We were then facing a quarter-final against Dublin and we hadn't a living hope because we were just basically falling over the line against weaker teams.

I found an avenue back in. I got my form back in training, and got back onto the team. We had Dublin and we were thinking... *Right, look nobody is giving us a hope here.* And I'd say it was one of the biggest games that I was ever involved in.

It was such a defining moment for the county... and we just blew it out of the water. We just absolutely annihilated Dublin that day.

That was huge to win an All-Ireland that year, because by right we should have lost to Sligo in Tralee and been well out of the championship.

There was a full attendance in Croke Park.

We were there, but the form had gone, we couldn't get anything going through the summer... we had lost to Cork in the Munster semi-final. At that time, there was complete turmoil. So many players weren't performing. It was about trying to find that fix to see what worked... that spark. We sparked. It was probably one of the best performances from all of us as a team. It set us up to win that All-Ireland.

Jack O'Connor was manager when I made my championship debut as a sub in 2006. In 2005, I was playing for the Kerry minors.

There were two mates of mine here at home, and I was chatting to a team over in San Francisco... Sons of Ború. They were going, 'Come over here... we'll look after you'. I asked about my two mates and they said, 'Yeah, we'll look after everybody'. The whole thing was being set up and I don't know did Jack hear about it or something, but he said something like, 'There is no way he is going... if he goes he mightn't come back'.

I got a call then in November to go to Castleisland to the training in 2005.

I wasn't out of the Kerry minors three months, so I was a part of that set up very, very early. When I got the call I was kind of thinking... *Is this a prank? Is there something going on here?*

It was an unbelievable journey.

I was *so* lucky. It was just mind-blowing stuff being part of that type of journey. I did 14 years with Kerry and I just don't know how I did it. When people ask, 'Do you miss it?'... I'm like, 'I miss it loads!'

99

DARRAN O'SULLIVAN
(& TOM O'SULLIVAN)

KERRY 1-24 DUBLIN 1-7
All-Ireland SFC Quarter-Final
Croke Park
AUGUST 3, 2009

Darran O'Sullivan lifts the Sam Maguire Cup high in 2009, but it was only that same summer that the flying forward graduated from being an impact sub and nailed down his starting place in the Kerry team.

★ **KERRY:** D Murphy; M Ó Sé, T Griffin, **Tom O'Sullivan (0-1)**; T Ó Sé (0-2), M McCarthy, K Young; D Ó Sé, S Scanlon (0-1); P Galvin (0-2), Declan O'Sullivan (0-3), D Walsh (0-1); C Cooper (1-7), T Walsh, **Darran O'Sullivan (0-3)**. Subs: T Kennelly (0-2) for T Walsh, P O'Connor (0-2) for D Walsh (48), S O'Sullivan for Darran O'Sullivan, A O'Mahony for Young, M Quirke for D Ó Sé.

★ **DUBLIN:** S Cluxton; D Henry, D Bastick, P Andrews; P Griffin, B Cullen, B Cahill (0-1); R McConnell, D Magee; P Flynn, D Connolly, B Brogan (0-3); A Brogan (0-3), C Keaney (1-0), J Sherlock. Subs: C Whelan for Magee, P Burke for Sherlock, C O'Sullivan for Cullen, A Hubbard for Henry, S Ryan for McConnell.

THE ACTION

After struggling through the backdoor, Kerry announced themselves on the All-Ireland stage in dramatic fashion as Jack O'Connor's men put the Dubs to the sword and destroyed their arch-rivals with 17 points to spare in what certainly goes down in history as one of the greatest performances ever seen from a Kingdom team in Croke Park.

Colm Cooper's goal after just 37 seconds set the tone for Kerry's supremacy, and they led by 1-14 to 0-3 at the break, with the 'Gooch' hitting 1-4 and skipper Darran O'Sullivan contributing with three points.

Conal Keaney netted a Dublin goal with 14 minutes to go, but the Kingdom, who were 1-19 to 1-7 up at this stage, never took their foot off the pedal and responded with the last five points of the game to compound Dublin's misery. Cooper finished with an impressive 1-7 tally, equalling the scoring abilities of the entire Dublin side.

Having witnessed their side lose to Cork in Munster, and struggle over the line against Longford, Sligo and Antrim in the qualifiers, Kerry fans travelled to Dublin in their numbers for this All-Ireland quarter-final, but without the heightened expectations of years gone by. But as throw-in fast approached on a dry and sunny August Bank Holiday Monday, there was a fire in Kerry that could be felt from the stands.

Kerry were seven points ahead after 15 minutes, and this advantage was doubled by the interval as Dublin only managed to score three points from play in the opening half... a Barry Cahill solo effort in the ninth minute, an Alan Brogan point seven minutes before the break, and a Bernard Brogan point.

Tom O'Sullivan, with his first and only Championship point, had even got on the scoresheet, and it was clear that this was not to be Dublin's day when they were twice denied by the woodwork.

The Brogan brothers got the first two scores after the restart, proving to be Dublin's only genuine scoring threat, but Kerry, determined to continue their display of compelling, enthralling and controlled football, got the next two scores as Seamus Scanlon and Cooper added to their side's impressive tally.

The second-half was another convincing victory on the scoreboard, 0-10 to 1-4.

★ ★ ★ ★ ★

66

WE WON BY 17 points, so it might not have been the best game to watch in terms of excitement, but for us, and for me as captain that year, it was a great game. I was only 22 and I was still in and out of the team… I was still seen as an impact sub.

The game before it, we got over Antrim in Tullamore but Colm Cooper and Tomás Ó Sé had both been left out of that game for disciplinary reasons. I was in… and I could very easily have been left off the team again for the quarter-final.

We hit Croke Park then… and I kicked three points in the first-half. I'd never kicked three points before. I was more of an assist guy, or I'd bang in a goal.

We obviously went on to win an All-Ireland that year but that game always stands out for me because it was just such a struggle in that championship. We were very lucky to have avoided getting knocked out against Sligo in Tralee. Diarmuid Murphy saved a penalty.

It was strange. We got to Croke Park, and we just exploded.

I think the Dubs fancied themselves that year, but obviously we had a serious calibre of player. And it was just like all of the poor performances previously were forgotten. We were back where we wanted to be in Croke Park.

For me, it was the start of becoming a regular for Kerry. I had been an impact sub up to then and that was it after that… I had my place in the team.

We went on to play Meath in the semi-final. I scored 1-1 in that game, including a penalty. It was a lucky penalty, but it went in. We beat Cork in the final.

Realistically, if I didn't start that Dublin game, I wasn't going to get anybody out of the team for the semi-final, because everybody just played so well. I wasn't very good against Antrim in the game before. I was okay… I wasn't the best, I wasn't the worst; I was kind of middle of the road.

Normally, the easy option back then was to say, 'Ah, he wasn't very good, so we'll put him on the bench… he'll definitely make an impact off the bench'.

I think the fact I got the nod to start was another show of confidence and that gave me a bit of belief… *Look, you're more than just an impact sub!* Even though I always felt that I was doing enough, that I should be on.

I think once you start feeling comfortable in the team in a certain position, everything is that bit easier after that. Up to that point, even though I felt like I should be on, my role was pretty much defined as the... *Impact sub.* That was the year I started nailing down a place, and that was the game where I showed that I was more than just a 20-minute man, who would burst through the middle a couple of times and set up a couple of scores.

As far as I remember, Croke Park was full.

Unless you are playing one of the big teams, it is not going to be full for a quarter-final, but that Dublin game was a packed house.

After that, I felt I kept getting better and better. The Meath game wasn't one of the most memorable games. I scored a penalty, but I wouldn't normally be taking penalties. Colm had a bit of a groin strain and I was told before the game I'd be taking a penalty if we got one. Even small things like that, being told that Colm had an injury and they wanted me to take it, just gave me that little bit more confidence.

I was captain, but the captaincy doesn't really mean anything... it is not going to put you on the team.

My performances after that were just steadily becoming more consistent and getting better. I was starting to develop proper relationships with the other lads on the team, where I could understand from the start where they were going to go and they could understand where I was going to go.

The chemistry of starting was good, whereas when I was coming off the bench it was hard to build chemistry with fellas because my role was literally just... *Solo... Go on your own, go through the middle... Then look for a pop pass or put it over the bar yourself.*

I had started championship games, but I hadn't really ever felt like... *Oh they are going to trust me now to do it.* I suppose it was easy to choose someone over me, a case of... *Well, we know what Darran can do off the bench. We know that if we are in trouble he can do X, Y, and Z.*

I was buzzing that day against Dublin, feeling like I had energy to burn. I remember one of the scores I got, I was going towards the Hill... running towards the corner flag, and shooting and it going in off the post.

It was one of those ones where you know the luck is with you, because on another day that might have hit the post and gone the other way... *Wide!*

When your confidence is up you try things that will come off and that's just the way it was for me that day. There just seemed to be a spread of players who did damage that day… everyone playing well, everyone feeling confident… and comfortable. It was weird. It was just like, we get to Croke Park and all of a sudden we were a different animal.

We had won the National League that year, beating Derry, and the championship started and we got hockeyed by Cork in a replay.

It was just like all of a sudden we were flat. We hit a wall or something, or maybe the motivation wasn't there because we'd been on the road for so long, but whatever it was I couldn't really explain it.

Whatever got us back into gear, it just seemed to be a big thing in a full Croke Park.

This is where we want to be and this is where we want to play.

All of a sudden… it was all go.

We didn't have much of a rivalry with Dublin at the time.

I suppose it was all Tyrone at the time, but we'd had a small victory over Dublin in 2007 where we beat them by a couple of points… it was tight.

This, in 2009, was only my second championship outing against them and they were very un-Dublin like… not the way Dublin are now. Back then, they were very loud in the media. They were all over the place, whereas now you hear nothing about them. Back then, you'd hear everything about them, but they weren't doing the business on the field.

It was a big win because they were being talked up. They were half-talking themselves up as well at the time.

After the game, we were just buzzing.

It was just like… BANG, all of a sudden the doom and gloom ended. The 'Kerry aren't what they used to be'… 'Kerry aren't this and that'… that talk was over all of a sudden.

'Kerry are back!'

'Who's going to beat them?'

That was it. The confidence was back after that and we couldn't wait to get back into training on the Tuesday night.

For me, another good thing about when you're starting is you know the

Tuesday night is going to be handy. You might do a bit of soccer or something, whereas if you aren't starting, no matter what you did coming off the bench, you are doing running on Tuesday night.

So even for someone like me who was used to doing the business on a Saturday or Sunday coming off the bench and making an impact, you still had to come to training on the Tuesday and do the runs. You feel... *This is a kick in the b*****ks.*

Knowing that you did the business from the start and you can go into training on Tuesday and do a proper recovery session, that filled me with more confidence, that gave me a little bit more purpose, and made me feel part of the core group of players.

To win an All-Ireland that year as captain... it was unreal. It is a bit of a blur.

The final itself... I don't remember a whole pile about it. I just remember coming off the field. I came off with a few minutes to go and the nerves only started to kick in then because I was thinking... *We are going to win this and I have to go up and talk in front of 80,000 people.*

It is one of those things that, no matter what I do in life, it will never replicate that feeling. I'm married and I have a child and it is amazing, but the excitement and fear of standing up and having to speak in front of 80-odd thousand live and more watching on TV... and picking up the cup, bringing it back to Glenbeigh... I could live for another thousand years and I'll never experience a feeling like that again.

And I come from such a small club. When I was brought in with Kerry, we were playing in Division 5. It is the great thing about Kerry. They don't care what club you are from, what division you are in... if you are good enough, they'll bring you in.

So, being able to come back to Glenbeigh and bring the Sam Maguire Cup... the young people able to say, 'Oh he's only from down the road, and he's back here now with Colm Cooper, the Ó Sé's and Declan O'Sullivan!'

It was a big thing for the young people in the area.

I always think that if I maybe was a bit cranky or threw the toys out of the pram, that I might been thrown into the team earlier, but how could I do that... I was doing my Leaving Cert, and sure, all these boys were my heroes.

I was just so happy to be there. And I felt important, I felt I was playing a role... and the boys obviously knew the role that I was doing; that made me feel good because I was just happy to be contributing.

We were getting to All-Ireland finals and we were contesting the biggest games of the year, every year, Maybe if we weren't getting to finals, I would have thought... *Hold on now a second, I'm not happy with this.* But the fact is, it was working. The role was suiting the team and it probably scuppered my own chances, the fact I didn't bother throwing my toys out of the pram... but when you are winning you just do it.

Unless you are winning, it's not worth it. That's the way I'd feel about it, but everyone is different. Some people just love being in there, and I did, I loved being in there, and I just wanted to make a difference. I wanted to make an impact every time I got thrown onto the field.

Even the Kerry fans, they appreciated the role I played.

The fact that I played with such legends as well and they appreciated what I was doing, and the credit the supporters used to give me... the love they'd give you coming out after games or if they met you on the street...all that stuff makes it easier to sacrifice your time.

I was in London until I was 12, so I came late. It was just a natural progression then.

Like that, football was the be-all and end-all. I started playing and I was pretty good; I was quick, and like that you try to get on the club team and the school team, and then you try and get to the next level.

And then all of a sudden, when you are coming to 15 or 16 you are thinking... *Jesus, wouldn't it be great to play with the Kerry minors?* Then you play with the minors, and you think... *Wouldn't it be great to play with the under-21s?*

I was lucky. I went straight from minor into senior, and I knew no different than sacrificing my time for training, like everybody does now.

It is a different ball game now with all the gym and stuff, but you just do it because that's what you want to do. If you want to play any sport you want to be at the top level. No matter what you're doing, you want to be up there with the best.

There is no point in doing something just to go through the motions. Down here, you are lucky enough that if you do get into the dressing-room you are going to be playing with the best players in the country.

I won an All-Britain championship with Tir Chonaill Gaels. I had represented London and every time we had come home on holidays, which was regularly, I would have played with Glenbeigh underage, so it wasn't like I was picking it up for the first time. I started my development over in London. I had a Cork man, Denis O'Leary as a trainer, and I was playing for a Donegal club. It was over there that I realised that I could play… obviously you bring a few of your soccer skills with you as well. I was used to playing at a decent level over there and I was used to playing with older groups as well, which toughened me up.

When I came back, it wasn't as if I was taking up a new sport… I was ready to go.

TOM O'SULLIVAN

Tom O'Sullivan breaks out of defence with the ball and away from Diarmuid Connolly, as Kerry smashed Dublin in the All-Ireland quarter-final in 2009.

“

WE WERE WRITTEN-off before that game.

We'd gone through the backdoor. We had played Sligo and we'd played Antrim; we nearly lost each game.

It was such a big game and we were playing Dublin… and we were written-off before it…. so that really stands out for me.

And, after about 10 minutes, I got my first point in championship football.

The build up to that game was tough; that was a *tough year* that year with Kerry. We were beaten early by Cork, and a lot of the punters were saying there was too much mileage on the clock.

We got Dublin then in the quarter-final.

We also got the hunger back… the bite back.

To beat Dublin, and produce a performance!

We just needed to find our hunger. If we had met any other team at that stage of the championship they would have beaten us.

But, we got into Croke Park, and we got Dublin!

Kerry supporters probably thought the Dublin game was our last game, and the Dublin supporters thought they were going to beat us.

Sligo had a chance to win by a point with a last minute penalty in the qualifier in Tralee, and most people thought the year was over at that stage, but Diarmuid Murphy made a great save. He kept us in the championship.

So many players were struggling to find their mojo after being beaten by Cork in the Munster semi-final.

I started off playing knockout championship; when you were beaten you were out, and that was it.

Then the backdoor came in.

But still, sometimes when you lose a championship game early… you are left in no man's land, even though there is a backdoor.

We had to go at it again. A lot of the time we were playing unfamiliar teams, that we weren't used to playing. It was hard to prepare for those types of games because you are unsure what type of player you are marking, for instance.

It is harder to do research on teams as well or do video analysis on them.

We struggled big-time against Sligo, and Antrim was a tight enough game as well. Those were games that Kerry supporters expected us to win well, but we didn't, so nobody expected us to beat Dublin. Some of us were playing championship a long time. I would say some players need big games to perform at times, and Dublin just came at the right time that year.

Mike McCarthy came back that year.

His first touch set up the 'Gooch' for the first goal of the game. That was a huge start for us. It was the perfect start really.

Everything fell into place the minute we heard we were playing Dublin, and from the start of the game players just seemed to click. Our forwards just didn't seem to miss on the day.

The backs did well.

Midfield did well. It was almost a perfect performance. *Out of nowhere!* As a team, we knew we hadn't gone away. We still had the same players who had been winning in the previous years.

I just think we needed that big team at the opposite end of the field. A big team on a big day is what we needed, and we got that in Dublin.

On that Kerry team that time, players had played in a lot of games. Sometimes when you play in a lot of games and when you've won a lot of trophies and medals, I think you need that… a big stage, and 82,000 watching.

When you can perform in front of 82,000 people, that's where you get the buzz from really.

Other teams might be the opposite, but that Kerry team at that time needed that big game just to get the engine going again.

It is a different ball game now, to be fair. Backs are coming out around midfield. It is just a different system of play at the moment.

If you were a corner-back before, you were back in the corner marking your man. You weren't expected to go up the field. You were always behind the 20-yard line really.

So many people have a huge influence on your career, family members and coaches in school. We had Jack O'Connor at under-21 level, then at senior we had Páidí Ó Sé… and Jack O'Connor as a selector. Jack was manager then for a good few years. Jack would have been one of my more influential coaches, along with Páidí. But underage coaches are so important as well.

I put so much into football, and I'm satisfied with the fact that I came out with so much, winning all those All-Irelands and eight Munster medals.

I think when you have those four All-Irelands, you want to have five.

There is just something about having five… I'm not being greedy now or anything, and having one was great, having three was great… but when you've four, it just seems that five is a better number.

But I always enjoyed playing, too. It wasn't all about winning every year, though it is easier to keep the hunger going to a certain level when you are on a winning team.

It is a lot tougher for players who are not winning All-Irelands in other counties. I was lucky really in that sense.

From underage up, I always seemed to fall into winning teams. We seemed to win an awful lot underage with the schools, and with my club as well. I seemed to grow up with a good group of players.

Players who aren't winning, they stay going to win, but players who are winning… they stay going because they want to win more. They want to try to emulate the players who have gone before them.

That was a big thing for us, trying to match the team of the 70s who won the four in-a-row. We were trying to match them.

It's just the competitiveness of it really. Gaelic football in Kerry is very competitive, and that's what makes Kerry so good.

I was in with Páidí back in 1998 and '99 and we won the All-Ireland in 2000. Páidí was a huge motivator. When you go in there first, you are really overawed.

You've Maurice Fitzgerald…. a lot of big players, so you are kind of going in there and keeping your head down, just trying to get by.

But, once you are in there, you want to be there for the biggest days.

The Munster final in Killarney is as big a day as playing the Dubs in Croke Park in an All-Ireland final. Those are the games.

Those are the three big days. That's the reality of it, really.

Munster final.

Cork in Killarney.

Full house.

A sunny day. You don't get much better than that.

Dublin in Croke Park.

Full house.

And then… All-Ireland final day.

Most players will name those three occasions as the biggest in their Kerry careers. Starting off, every day is a big game.

But, as you get older, and as you get used to being there, those are the three days you want.

99

KIERAN DONAGHY
(& EAMONN FITZMAURICE)

KERRY 3-16 MAYO 3-13
All-Ireland SFC Semi-Final Replay
Gaelic Grounds, Limerick
AUGUST 30, 2014

The road to the Hogan Stand and lifting 'Sam' in 2014 was a long and painful one for Kieran Donaghy, who thought his career might have been over 12 months earlier through injury.

★ **KERRY:** B Kelly; P Murphy, A O'Mahony, S Enright; K Young (0-1), P Crowley, F Fitzgerald; A Maher, D Moran; M Geaney, J Buckley, D Walsh; **K Donaghy (1-0)**, P Geaney (0-4), J O'Donoghue (2-6). Subs: M Ó Sé (0-1) for Enright, BJ Keane (0-2) for P Geaney, D O'Sullivan for Buckley, K O'Leary for M Geaney, J Lyne (0-2) for Walsh, B Sheehan for O'Mahony.

★ **MAYO:** R Hennelly; T Cunniffe, G Cafferkey, K Higgins; L Keegan, C Boyle, D Vaughan (0-1); B Moran, S O'Shea; K McLoughlin (0-1), A O'Shea, J Doherty (0-3); C O'Connor (2-5), A Moran (1-1), A Dillon. Subs: T Parsons for B Moran, A Freeman (0-1) for A O'Shea (Blood), M Conroy (0-1) for Dillon, K Keane for Cafferkey, R Feeney for A O'Shea, Freeman for A Moran, B Harrison for Vaughan, C Barrett for Boyle.

THE ACTION

AS EPIC SEMI-FINALS go, this was one of the most incredible games of the decade, if not one of greatest games of all time. A truly great Mayo team fell short of returning to the All-Ireland final for the third year in-a-row as two converted penalties from James O'Donoghue helped send Kerry through after extra time in a dramatic semi-final replay at the Gaelic Grounds in Limerick.

Mayo goalkeeper Rob Hennelly had a chance to win it for the Connacht champions with the final kick of normal time, but came up short with a last gasp free. As Kieran Donaghy cleared for the Kingdom, referee Cormac Reilly blew for full-time.

Mayo led 2-5 to 1-5 at the half-time break after a rip-roaring opening 35 minutes, but it took a late point from Mayo wing-back Donal Vaughan to force extra time, with the scores 3-11 each.

The sides were then level at 3-13 apiece at the extra time interval, before Kerry pushed on to secure a place in the final.

In the second period of extra time Mayo ran out of road as a fresher looking Kerry team lasted the distance in a truly titanic clash. Substitute Jonathan Lyne put Kerry in front, before Paul Geaney and a second Lyne score sealed an All-Ireland final place for Eamonn Fitzmaurice's side. Further salt was rubbed into Mayo's wounds when Cillian O'Connor saw red in the dying moments.

As a game it had it all; six goals, a red card, extra time, breathtaking scores, a controversial pitch invasion, frees dropping agonisingly short, and colleagues clashing heads. This truly remarkable joust will go down as one of the finest displays of gaelic football ever played.

Six days previously in a similarly fascinating encounter in Croke Park Kerry ultimately required a superb contribution from Donaghy, who was brought off the bench with 11 minutes of normal time remaining, to earn the Kingdom a draw.

★★★★★

66

I NEARLY CALLED it a day the year before with an injury called Osteitis Pubis. It is a hard to diagnose injury, really. Basically, it prevents you from running flat out. You walk around and nobody would know you're injured... you've no crutches and you've no brace on your leg. You can jog and you can do all the other things, but you actually can't run flat out and kicking a ball is obviously an issue with it as well.

It was hard. I was dropped in 2013 before the Munster final and brought on against Dublin in that famous All-Ireland semi-final. I was brought on in many ways on similar terms to the first Mayo game in 2014... when you put the big fella in full-forward and hope he pulls a ball or two out of the sky.

But that day against Dublin, unfortunately, I didn't.

Then, I played in a town league final for Austin Stacks against Kerins O'Rahilly's at the end of that year and I remember putting my right hand behind my right leg, and I had to lift my leg forward when I was walking away from the pitch that day back to the car.

And I remember thinking... *I'm bang in trouble here, this is probably the end!*

That's where I was at the end of 2013.

The All-Ireland semi-final replay in Limerick in 2014 against Mayo really stands out in my memory.

In many ways, if we'd won that first game in Croke Park, if Bryan Sheehan had scored the 70-yard free at the end, the All-Ireland final could have been different. It would have been a remarkable kick obviously... he had it in the locker, but it just dropped short. It was a huge effort.

But, I often feel the replay made us bullet-proof going into the final. It made me bulletproof as well because I got such confidence out of the second day.

Eamonn Fitzmaurice came up to me in the team meeting two hours after the first Mayo game – the drawn game in Dublin – and said, 'Look, we're going with you in the replay. It's going to go in on top of you... early and often! And we're going to live or die by it... you are starting to move well!'

At the end of 2013, I was struggling with the leg. I went up to Santry and I got great advice up there as always. It was just slow coming along and Ger Keane, the

Kerry physio at the time, had put Trojan work into getting me right. I remember we were doing runs out in An Riocht – the running track in Castleisland – and I just couldn't get into fifth gear. Then Ger came up with a new type of exercise to try and strengthen the area, and that helped a lot.

I was also up with Seán Boylan, drinking the herbs above in Dunboyne, and he was doing bits of sessions with me as well, trying to help me get back. He has a huge understanding of the human body and blood flow. He was trying to get more of a blood flow into the area at the time.

Between the two lads, I started coming on and we had a training holiday out in Portugal... though I didn't actually bring much gear. I was starting to get back out onto the pitch but I wasn't really kicking in games.

Next thing, you are living like a professional which is why those training camps are so good for GAA teams. All of a sudden, you are living like a pro... you've no job, you've no outside pressures of family life or work commitments... you get to relax, and you get treatment on your body from the physios. I wouldn't call it a training holiday for the physios because they get absolutely murdered on those training trips. All they are doing is trying to get people right and keep fellas right with rubs. They'd be there at 11.30pm and midnight, and lads would still be getting sessions with them.

I didn't even plan on training out there.

I was there purely to get three physio sessions a day between Eddie Harnett and Ger Keane, and to get as much done as I could in terms of recovery in warm weather... and getting into the sea. As the week went on, I started getting stronger on it and eventually a year later... it was about a year later to the day... the pain started to ease.

I was out doing a warm-up with the lads... I wasn't doing any contact. The warm-up finished and I thought... *Jesus, I didn't think of that injury at all!*

I was doing a good bit of twisting and turning, and a good bit of running on it.

A decision was taken to let me out on the pitch and I played well in a little cameo of 30 minutes of football. Then I came back and I was a sub against Clare, and a sub against Cork... and then the Galway game was the big one, where I didn't play at all.

It was a tight game, and it was my first time being an unused sub for Kerry when I was fit, in eight or nine years. I was very disappointed after the game. I felt I was after putting in nearly 13 or14 months in getting this right and… *Now I'm not even being brought on.*

I'll be honest, I was in a bad place. My confidence was low. I was kind of half-doubting myself. *Could I still do it? Could I go on and help the team?*

The career was probably on the line. *If I can't get into the team, I'm not going to be playing… My career is finished at the top level.* That's where I was at.

I was a bit upset. I brought it to training on Tuesday night and I talked to Eamonn. I kept very calm.

'Eamonn, what's the story? Am I in the plans?'

He said, 'Oh you are! That's just the way the game goes. It just didn't suit the last day, but look… just keep going. It's starting to come'.

I worked very hard for the next three weeks before that first Mayo game. I didn't get to start but saying that, Paul Geaney and James O'Donoghue were going unbelievably well. With Colm Cooper down with the injury, I was hoping that it would be me, Paul and James inside.

It was a frustrating three weeks but I enjoyed it, because I was able to put it up to the management and then I'd to go and back it up with every session… I like that bit of pressure and I was able to do that.

I came on. Eamonn said, 'It's going to go in early and it's going to go in often'.

So I went from not playing three weeks before that to, all of a sudden, being the focal point of the attack. That was a difficult week, even in my own headspace.

I came on and caught a few balls, and we came from five points behind and now, all of a sudden, it was dawning on me that I was playing in the replay. There was a lot of pressure and weight on my shoulders going into the game to deliver down in the Gaelic Grounds against an excellent Mayo side.

It was a great feeling after the replay. I was very proud of myself for sticking in there and going through it, because it was hard.

The boys could see me about the training ground and the boys could see me in Fitzgerald Stadium, in Austin Stacks Park in Tralee… and they could see me *looking fit* and healthy! You are walking around as if you are fine, but constantly telling fellas that you aren't right yet, that you can't run properly yet… and you can't kick yet. That was a stressful time.

The build-up to the game in Limerick was great. There was a bit of a furore around the game because it had to be played in the Gaelic Grounds as there was an American Football game being played in Croke Park on the same day.

But the atmosphere was something else... obviously there were 40,000 supporters packed into the place.

It was such a mad game. I was looking over after about 20 minutes and Mayo were winning by seven points, 2-3 to 0-2, and I was thinking... *Yeah, this isn't really working for any of us.*

And I remember, I won a free.

It was a ball played in by James O'Donoghue, a low ball across the edge of the square. Ger Cafferkey was holding one of my hands and I won the ball with my left hand. I tried to turn him, and he pulled me down... and I tumbled on the ground. I got up and I gave a big fist pump to the crowd, but it was more a fist pump to myself and to the fans, to be honest. It was to say... *Let's go, we need ye, we need momentum!*

I know the role I played with the Kerry supporters. Our fans usually responded to me so that fist pump was more to get the crowd going, and get a bit of momentum going.

Two minutes later I got the volley to bring us back to within three and you could just tell that the momentum was starting to shift, and that this game was going to be special... and that this day was going to be special.

It was a dry day, two great teams going hammer and tongs... big hits, big collisions, six goals, penalties, drama... and Aidan O'Shea and Cillian O'Connor clashed heads. David Moran put in one of the greatest displays by a Kerry midfielder ever... including Darragh Ó Sé, Jacko and all those boys.

Moran and Anthony Maher gave us a great foothold. James O'Donoghue was just magical on the day as well.

Even being on the pitch afterwards.... my uncle Anthony was down from the North, my cousin Ronan Fitzgerald who had a bad injury playing rugby...he was out onto the pitch afterwards and came up to me with my uncle.

Seeing all those people, having been where I was for the previous 15 months... and all of a sudden to be getting ready for another All-Ireland final out of nowhere and trying to make up for the disappointments and the losses. Getting another chance, which I didn't think I was going to get when I in the doldrums with that injury. It was just amazing.

I remember going over to hug David Moran… and his dad 'Ogie' just running in ahead of me and hugging him. And then me hugging David.

And then me hugging 'Ogie'.

What people don't realise really is what family members go through in *our* journey to try and be inter-county footballers. They have to listen to stick from the crowd… people giving out about their family members, and they have to deal with disappointments when things go bad. They are always there and they feel every part of the journey emotion-wise with us.

My father-in-law Frank Stephenson couldn't take in the game in the Gaelic Grounds, so before it went to extra time he went away. He was walking down the road and there were a few cheers from the crowd when it was still in normal time – it was the Robbie Hennelly free, the one that looked like it was going over to send Mayo to the final. Tom Parsons batted it but I jumped with him like a volleyball player and knocked it down.

Frank was walking down the road and heard the cheer of Mayo fans. He says to the guy inside in a chip van, 'What's the story?' The radio was on and your man said, 'Mayo have a free to win it'

Frank had a picture in his head, that it was Cillian O'Connor from 25 yards. So he walked off in a bit of a huff, he got into the car down the road and he headed off.

It dawned on him to turn on the radio to listen to the interviews after the game but when he did that, the game was still in full flow. He nearly felt like turning around but he couldn't so he pulled into the Clayton Hotel there by the river in Limerick and he went in and watched the rest of the match in the hotel bar.

That's my father-in-law, so that shows you! Imagine what the mums and dads go through! It is a very emotional and stressful time for us as players in the middle of it, but definitely for family members as well who don't have any control over the situation. All they can do is look on and hope.

There was a jump ball in the last play of the game.

I won the ball but I got a bad fist, a rap into the back of the head, from one of the Mayo fellas who knocked the ball out of my hand. The whistle went and I was kind of startled by it and I turned around going… *Who punched me?*

But then I was like… *Who cares, the game is over!*

It had just dawned on me that the game was over and I took off running to the crowd with the ball under my hand… and kicked it as far as I could up into the crowd and let out a roar because the pressure on me going into the game was incredible.

To deliver a good performance, play as well as I did, and for us to get a huge win… it was *the* most emotional semi-final I was ever involved in. It kind of had the feeling of a final, but we had to dust ourselves down fairly rapidly with Donegal on the horizon.

It was a great buzz. We had a few pints after it, and that was enjoyable as a team… but we had to start into the business end of trying to win the All-Ireland.

The game had everything.

It just was a game that had every bit of class and skill, and skulduggery – just two teams absolutely desperate to win.

It could have changed at any moment. I remember Mayo were going through on goal at the start of the first period of extra time… they were after getting the first two points. Lee Keegan had a goal chance and Peter Crowley came out of nowhere to intercept the ball. That was a huge changing point in the game because we got two frees after that to level it.

And then Jonathan Lyne came on and kicked two massive scores to give us the momentum back again.

At times we felt the game was gone… numerous times. When they were seven points up we thought it was *gone*.

You really do take notice of the crowd and the atmosphere… it definitely makes a difference.

I would have always been very aware of the crowd, and that's why I think I would have struggled playing in the lockdown period in the past year without fans.

I would have always played for the crowd and I was very aware that if I did something on the field… I'd try and connect with the crowd and lift the team's spirits even more.

I remember telling David Clifford, when he came into the scene first… I said, 'Dave, celebrate your goals, because you are going to be an icon for the next number of years… If you get that big goal, and you celebrate with the crowd, they will then give you more energy and give everyone a lift'.

The Underdogs TV series was a great experience for me in 2005. It gave me another platform to show what I could do but I still think I was going to make it whether I was part of the *Underdogs* or not. I was pushing hard the year before.

I had been on the Kerry squad the year before.

That gave me great experience and the *Underdogs* was another lift for me. Jack O'Connor put me in with 14 minutes to go in the Munster final in 2005 when the game was in the melting pot. That was the first time I felt I could actually play with Kerry. *But did I think I'd go on to have the career I had?* No!

I had a unique set of skills but I was by no means a world-beater as a footballer.

Just like most of the things I do in my life, if I get a chance I'll try and grab it with two hands and give it everything and see how it goes… if it works, it works … and if it doesn't, it doesn't. That is kind of the way I would approach everything.

I am very proud looking back… I was very lucky.

I got 10 Munster medals… the first one in 2005. It ended up being a disappointing year because I wasn't brought on in the All-Ireland final against Tyrone.

But winning the All-Ireland then in 2006 and having the year I had in '06… going from being a solid midfield partner with Darragh Ó Sé… to being an All Star and Player of the Year playing full-forward with Kerry gave me huge confidence to go on and try and be the player that I could be… to try and be a leader for Kerry, and to try and deliver for Kerry and for the people of Kerry.

We are all very grounded players in Kerry.

Four All-Irelands, three All Stars and a Player of the Year is great and all… but Jack O'Shea has four Players of the Year, seven All-Irelands and six All Stars so you are not allowed run away with yourself in Kerry ever. No matter who you are!

EAMONN FITZMAURICE

Kerry Manager Eamonn Fitzmaurice and Mayo's James Horan shake hands after their drawn All-Ireland semi-final in 2014, with neither knowing the 'Battle of all Battles' lay ahead of both of them in the replay in Limerick.

"

THE ALL-IRELAND SEMI-FINAL replay against Mayo in 2014, when I was manager, stands out for a good few reasons. It was such an epic battle.

There was a point in the first-half when we were seven points down and we brought it back to three at half-time. We were level at the end of normal time, and the Mayo goalkeeper Robbie Hennelly had a free to win it right at the end. He was straight in front of where I was standing... his kick was in my eye-line the whole way.

It split the posts... it was straight between the posts, but it was a small bit short.

My heart was in my mouth. We were playing very well and I knew we had more in the tank... that if the game went to extra time...

But for a split second, it looked like we were going to be out.

In extra time we ended up winning by three. The thing that was most satisfying about that night was that the whole panel got to contribute... with the game going to extra time. Players who hadn't played any football at all that year got to come on... held their own, and played their part.

There was a fierce collective spirit that evening.

The atmosphere was incredible.

It was a full house that day. It was a Saturday evening game so that added to the atmosphere because people probably had the few pints beforehand and everyone was full of the joys of it... so there was serious noise there.

There were also a lot of things that happened behind the scenes that added to the occasion. I was reluctant to go to Limerick the day before. I felt we'd have an awful lot of waiting around on the day of the game, when it was an evening throw-in.

The team stayed in Killarney together, and we got an escort up to Limerick the day of the game. There was a fierce buzz on the way up. You could see all the Kerry cars... there was a lot of support coming up from Kerry for the game.

When we got there, we were out on the pitch beforehand doing our warm-up... and the dressing-rooms flooded. We had to get a plumber to fix the dressing-room. They sorted that out, but as we were approaching half-time then, the County Board secretary Peter Swiss came up to me and said we couldn't go into our dressing at half-time because one of the stewards was after having a heart attack in the tunnel.

He said we'd to go into the old dressing-rooms under the main stand.

I understood, but I told him, 'We have all our energy drinks... everything the players need at half-time in the dressing-room... we're going to have to go and get that moved'.

Then, he came to me then and said, 'No... it's okay, your man is okay!

The players ran in... and the steward was on the ground.

He was surrounded by medical personnel, but he was actually okay. I noticed him... as I knew about it, but the players didn't even spot him.

It was very funny then. We were inside and I was just about to get ready to start talking to the lads... and Mike Finnerty, our doctor, burst in the door.

'Your man is grand lads… HE'S ALIVE!'

All the players were looking at him, thinking… *What's he on about?*

The players had no idea!

There was just so much going on… and there was so much going on in the game. We went down and we came back, and we were hanging on in the end.

There were yellow cards and red cards.

The Mayo supporter came onto the pitch at the end. There was just so much that went on. It was just one of those amazing days, but it was a great one to come out on the right side of.

In the first day in Croke Park, we played very well in the first-half but Lee Keegan was sent off coming up to half-time and it actually spurred them on more than it helped us. Mayo dominated the second-half.

We needed Kieran Donaghy to catch the ball at the end, and James O'Donoghue to get the goal. Kieran O'Leary got the equalising point. We were five points down with time almost up and we ended up getting a draw out of it.

I was delighted with the lads that they showed such resilience and fight that first day.

The replay was nerve-racking but the thing I enjoyed the most about that day was that it felt as a group we really came of age. The younger players really started to stand up, and then you had the older statesmen… the likes of Kieran Donaghy, Aidan O'Mahony, Marc Ó Sé and Killian Young. Players who had been around the block a good few times… they were able to bring the new generation of guys through with them as well.

Everyone to a man played well that day. Players that came off the bench who hadn't played in previous games… the likes of Pa Kilkenny, Mark Griffin… and Jonathan Lyne who got two massive points. It was a great statement from the whole panel that they were all able to contribute on the day when we needed it the most.

Limerick was a novel venue as well.

You'd have to go back a long time before the last All-Ireland semi-final was played outside of Croke Park… and it probably won't happen again for a long time. There was just so much about it.

It was just one of those games that was a great one to win, but it would have been a tough one to lose. A good few of the Mayo players who have retired since have mentioned that game as a defeat they really found hard to take at the time, that it was a real tough one for them.

That evening, we went out to the Woodlands Hotel in Adare for our bit of food. The players went back down to Kerry, but the management stayed there that night because we went up to Dublin the following morning for the Dublin and Donegal game. We definitely didn't think watching that game that day, or on the way down afterwards, that Dublin would become the team they became. It just goes to show how good they have been.

There were other years that we were quite close to Dublin but we just couldn't get the job done. They are a serious team and at the time, and certainly after winning the All-Ireland in 2014, we didn't think it would be a long wait before we'd win it again. We got to the final in 2015, but we didn't play as well as we could play. We were very close in 2016 and '17, and in '19 when it went to a replay we were very, *very* close. Three of those years, we've been very close… but just that slight bit off getting it done.

The Kerry way has been to stick to it and keep going.

And we'll get there again.

I am very happy with the way it all worked out. To be from Lixnaw and to have played with Kerry was a huge thing. I never had these massive ambitions to play football for Kerry. It was just something that happened as the years went on.

The same as becoming a manager. The whole time I was playing with Kerry, I never thought in a million years that I'd end up being entrusted with that role and having the privilege of being in that role.

I look back on it as a fantastic period in my life. I really enjoyed it. I was there for six years. I feel that while I was there we gave it absolutely everything we had. It was good enough one year, it wasn't good enough the other years, but we certainly gave it everything and I can look in the mirror and say that there isn't too much I'd change.

It was a hugely enjoyable time in my life, and obviously the fulfilment comes with winning and being involved with players and seeing them developing and improving.

By the end of 2018, it was clear that it was time for me to move on, and the players could do with a new voice… and a change of direction.

I have no regrets leaving… I knew it was the right decision.

When I was young, I never really thought about playing for Kerry that much. I think sometimes when you are from the traditional football areas it is something you really focus on, and you go to the traditional football schools. But for me, it was a bit different. I was just kind of playing my way up through the ranks.

I was aware there were local people that had played with Kerry, but it wouldn't have been the be-all and end-all for me when I was young.

I went to secondary school in Tralee… I went to the Gaelcholáiste Chiarraí. It was a new school at the time so it wasn't like going to the Green or the Sem… one of the big football schools. If you were playing well in one of those school teams and playing well in the Corn Uí Mhuirí, it would give you that kind of indication that maybe you were able to survive at that level.

The fork in the road for me was back when I was playing under-16… they had this coaching couple of days in UL called Óg Pheil.

There were three players picked from all the different districts around Kerry to go as a Kerry team up there for the three days. I was one of the lads picked from North Kerry and we went up and we played, and we stayed in the student accommodation in UL. We had sessions all day for the three days.

The best coaches from all over Munster were there, giving us different sessions, and I felt comfortable up there. There were players from all over the county… and you'd know they were serious footballers. I was able to hold my own in that company, and that was a turning point for me then.

The football bug really hit after that. I had ambitions to play for Kerry after coming back from that camp, whereas before I went… I was playing with my club, I was playing hurling, and I wouldn't have really been looking that far forward into the future.

The following year I was on the Kerry minor panel when we won the All-Ireland in 1994, and I was minor again the following year in '95. Football started to take up more of a prominent position then in my life. In 1995, we lost to Cork in a replay in Munster. We drew with them in Tralee and they beat us in the replay in

Páirc Uí Chaoimh. I learnt an awful lot in those two years.

I went to UCC. We won a Freshers All-Ireland in my first year. I was getting to play with fellas from other counties, and getting exposed to a very good level of coaching all helped me to develop. I was on the under-21 panel in 1996 and we won the All-Ireland, beating Cavan in the final. I played in that game. It was a quick enough trajectory really, because only a couple of years previously I wouldn't have thought I would have been at that level.

I still kept playing hurling right up until the end... until I retired, but football was number one. I tried to play as much hurling as I could around the football, but there were years I didn't get to play with Lixnaw at all.

I made my debut for the senior team in 1996. My first appearance... I came on as a sub against Meath in the 1996-97 League... in November '96. I played in a couple of league games in '97 but I wasn't on the championship panel that year. I was in and out for training games. I was on the junior team.

We got to a Junior All-Ireland final where we were beaten by Mayo by a point. I was on the fringes of the championship squad in 1997, and after Kerry won the All-Ireland in '97 I was in playing league games again.. We won the under-21 All-Ireland again in 1998... and then I got on the Senior Championship squad that year, making my championship debut against Cork.

It was a proud moment, but when you are going through it you kind of take no notice of it because it is just the next step. When you get the jersey, you want to hold on to it, and you want to try and improve.

When you look back at things, you can have that sense of satisfaction, but at the time you are very focused on just keeping going. For my championship debut, I came on as a sub at half-time against Cork in 1998 in Killarney... straight knockout.

It was a huge game. Kerry were All-Ireland champions. I really enjoyed it... I felt at home, I felt like I could do a job.

In 2000, when we won the All-Ireland, the replayed final was a special day but the game that stands out for me that year was the semi-final replay against Armagh. I played well myself and it was a great win for the team after extra time. There were also great battles the following year when we played Dublin in Thurles in the All-Ireland quarter-final.

The 2004 final when we beat Mayo was another big game, because we were after a couple of tough years. When you think back on those games, they were very special for sure.

From a club perspective, we won an All-Ireland junior title with Finuge in 2005, which was fantastic. There were a couple of county hurling championships with Lixnaw. There was a county football championship with Feale Rangers... that was a great win. I won a county championship with UCC in Cork against Nemo Rangers in 1999... again, a great win.

The stronger football is in schools in Kerry, the better. It is a step up from club football and it gets players ready to step up to the inter-county scene if and when they get an opportunity.

I see it as a huge part of what we have in Kerry always, and the more schools we have with a vibrant football scene, the better.

We had a golden era in Pobalscoil Chorca Dhuibhne. Looking at the traditional football schools, the likes of the Green and the Sem, it was a huge motivation for us to try and put it up to them, to try and beat them... and put our school on the map. Coláiste na Sceilge achieved something similar in South Kerry.

We are fortunate in Kerry that there are a lot of ex-players teaching and involved in the schools. They are able to have a positive influence then on the young lads to get them interested and keep them going.

This is even more important than in a club, because in a club you are only going to have your couple of nights a week together, but in a school situation you are meeting the lads every day

If you've a game the day before and if something has gone well or something hasn't gone well, you can meet a player the following morning... just bump into them in the hall.

'How are things?'

'Listen if you are doing that again, in that game... you might do it this way'.

You can have a huge influence on the players. You are meeting them so often in a good environment.

Football is a time consuming pastime. It takes up a lot of your mental energy too because you are thinking about it so much... as both a player and being involved in the management capacity. But it is a hugely enjoyable part of your life.

It is a very fulfilling to be involved with a group of people who are very driven, very dedicated, and who are trying to achieve big things. That is true in whatever county you are from, but when you are from a county like Kerry, with the tradition and the history that comes with it… the responsibility that goes with wearing the jersey and representing Kerry, that all brings an extra layer with it.

When you finish up and you look back at it, you'd be pinching yourself and thinking… *Was I really involved in that, at that level for so long?*

I was involved in different capacities. I was involved as a player starting every game, and then towards the end of my career as a sub coming on in games… getting an insight into what the sideline was like.

I was involved as a selector with Jack O'Connor, and then I was a manager myself, so I've seen it from a lot of different sides.

I consider myself very, *very* fortunate. We had a degree of success and we've had plenty of tough days as well, but certainly when you look back at it… coming from where I came from, with the abilities I had?

If I'd been told 25 years ago that this was the way things were going to pan out, I'd have certainly taken it.

FIONN FITZGERALD

DR CROKES 2-11 COROFIN 0-8
All-Ireland Club SFC Semi-Final
Gaelic Grounds, Limerick
FEBRUARY 11, 2017

Although he had the ultimate honour of lifting the Sam Maguire Cup as Kerry captain, Fionn Fitzgerald remembers the Dr Crokes colours on his back when he names the most defining day of his brilliant career.

★ **DR CROKES:** S Murphy (0-1); J Payne, M Moloney, **F Fitzgerald**; D O'Leary, G White, L Quinn; A O'Donovan, A O'Sullivan; J Buckley, G O'Shea (1-0), B Looney (0-1); C Cooper (0-1), D Casey (0-2), K O'Leary (0-5). Subs: S Doolan for White, White for Doolan, M Burns for Looney, J Kiely (1-0) for O'Shea, T Brosnan (0-1) for Casey, Doolan for O'Leary, M Milner for Cooper.

★ **COROFIN:** B Power; C Silke, K Fitzgerald, L Silke; K Molloy, C McGrath, C Cunningham; D Burke, R Steede; G Sice (0-2), D Wall (0-2), J Leonard (0-2); I Burke (0-1), M Farragher (0-1), M Lundy. Subs: G Higgins for C Silke, A Burke for Molloy, B O'Donovan for Cunningham, C Brady for Wall.

THE ACTION

DR CROKES MARCHED into the All-Ireland Senior Football Championship final on St Patrick's Day 2017 with a deserved win over 2015 champions Corofin at the Gaelic Grounds in Limerick.

The nine-point victory made for sweet redemption after the Killarney outfit had fallen short at this very hurdle in 2012, '13 and '14. A goal from Gavin O'Shea helped the Kerry champions lead by double scores, 1-7 to 0-5 at the interval. And when Corofin hit back after the restart, Crokes pulled away again with substitute Jordan Kiely getting the decisive goal.

Former Kerry captain Kieran O'Leary sent out a timely reminder to the Kingdom manager Eamonn Fitzmaurice with a superb display, shooting five points from play in the opening half.

O'Leary was involved yet again, setting up the goal for O'Shea four minutes from the break when he kept an effort from Colm 'Gooch' Cooper in play and passed outside to O'Shea, whose shot for a point dipped into the top right corner. There was an element of fortune to the goal from O'Shea, son of manager Pat, but the Killarney side were well worth their lead.

Corofin reacted well after the half-time break but despite the Galway champions getting three points without response in the third quarter to reduce Crokes' winning margin to four, the game was wrapped up on 49 minutes when Kiely notched their second goal.

Dr Crokes went on to win the All-Ireland title by defeating Slaughtneil of Derry 1-9 to 1-7 in Croke Park.

★★★★★

"

THE GAMES THAT go right down to the wire are the most memorable ones.

The stand-out games from a Kerry perspective were the 2014 All-Ireland semi-final against Mayo, and the semi-final against Dublin a year earlier, though we came out on the wrong side that day.

The game against Mayo went to extra time, and in 2013 Dublin got a goal in the last minute… but it was nip and tuck all the way.

The 2014 match was a huge game – funnily enough the final was probably a little bit of a let-down, even though we won. It wasn't really a great game.

In 2017, our win in the All-Ireland club final, wasn't a thriller either. But our semi-final against Corofin was a huge game… because we had lost three semi-finals in-a-row before that. We just about got over the line in the final. It was all about winning.

Whereas, symbolically and psychologically, the game against Corofin was a *big* game. We won comfortably in the end, by nine points… but the winning margin wasn't important. It was the *act* of winning.

We had lost three semi-finals previously when we were hot favourites for some of them. We lost to Crossmaglen, Castlebar and Ballymun… and we felt our opportunity had gone. We had a lot of success in Kerry and in Munster, but we just couldn't crack the All-Ireland semi-final stage.

One of the unique parts of it was the fact you played the Munster final in December… and the semi-final wasn't on until February. Almost a three-month lull. We had some big performances in Munster. We were almost on a roll in Kerry and Munster for a few years, but whatever it was we seemed to lose momentum.

We were beaten by better teams maybe… fitter teams maybe or hungrier teams maybe, I don't necessarily know. But psychologically, there was definitely some form of a stumbling block there.

We knew we were good enough to compete, but we just didn't do it.

Pat O'Shea was over us as manager at that stage, so we were extremely well-organised. He had come back in as the manager and there was literally no stone left unturned.

We trained a huge amount. I remember cancelling a holiday at the start of January and we just agreed… *It was now or never.*

We never knew if we'd get back into that position again and we also knew we were coming up against probably the best club team of all time. They were after winning two of the previous three All-Irelands.

We knew that we'd have to be at our best.

Corofin maybe felt that we caught them on the hop a bit, or they didn't perform on the day. I know they made up for that two years later in a big way and they gave us a nice clipping in the All-Ireland final.

We had a lot of heartache with injured players, and just different setbacks in a lot of the games. I've bad memories of the likes of Portlaoise and Semple Stadium. We played in some of those pitches and we had lots of stumbles… some big losses, but it was just a relief really to get over the line and a relief then to get to the All-Ireland final.

Pat was a master tactician in regard to getting us ready for a game, even though we were considered underdogs.

He convinced us that we had nothing to lose… that was how he presented the game to us.

We knew how we were playing… and we were very well coached, and we knew how to play the game in different ways. We just had a really good balance in our team. Everybody really knew what they were about, and our bench was very strong. We had a couple of players coming off the bench that year that were on the Kerry panel at that time.

Everyone bought into what we were doing.

There was collective team effort, all the way throughout the year. You could almost feel something bubbling in the background. There was apprehension going into that semi-final, but we got into it anyway and we played some very measured football.

Corofin were an extremely well-coached team as well. But we hit the ground running in a very primitive and basic way. We had a game plan, we knew what we were doing… and we had a raw hunger as well. We probably didn't have that some of the other days that we were caught.

If we hadn't done that… it would have been a major black mark on a lot of our careers. We would have felt we'd under-achieved if we hadn't won an All-Ireland medal.

Both teams had extremely talented forwards.

We were all marking inter-county forwards. I was on Ian Burke, and they had Michael Farragher and Michael Lundy... top players. It was very much man-on-man football... each of us dealing with our man.

When we played Corofin two years later it was a similar enough side really, but they gave us a lesson whereas we gave them a bit of a lesson that time in 2017. They learned, and two years later gave us a footballing lesson insofar as they played good football exactly the way traditionalists would like it to be played.

We went at it in 2017 like our lives depended on it, really! And it worked out quite well.

We got a goal in the first-half, but we were probably a little bit fortunate with that score. We were up by a couple of points at half-time and we were expecting an onslaught, but one of the key things for us that year was we had a *huge* bench. We had Jordan Kiely, Micheál Burns and Tony Brosnan all coming off the bench... and they gave us a huge lift.

I remember distinctly towards the end of the game, the 'Gooch' was playing back almost in the defence and Daithí Casey made a massive run to literally put the ball on the plate for Jordan Kiely to get a nice goal... that's what probably clinched it for us in the very end.

It was a real industrious performance but also we were composed, and everything we had done over the previous year – and you could argue over the 10 years, but the previous year in particular – we carried it through and we delivered when it mattered most.

Kieran O'Leary did exceptionally well even though he played very deep on the day. It just clicked for a lot of guys. The likes of Ambrose O'Donovan in the middle of the field... and Alan O'Sullivan put in huge shift around the middle too.

The standout game for me in a Kerry jersey was the 2014 All-Ireland semi-final replay.

There were so many aspects to it. First of all, it was that it was a replay. Secondly, it was the novelty of an All-Ireland semi-final being out of Croke Park because there was an American Football game on at the time.

The whole thing of going to Limerick… that kind of thing in GAA is unusual. There were Munster hurling finals on in Killarney over 30 years ago… it's similar to that type of stuff.

It is those types of games, whatever it is, they tend to bring a whole new lease of life to the game… and the whole background to the story is very different.

We were down by a couple of goals at the start. Mayo started with fierce gusto altogether and we were under pressure straight away, but we just hung in there… and got a couple of goals back then.

It was a real end-to-end game of football.

It was memorable for me in other ways too, because I got a black card and I was watching the end of the game through my fingers. It was an absolute nail-biting game to be involved in and to watch, but one of the most satisfying ones. There were fellas on both sides just dropping at the end. There was literally nothing left in us.

The year previously, we had played in a similar end-to-end free-flowing game against Dublin where they came out on top. We were right in the mix right until the end of that game but they came out on the better side, and went on and won the All-Ireland that year.

They are the kind of games you remember obviously. When you win it is probably a bit more memorable… not so much when you lose, but at the end of the day there are not too many of those types of games that you get to play in your career.

You play a load of championship games, but there might only be 10 or 15 of those games in your whole career, between club and county, where there is end-to-end football. That Mayo game in particular… you could feel the energy from the crowd…. *the tension.*

Those games don't happen as often as you would like and you can't manufacture them. You would think that Kerry and Dublin in the 2015 All-Ireland would have had the makings of a fantastic game. Dublin won, but it was still a poor game on a wet day.

Overall it was a let-down of a game for most people to watch.

Whereas the game against Dublin in 2013 was a *far* more enjoyable to play in and a lot more entertaining to watch.

It was my brother's 21st the night after the Mayo game, and I came back down afterwards.

I remember getting on the bus and the Kerry supporters were lined up outside Limerick. We had a loyal band of Kerry supporters who followed us over the years, went to all the league games and all that… they had a serious *connection* with that team.

Mayo have incredible supporters too. They brought the full cavalry as well… and that's probably what made the occasion. If it was in Croke Park, I'm not sure it would have been the same type of game with the atmosphere and everything.

Even at club level, when you look at Austin Stack Park… if you get a good crowd it tends to be by far a greater place for a close game than maybe Fitzgerald Stadium. Unless you had a full house, which would be rare in Fitzgerald Stadium. That type of an atmosphere is at its greatest in a setting like that.

The evening throw-in really helped that day against Mayo too. Even the arguing about pitches, and Mayo not happy about it… there was plenty of background noise to the game. It added to the whole mystique of it.

Maybe we're biased… maybe I'm saying all that now because we won, but even the 2013 game against Dublin which we lost stands out as being one of those games where you just want it to keep going on and on. It was like a game of table tennis… up and back, and had a bit of everything from the start.

Later that year Paul O'Connell came up to myself and James O'Donoghue at the RTÉ Sports Awards and said that the Mayo game was one of the best games he'd ever seen played in Limerick.

Mayo were very unlucky, in fairness to them. It was just one of those games where they went at it with everything they had, and so did we, and we just barely fell over the line.

We should have lost it a load of times but when you get through it, there is almost a sense of… *This is our time now.* There was that type of feeling after the game. Even though the Donegal game in the final was a bit of a let-down.

We knew what we were trying to do and we did it, and it got us over the line. A lot of the time that's what finals are like. A lot of the classics tend to be quarter-finals and semi-finals, whereas in the final it is just a matter of getting the job done.

Even the All-Ireland club final as well, that wasn't exactly a thriller of a game. Both teams were a bit tentative… there's a lot on the line. Maybe Croke Park does that to you too on All-Ireland final day… that's the reality of it.

It is strange how becoming captain in 2014 came about. I'd always be the first to say that it was Kieran O'Leary who they gave it to first of all.

How it came about is that 'Gooch' got injured in the All-Ireland club semi-final that we lost to Castlebar Mitchels in 2014. He did his cruciate ligament and it was disastrous for Crokes, for Kerry, and for him.

He was going to be the captain for Kerry that year. Then Kieran O'Leary was going to be captain, but Kieran wasn't starting and I was starting at the time. Johnny Buckley was involved as well, but I was the next in line.

I ended up starting all the games for the rest of the year and that's how I ended up being co-captain. Kieran in my eyes was the *real* captain. He dealt with the whole thing very well. It was great for the two of us because we'd be good buddies. The way it unfolded, it was almost the stars were lined the way it worked out in the end, but it wasn't necessarily planned that way.

And I know myself I was actually official captain in 2018, and it just wasn't working out for me. I wasn't making the team, and you had the same situation where you had some of the younger guys standing in as captain… Gavin White and Shane Murphy. I saw it from both sides of falling into the captaincy… and having it, and then losing it.

But it was huge, it was massive.

Some people can get very hung up on the captaincy, but it was a massive honour to be the captain along with Kieran.

I started playing football in Fitzgerald Stadium, in the small field there with Dr Crokes… we didn't have our main field ready at the time. So, I played most of my football in Fitzgerald Stadium from five or six up. A lot of the club games would still go on in Fitzgerald Stadium. I am very, *very* lucky in that regard.

I went to school then in the Sem which has a huge tradition of football. At Crokes we had decent underage teams. We were not exceptional but a lot of effort was put in at that level which paid off eventually for the club when we got to senior level.

I was one of those lads who got bitten by the bug early. I made teams and I didn't make teams… and eventually I got to play senior. But I had a longer route… I was 22 or 23 when I started to break into the starting team. It is extremely competitive in Kerry and there is a really high standard of football at club level.

I was okay with the way my Kerry career ended. I'm still young enough to be playing. In the last year or two I wasn't particularly happy with how I was playing and basically the decision was made, and I was gone from it. I wouldn't be one to hang around.

I did a small bit of coaching here and there afterwards, and I really enjoyed my club football. At the time we were on a roll with the Crokes. We got back to the All-Ireland club final after that and I just moved with it. I went to America the following summer so there wasn't much point in looking back on it… having any major hang-ups.

The following year Kerry got to the All-Ireland final.

Sure, I'd love to have been playing, but I am honestly very grateful and lucky to have been given the opportunities I got. There are loads of others and people around me at the time that would have loved to have those opportunities, and I was very lucky at times… and maybe unlucky at other times.

I didn't necessarily think Kerry would take over after 2014, but I didn't expect that we wouldn't go on and win another All-Ireland since.

Printed in Great Britain
by Amazon